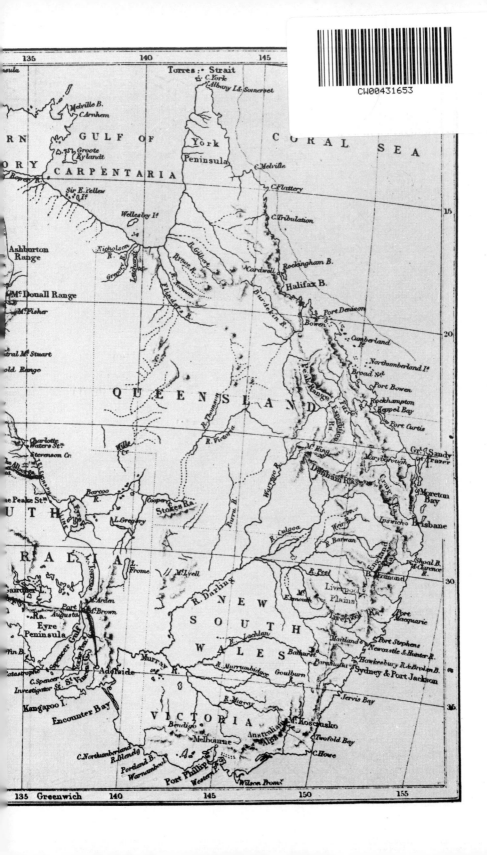

BEYOND THE BLACK STUMP

BEYOND THE BLACK STUMP

Tales of Travellers
to Australia
1787-1850

MICHAEL FOSS

MICHAEL O'MARA BOOKS LIMITED

First published in Great Britain by
Michael O'Mara Books Ltd
20 Queen Anne Street
London W1N 9FB

British Library Cataloguing in Publication Data

Foss, Michael
    Beyond the black stump: tales of travellers
    to Australia, 1787–1850.
    1. British—Australia—Social
    life and customs   2. Australia—Emigration and
    immigration—History
    I. Title
    994'.00421   DU122.B7

    ISBN 0-948397-47-0

Edited by Anne Norton

Typeset by Florencetype Ltd, Kewstoke, Avon
Printed and bound in Great Britain
by The Bath Press, Bath

CONTENTS

CHAPTER ONE

DISCOVERY

Many strange, haphazard circumstances have given rise in our long past to the birth of a nation. Nomadic wanderings and mass migration, tribes bursting out of bounds, casual wars, deliberate campaigns of conquest, religious explosions, settlements that followed trade: out of events like these familiar countries emerged. But few nations have been formed out of negligence, despair and a community of sinners. That peculiar distinction belongs to Australia; and to transcend such dubious birth-rites, within two short centuries, is the impressive measure of her achievement.

From the first, the *Australis Terra* – the Southernmost Land – was a place that European explorers were reluctant to find; and when they did find it, the region, or so it seemed, was one that nobody wanted. When the age of western maritime discovery began in the fifteenth century, sailors and traders were ready to snarl, fight and cheat each other over every scrap of sand, rock and turf that they encountered on the golden path to the Indies. But in the face of a vast continent, held by international rumour to occupy the southern parts of the Pacific, they were unaccountably shy. Nor did this shyness result from ignorance of the possibilities or from lack of means. Marco Polo, whose *Travels* became the fabulous sourcebook for western imagination and western greed, had mentioned 'Greater Java', the biggest island in the world. And in the mysterious way of cartographers a large territory called 'Iave la Grande', rather vague as to its coast-line and geographical position, had been dumped onto the southern parts of sixteenth century maps which might otherwise have seemed embarrassingly vacant. And this territorial conjecture was not much out of the way of known routes. It was placed only a few degrees, at the most, to the south of the islands of the East Indies, which had been pierced and trampled and thoroughly documented over many a long year by Portuguese and Dutch adventurers, with some

1

help also from the Spanish, the French and the British. To turn aside, bending a little to the south, in quest of a larger land and greater riches would have been no difficult task for navigators who had already mastered the East Indies.

By the end of the sixteenth century, it was the opinion of some geographers that such journeys had in fact been made. In 1597, the Dutchman Cornelius Wytfliet stated confidently:

> The Australis Terra is the most southern of all lands. It is separated from New Guinea by a narrow strait. Its shores are but little known, since, after one voyage and another, that route has been deserted, and seldom is the country visited, unless when sailors are driven there in storms. The Australis Terra begins at two or three degrees from the equator, and is maintained by some to be of so great an extent that, if it were thoroughly explored, it would be regarded as a fifth part of the world.

If Wytfliet was correct, as is likely, why were the voyages on which he based his case neither made known nor followed up? Was there something about *Australis Terra* that resisted full discovery and exploration?

Clues began to accumulate. Around March 1606, the Dutch ship *Duyfken* made a landfall and charted about 200 miles in a new region that proved to be part of the coast to the west of the modern Cape York peninsula. This was the first authenticated European landing on the island continent of Australia. The men of the *Duyfken* were not enthusiastic. An account related gloomily that 'in sending their men on shore to intreat of trade, there were nine of them killed by the heathens, which are man-eaters; so they were constrained to return, finding no good to be done there.'

The despondency induced by this first Australian landfall seemed to infect all the voyagers who followed after the *Duyfken*. About six months after the journey of the *Duyfken*, two Spanish captains named Luis de Torres and Diego de Prado passed through the strait off the northern tip of Australia which is now named after Torres. Neither of the captains was complimentary. Prado spoke of 'a big barrier of shoals', of water that was 'very foul', of an island where 'all the night the dogs howled'. Torres' letter to the King of Spain was equally dispiriting:

> There were very large islands, and they seemed more on the side of the south: they were inhabited by black people very stout naked: they have as weapons very thick long spears many arrows stone clubs very misshapen, none of their weapons could we use: I captured in all this land twenty persons of different peoples, in order with them to give a better account to Your Majesty they give much notification of other peoples, although up to now they do not make themselves understood well: we went over this shallow two months, at the end of these we came into 25 fathoms of depth, and in five degrees of latitude, and ten leagues from the coast and having gone 480 leagues here the coast goes stretching back to the north-east: I did not get to it because the shallow got very shoal.

Tentative feelers of discovery advanced from Europe, but when they touched the barrens of the northern Australian coast they shrank back discomforted. How tedious every prospect seemed. Fine beaches and sunlight perhaps, but no glory, no riches, and hardly a decent harbour. In 1623, Jan Carstensz, the Dutch captain of the *Pera*, summarized the result of his investigations:

> The land from 13° to 17°8' is a dry and poor district, without any fruit trees or what men could derive benefit from; it is low and uniform without hills or heights, wooded in various places with undergrowth and brush; with little fresh water; and what is to be got, must be gathered in dug pits; there are also no points or inlets other than a very few bays, but not sheltered against winds from the sea and it extends mainly north-east and south-west with shallow clay and sand bottoms, with many and various salt rivers, which extend inland where their women and children are taken over with dry timber or boughs from trees. The men are in general barbarous and of one shape of body and fashion of face pitch black and quite naked with a woven net on the head or neck, therein they seek their food and what they chiefly live on (so far as we could see) are certain roots, which they dig out of

the earth very bad in odour. We judge their house or dwelling-places in the east-monsoon are on the strand, there we saw many and various huts, made of dry hay; also a multitude of dogs, herons and water curlews, and other wild fowl, as also very tasty fish, which can be easily taken with a dragnet; they have absolutely no knowledge of gold, silver, tin, iron, lead, or copper, and also of nutmegs, cloves and pepper all of which were shown to them on various occasions and visits, without any notice or use being made of them; from this as in all the other information found it can be gauged, they are indigent and miserable men and the most use to be made there is of iron and corals. Their weapons are shields, spears and *callawaijen*, the length of 1½ fathoms, made of light wood and cane, some with fish-bones and others with human bones attached, as ascertained, which they know how to throw by a special technique with a piece of timber the length of ½ a fathom, to the forepart of which a hook is tied (and the *callawaij* or spear set above).

It was a litany of woes: hard country and bad water; contrary winds and tricky moorings; sufficient game and fish, but no metals either precious or useful, no valuable spices. And as for the natives, they were a species of primitive barbarian beneath contempt, hardly a people but something exotic to be caught and caged for the freakshows of Europe. Carstensz, 'wishing to return with something' for the Dutch East India Company, on 18 April 1623 came among a large party of Cape York natives:

After noon, the boats having come back, we were informed by the skipper, when he had landed with the party, a great lot of blacks (some of them armed and others not) came up to them, and were so forward and appeared so bold that they grasped the muskets of our men and wanted to take them from their shoulders and everything they saw was attractive to them; therefore they were enticed with some iron and corals, and so our people seeing their opportunity, caught a black by a string which was attached round his neck and brought him on board; the rest, who remained on the beach, made a great clamour and hubbub, and others, who were still in the bushes, stayed there; the aforesaid people are pitch black, thin of body and quite naked, with a woven basket or net on their head.

Further voyages appeared merely to confirm the bad opinion. In 1629 François Pelsaert, wrecked in the *Batavia* on Houtman Rocks off the west coast of Australia, set out in a ship's boat for Java by way of the continental coast. His opinion of this more western territory was no better than that of Carstensz on Cape York:

Our people searched till evening for water, but found none, they also saw four men, who came creeping on hands and feet, to get near our people, then our men unseen by them out of a low place to the high came close, they sprang up and ran away at full speed, which we saw sufficiently from the boat; they were black men, quite naked, having no covering, and in the evening our people came back on board swimming, much hurt by the rocks, on which they were cast by the breakers, thereupon we pulled up anchor, to look for a better location, and sailed by night with little sail, close along the shore outside the breakers.

On the 15th in the morning, we were near a point where a great reef stretched, about four miles to sea, then we ran between the landward, and seaward reefs, which we estimated to lie in 23°, and sailed thus along the coast, there a reef stretched away along it, where the land was very bad, and there seemed to be calm water; we did our best, to get in there, then found no opening and about noon saw an entrance, where there were no breakers, we ran into it but it was very rocky, and sometimes only one or two feet of water. This coast had a foreland with dunes, about four miles broad, before one comes to the high land, we there began to dig in various places, but the water was salt; a party went to the high land, there by luck they found some holes in a rock, where sweet water from the rain had been left, it seemed that a short time before there had been blacks, since bones of crabs lay there, and ashes from a fire near by. Here we quenched a little our great thirst, since we were almost at the end of our endurance, and since leaving the ship had had only one or two small measures a day. Without any wine or other drink. Here we gathered above what we drank, about 80 cans of water, and stayed here for the night.

On the 16th we in the morning went farther, to see if there were more holes in the hills, but our seeking was in vain since it seemed not to have rained there for a long time, and there was no sign of running water, and moreover the high land was very bad, and the land was dry, without trees, leaves, or grass, and everywhere high ant-hills, of earth thrown up, which from afar were not unlike men's huts.

There were also such swarms of flies which got about our mouths, and in our eyes, so that we could not get away from them. Here we saw also 8 black men, who each had a stick in the hand, and approached about a musket-shot of us, then as we went toward them, they ran away, and we could not make them stay, until we could come to them. Towards noon as we saw that no more water was obtainable, we set sail, and ran through another opening in the reef, which lay somewhat farther to the north. Here we had the latitude of 22°17'. I had the intention of running for Jacop Remmessen's river, but the wind went to the north-east so that we could not hold to the coast, we were forced, since now the people were left more than 400 miles from us, and so far we had found no water to assist them, but only so much for ourselves that we might have two small measures a day, to resolve to do our best to prosecute our voyage, in the name of God, as speedily as possible to Batavia, so that any orders by the Governor-General, or means of rescue might be put into operation.

By the middle of the seventeenth century, a body of opinion had been gathered from all parts (but mainly Dutch) regarding the north and west coasts of the giant new land. The conventional view, which was depressing, was set out in the instructions prepared for Abel Tasman in the early 1640s:

The *jacht* the Duyffken discovered the unknown South and West coasts of Nova Guinea for about 880 miles from 5 to 13¾ degrees south latitude, and merely found, that there was much land for the most part waste, and various places inhabited by wild, cruel dark barbarous men, who killed some of our sailors, so that the true location of the land and what might be produced or desired could not be understood, but through lack of provisions and other needs they turned back from the discovery thus begun.

In two expeditions between 1642 and 1644, Tasman did much to remedy the deficiencies of Australian discovery. He did careful and impressive work in the land at first named for Governor Van Diemen and later called Tasmania after the explorer himself. On the second voyage he covered some 10 degrees of northern Australian coast between Port Darwin and the Gilbert River in the Gulf of Carpentaria. But he quite failed to undo the prejudice of former expeditions. It was a hard, wretched, unproductive land. Tasman's masters in the Dutch East India Company, a body of Europeans thoroughly devoted to profit and exploitation, were not well pleased with him.

So matters rested for nearly a century and a quarter. The north, west and south coasts of the land generally know as 'New Holland' had been seen, more or less, and rejected as unprofitable. Exploration gave way to slumber; the unknown east coast did not seem worth the effort of an expedition.

Then one of the greatest names in the whole history of navigation took a hand in the work of discovery. When Captain James Cook set out for the South Seas in the *Endeavour* in 1768 he went, not as a profiteer or servant of commerce, but as a man of the European Enlightenment, the leader of a carefully planned and well-founded scientific expedition. Few men were better qualified than the great navigator and few since have carried the burden of scientific curiosity with such diligence, judgement and good sense.

By early 1770, Cook had finished his work in New Zealand. On a low, wet day in March he departed, heading westward for New Holland in a cloudy drizzle. Gales and a southerly sea swept him further north than he intended. In the early morning of 19 April, turning in towards the land, he saw his first point of the continent, at the place now called Cape Everard in Victoria.

For more than four months the *Endeavour* crept up the east coast of Australia, a deliberate progress recorded in the captain's sober prose. James Cook was not a fast man with the pen, and his purpose was anything but sensationalism, but among the dry bones of the observations, bearings and soundings appeared the flashes of a passionate intelligence driven to irritability, amazement or humour. And behind all the careful language there still gleamed the light of that strange romance which is revealed as a new land unfolds to astonished eyes.

How familiar, even banal, the old names are today. Yet there was a moment of magic at first acquaintance. The ship rounded a point, a cape, a bluff; there was a bay or a river, with reefs and shoals perhaps; the country spreads out quietly; is it friendly or hostile? The geography is charted, the name noted, and the *Endeavour* passes on, leaving the place to unfold in time, passing from mystery to familiarity. Here are the first moments in the life of Botany Bay and Port Jackson:

SUNDAY 6*th* (May). In the evening the yawl return'd from fishing having caught two Sting rays weighing near 600 pounds. The great quantity of New Plants &c^a Mr Banks & Dr Solander collected in this place occasioned my giveing it the name of *Botany Bay*. It is situated in the Latitude of 34°0′ S, Longitude 208°37′ West; it is Capacious safe and commodious, it may be known by the land on the Sea-coast which is of a pretty even and moderate height, rather higher than it is farther inland with steep rocky clifts next the Sea and looks like a long Island lying close under the Shore: the entrance of the harbour lies about the Middle of this land, in coming from the Southward it is discoverd before you are abreast of it which you cannot do in coming from the northward; the entrance is little more than a Mile broad and lies in WNW. To sail into it keep the south shore on board untill within a small bare Island which lies close under the north shore, being within that Island the deepest water is on that side 7, 6 and five fathom a good way up. There is shoal'd water a good way off from the South Shore from the inner South point qu[i]te to the head of the harbour, but over towards the north and NW shore is a channell of 12 or 14 feet water at low water 3 or 4 leagues up to a place where there is 3 & 4 f^m but here I found very little fresh water. We anchord near the south shore about a Mile within the entrance for the conveniency of sailing with a Southerly wind and the getting of fresh water but I afterwards found a very fine stream of fresh water on the north shore in the first sandy cove within the Island before which a Ship might lay almost land lock'd and wood for fual may be got every where: altho wood is here in great plenty yet there is very little variety, the largest trees are as large or larger than our oaks in England and grows a good deal like them and yields a redish gum, the wood itself is heavy hard and black like Lignum Vitae; another sort that grows tall and strait some thing like Pines, the wood of this is hard and Ponderous and something of the nature of American live oaks, these two are all the timber trees I met with. There are a few sorts of Shrubs and several Palm trees, and Mangroves about the head of the harbour. The Country is woody low and flat and as far inland as we could see and I believe that the soil is in general sandy, in the wood are a variety of very boutifull birds such as Cocatoo's, Lorryquets, Parrots &c^a and Crows exactly like those we have in England. Water fowl are no less plenty about the head of the harbour where there are great flats of sand and Mud on which they seek their food, the most of these were unknown to us, one sort especialy which was black and white and as large as a goose but most like a pelican. On the Sand and Mud banks are Oysters, Muscles, Cockles &c^a which I believe are the chief support of the inhabitants, who go into shoald water with their little Canoes and pick them out of the sand and Mud with their hands and sometimes roast and eat them in the Canoe, having often a fire for that purpose as I suppose, for I know no other it can be for. The Natives do not appear to be numberous neither do they seem to live in large bodies but dispers'd in small parties along by the water side; those I saw were about as tall as Europeans, of a very dark brown colour but not black nor had they wooly frizled hair, but black and lank much like ours. No sort of cloathing or ornaments were ever seen by any of us upon any of them or in or about any of their hutts, from which I conclude that they never wear any. Some we saw that had their faces and bodies painted with a sort of white paint or Pigment. Altho I had said that shell fish is their chief support yet they catch other sorts of fish some of which we found roasting on the fire the first time we landed, some of these they strike with gigs and others they catch with hook and line; we have seen them strike fish with gigs & hooks and lines were found in their hutts. Sting rays I believe they do not eat because I never saw the least remains of one near any of their hutts or fire places. However we could know but very little of their customs as we never were able to form any connections with them, they had not so much as touch'd the things we had left in their hutts on purpose for them to take away. During our stay in this Harbour I caused the English Colours to be display'd ashore every day and an inscription to be cut out upon one of the trees near the watering place seting forth the Ships name, date &c^a. Having seen every thing this place afforded we at day light in the Morning weigh'd with a light breeze at NW and put to sea and the wind soon after coming to the Southward we steer'd along shore NNE and at Noon we were by observation in the Latitude of 33°50' S about 2 or 3 Miles from the land and abreast of a Bay or Harbour wherein there apper^d to be safe anchorage which I called *Port Jackson*. It lies 3 Leag^s to the northward of Botany Bay. I had almost forgot to mention that it is high water in this Bay at the full and change of the Moon about 8 o'Clock and rises and falls upon a perpendicular about 4 or 5 feet.

'During our stay in this Harbour I caused the English Colours to be displayed ashore every day and an inscription to be cut out upon one of the trees.' Did this constitute an act of possession, and if so by what right? Perhaps it was beyond Cook to answer. He acted merely out of convention and hope. By the next day he was gone.

Progress was steady and without any great alarms. The scientists of the expedition, Dr Solander and Mr Joseph Banks, went busily ashore in search of flora and fauna. The natives were evasive. By 25 May the *Endeavour* was at the Tropic of Capricorn, on the east coast of Curtis Island. Then more difficult times began, since they were entering the vast dangerous tracts of the Barrier Reef. The weather was sultry and subject to sudden storms. The land became low-lying and the coast was deceptive, retreating into mangrove swamps. Fresh water was scarce. The channels were hard to find and the navigation extremely tricky. On the night of Trinity Sunday, 10 June 1770, when the officers were rising from supper, the ship went within a few moments from seventeen fathoms to zero and grounded. She was stuck fast on the coral of the Barrier Reef, off the point that Cook called Cape Tribulation 'because here begun all our troubles'.

Some desperate work by the crew freed the ship and leaking badly she limped to land. For two further months the *Endeavour* remained caged in by the hidden teeth of the reef, 'in which time we have sailed 360 leagues without ever having a man out of the chains heaving the lead when the ship was under way, a circumstance that I dare say never happened to any ship before and yet here it was absolutely necessary.'

A Reef such as here spoke of is scarcely known in Europe, it is a wall of Coral Rock rising all most perpendicular out of the unfathomable Ocean, always overflown at high-water generally 7 or 8 feet and dry in places at low-water; the large waves of the vast Ocean meeting with so sudden a resistance make a most terrible surf breaking mountains high especially as in our case when the general trade wind blowes directly upon it.

With a sigh of relief, on 13 August, Cook was at last free of the reef and able to reflect on the compulsion that drove men of his disposition and curiosity into such ugly dangers:

Was it not for the pleasure which naturly results to a Man from being the first discoverer, even was it nothing more than sands and Shoals, this service would be insuportable especialy in far distant parts, like this, short of Provisions and almost every other necessary. The world will hardly admit of an excuse for a man leaving a Coast unexplored he has once discover'd, if dangers are his excuse he is than charged with *Timourousness* and want of Perseverance and at once pronounced the unfitest man in the world to be employ'd as a discoverer; if on the other hand he boldly incounters all the dangers and obstacles he meets and is unfortunate enough not to succeed he is than charged with *Temerity* and want of conduct.

By now, Cook considered that his debt to science and discovery was fully paid so he fled away from that bad land and worse sea. There was one last duty to be done on behalf of King George III:

Having satisfied my self of the great Probabillity of a Passage, thro' which I intend going with the Ship, and therefore may land no more upon this Eastern coast of *New Holland*, and on the Western side I can make no new discovery the honour of which belongs to the Dutch Navigators; but the Eastern Coast from the Latitude of 38° South down to this place I am confident was never seen or viseted by any European before us, and Notwithstand[ing] I had in the Name of His Majesty taken posession of several places upon this coast, I now once more hoisted English Coulers and in the Name of His Majesty King George the Third took posession of the whole Eastern Coast from the above Latitude down to this place by the name of *New South Wales*, together with all the Bays, Harbours Rivers and Islands situate upon the said coast, after which we fired three Volleys of small Arms which were Answerd by the like number from the Ship.

Then, with a final malediction cast towards the everlasting shoals, on 23 August 1770 Captain Cook headed northwest by west from the tip of Cape York and quit Australia without much regret.

*

But what was the nature of this 'New South Wales' that Cook had discovered for Europe? No one was better placed to answer this question than the great navigator himself, and this he set out to do in his thorough-going, methodical manner:

In the Course of this Journal I have at different times made mention of the appearance or Aspect of the face of the Country, the nature of the Soil, its product &c^a. By the first it will appear that to the Southward of 33° or 34° the Land is in general low and level with very few Hills or Mountains, further to the northward it may in some places be called a Hilly, but hardly any where can be call'd a Mountainous Country, for the Hills and Mountains put together take up but a small part of the Surface in comparison to what Planes and Vallies do which intersect or divide these Hills and Mountains: It is indefferently well watered, even in the dry Seasons, with small Brooks and springs, but no great Rivers, unless it be in the wet Season when the low lands and Vallies near the Sea I do suppose are mostly laid under water; the small brooks may then become large Rivers but this can only

Cook's chart of the east coast of Australia

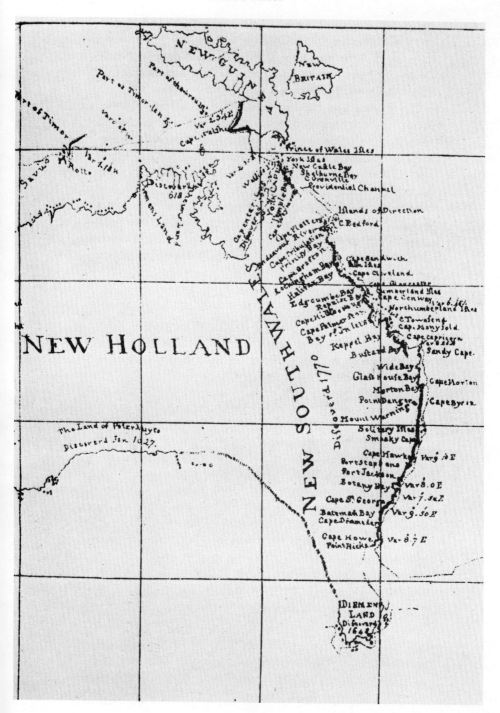

happen with the Tropick. It was only in *Thirsty Sound* where we could find no fresh Water, excepting one small pool or two which Gore saw in the woods, which no doubt was owing to the Country being there very much intersected with Salt creeks and Mangrove land.

The low Land by the Sea and even as far in land as we were, is for the most part friable, loose, sandy Soil; yet indefferently fertile and cloathed with woods, long grass, shrubs, Plants &c^a. The Mountains or Hills are Chequered with woods and Lawns. Some of the Hills are wholy covered with flourishing Trees; others but thinly, and the few that are on them are small and the spots of Lawns or Savannahs are Rocky and barren, especially to the northward where the country did not afford or produce near the Vegetation that it does to the southward, nor were the Trees in the woods half so tall and stout.

The Woods do not produce any very great variety of Trees, there are only 2 or 3 sorts that can be call'd Timber; the largest is the Gum Tree which growes all over the Country, the Wood of this Tree is too hard and ponderous for most common uses. The Tree which resembles our Pines, I saw no where in perfection but in Botany Bay, this wood as I have before observed is some thing of the same nature as America Live Oak; in short most of the large Trees in this Country are of a hard and ponderous nature and could not be applied to many purposes. Here are several sorts of the Palm kind, Mangro[v]es and several other sorts of small Trees and shrubs quite unknown to me besides a very great Variety of Plants hetheto unknown, but these things are wholy out of my way to describe, nor will this be of any loss sence not only Plants but everything that can be of use to the Learn'd World will be very accuratly described by Mr Banks and D ^{r} Solander. The Land naturly produces hardly any thing fit for man to eat and the Natives know nothing of Cultivation. There are indeed found growing wild in the woods a few sorts of fruits (the most of them unknown to us) which when ripe do not eat a miss, one sort especially which we call'd Apples, being about the size of a Crab-Apple, it is black and pulpy when ripe and

Cassewary. From John White, *Journal of a Voyage to New South Wales*, 1710

Cassowary of New South Wales.

London Published Dec 29. 1789 by J.Debrett.

tastes like a Damson, it hath a large stone or kernel and grows on Trees or Shrubs.

In the Northern parts of the Country as about *Endeavour River*, and probably in many other places, the Boggy or watery Lands produce Taara or Cocos which when properly cultivated are very good roots, without which they are hardly eatable, the tops however make very good greens.

Land Animals are scarce, as so far as we know confined to a very few species; all that we saw I have before mentioned, the sort that is in the greatest plenty is the Kangooroo, or Kanguru so call'd by the Natives; we saw a good many of them about Endeavour River, but kill'd only Three which we found very good eating. Here are like wise Batts, Lizards, Snakes, Scorpions, Centumpees &c^a but not in any plenty. Tame Animals they have none but Dogs, and of these we saw but one and therefore must be very scarce, probably they eat them faster than they breed them, we should not have seen this one had he not made frequent Visets while we lay in Endeavour River.

The Land Fowles are Bustards, Eagles, Hawks, Crows such as we have in England, Cockatoes of two sorts, white and brown, very beautifull Birds of the Parrot kind such as Lorryquets &c^a, Pidgeons, Doves, Quales, and several sorts of smaller birds. The Sea and Water Fowls are Herons, Boobies, Nodies, Guls, Curlews, Ducks, Pelicans &c^a and when Mr Banks and Mr Gore were in the Country at the head of Endeavour River they saw and heard in the night great numbers of Geese. The sea is indifferently well stock'd with Fish of various sorts, such as Sharks, Dog-fish, Rock-fish, Mullets, Breames, Cavallies, Mackarel, old wives, Leather-Jackets, Five-fingers, Sting-Rays, Whip-rays &c^a – all excellent in their kind. The Shell-fish are Oysters of 3 or 4 sorts, viz Rock oysters and Mangrove Oysters which are small, Pearl Oysters, and Mud Oysters, these last are the best and largest; Cockles and Clams of Several sorts, many of these that are found upon the Reefs are of a Prodigious size: Craw-fish, Crabs, Musles, and a variety of other sorts. Here are also among and upon the Shoals & reefs great numbers of the

Implements and weapons of the Aborigines. From John White, *Journal of a Voyage to New South Wales*, 1790

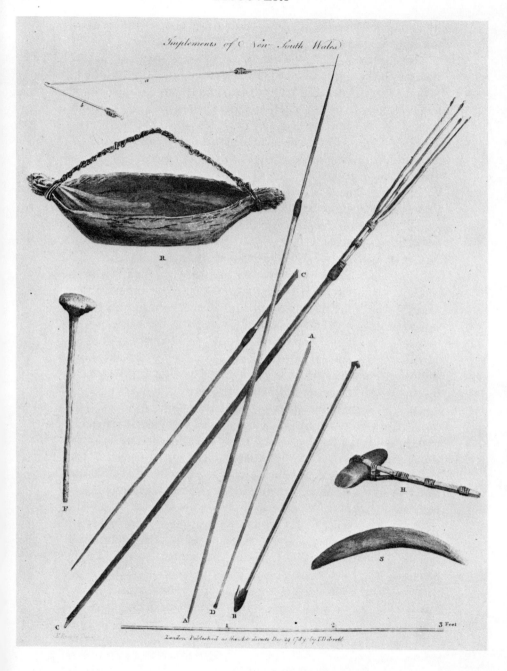

Implements of (New South Wales)

finest Gree[n] Turtle in the world and in the Rivers and salt Creeks are some Aligators.

The Natives of this Country are of a middle Stature straight bodied and slender-limbed, their skins the Colour of Wood soot or of a dark Chocolate, their hair almost black, some lank and others curled, they all wear it crop'd short, their Beards which are generaly black they like wise crop short or singe off. Their features are far from being disagreeable and their Voices are soft and tunable. They go quite naked both Men and women without any manner of Cloathing whatever, even the Women do not so much as Cover their privities. Altho none of us were ever very near any of their women, one gentleman excepted, yet we are all as well satisfied of this as if we had lived amonng them. Notwithstanding we had several interviews with the Men while we lay in Endeavour River, yet whether through Jealousy or disrigard they never brought any of their women along with them to the Ship, but always left them on the opposite side of the River where we had frequent opportunities [of] Viewing them through our glasses. They wear as Oraments Necklaces made of shells, Bracelets or hoops about their arms, made mostly of hair twisted and made like a cord hoop, these they wear teight about the upper parts of their Arms, and some have girdles made in the same manner. The men wear a bone about 3 or 4 Inches long and a fingers thick, run through the Bridge of the nose, which the Seamen call'd a sprit sail yard; they like wise have holes in their ears for Earrings but we never saw them wear any, neither are all the other oraments wore in common for we have seen as many without as with them. Some of those we saw on Posession Island wore Breast Plates which we suppose'd were made of Mother of Pearl shells. Many of them paint their bodies and faces with a sort of White paist or Pigment, this they apply different ways each according to his fancy. Their Offensive weaphons are Darts, some are only pointed at one end others are barb'd, some with wood others with the Stings of Rays and some with Sharks teeth &c[a], these last are stuck fast on with gum. They throw the Dart with only one hand, in the doing of which they make use of a peice of wood about 3 feet long made thin like the blade of a Cutlass, with a little hook at one end to take hold of the end of the Dart, and at the other

end is fix'd a thin peice of bone about 3 or 4 Inches long; the
use of this is, I beleive, to keep the dart steady and to make it
quit the hand in a proper direction; by the help of these
throwing sticks, as we call them, they will hit a Mark at the
distance of 40 or 50 Yards, with almost, if not as much
certainty as we can do with a Musquet, and much more so
than with a ball. These throwing sticks we at first took for
wooden swords, and perhaps on some occasions they may use
them for such, that is when all their darts are expended, be
this as it may they never travel without both them and their
darts not altogether for fear of enimies but for killing of
Game &cᵃ as I shall shew hereafter. Their defensive weapons
are Shields made of wood but these we never saw use'd but
once in Botany Bay. I do not look upon them to be a warlike
People, on the Contrary I think them a timorous and inoffensive race, no ways inclined to cruelty, as appear'd from
their behaviour to one of our people in Endeavour River
which I have before mentioned. Neither are they very numerous, they live in small parties along by the Sea Coast, the
banks of Lakes, Rivers creeks &cᵃ. They seem to have no fix'd
habitation but move about from place to place like wild
Beasts in search of food, and I beleive depend wholy upon
the success of the present day for their subsistance. They
have wooden fish gigs with 2, 3 or 4 prongs each very
ingeniously made with which they strike fish; we have also
seen them strike both fish and birds with their darts. With
these they like wise kill other Animals; they have also wooden
harpoons for striking Turtle, but of these I beleive they got
but few, except at the Season they come a shore to lay. In
short these people live wholy by fishing and hunting, but
mostly by the former, for we never saw one Inch of Cultivated land in the whole Country; they know however the use
of Taara and sometimes eat them. We do not know that they
eat any thing raw but roast or broil all they eat on slow
small fires.

Their Houses are mean small hovels not much bigger than
an oven, made of peices of Sticks, Bark, Grass &cᵃ, and even
these are seldom used but in the wet seasons for in the dry
times we know that they as often sleep in the open air as any
where else. We have seen many of their Sleeping places
where there has been only some branches, or peices of bark

ris about a foot from the ground on the windward side. Their Canoes are as mean as can be conceived, especially to the southward where all we saw were made of one peice of the bark of Trees, about 12 or 14 feet long, drawn or tied together at one end as I have before made mention. These Canoes will not carry above 2 people, in general their is never more than one in them, but bad as they are they do very well for the purpose they apply them to, better than if they were larger, for as they draw but little water they go in them upon the Mud banks and pick up shell fish &c^a without going out of the Canoe. The few Canoes we saw to the northward were made of a log of wood hollow'd out, about 14 feet long and very narrow with out-riggers, these will carry 4 people. During our whole stay in Endevour River we saw but one Canoe and had great reason to think that the few people that resided about this place had no more; this one served them to cross the River and to go a fishing in &c^a. They Attend the Shoals and flatts one where or a nother every Day at Low-water to gather Shell fish or what ever they can find to eat, and have each a little bag to put what they get in: this bag is made of net work. They have not the least knowlidge of Iron or any other Metal that we know of; their working tools must be made of stone, bone and shells, those made of the former are very bad if I may judge from one of the Adzes I have seen.

Bad and mean as their Canoes are they at certain Seasons of the Year, so far as we know, go in them to the most Distant Islands which lay upon the Coast, for we never landed upon one but what we saw signs of people having been there before. We were surprised to find Houses &c^a upon Lizard Island which lies 5 Leagues from the nearest part of the Main, a distance we before thought that they could not have gone in their Canoes.

The Coast of this Country, at least so much of it as lays to the Northward of 25° of Latitude, abounds with a great Number of fine Bays and Harbours, which are shelter'd from all Winds. But, the Country it self so far as we know doth not produce any one thing that can become an Article in trade to invite Europeans to fix a settlement upon it. However this Eastern side is not that barren and Miserable Country that *Dampier* and others have discribed the western side to be. We are to Consider that we see this Country in the pure state of

Nature, the Industry of Man has had nothing to do with any part of it and yet we find all such things as nature hath bestow'd upon it in a flourishing state. In this Extensive Country it can never be doubted but what most sorts of Grain, Fruits, Roots &c^a of every kind would flourish here were they once brought hither, planted and cultivated by the hand of Industry, and here are Provender for more Cattle at all seasons of the year than ever can be brought into this Country.

When one considers the Proximity of this Country with New-Guiney, New-Britain and several other Islands which produce Cocoa-Nutts and many other fruits proper for the Support of Man, it seems strange that they should not long ago have been transplanted here; by its not being done it should seem that the Natives of this Country have no Commerce with their neighbours the New-Guinians, it is very probable that they are a different people and speake a different Language; for the advantage of such who want to clear up this point I shall add a short Vocabulary of a few words in the New-Holland Language which we learnt when in Endeavour River. . . .*

From what I have said of the Natives of New-Holland they may appear to some to be the most wretched people upon Earth, but in reality they are far more happier than we Europeans; being wholy unacquainted not only with the superfluous but the necessary Conveniences so much sought after in Europe, they are happy in not knowing the use of them. They live in a Tranquillity which is not disturb'd by the Inequality of Condition: The Earth and sea of their own accord furnishes them with all things necessary for life, they covet not Magnificent Houses, Houshold-stiff &c^a, they live in a warm and fine Climate and enjoy a very wholsome Air, so that they have very little need of Clothing and this they seem to be fully sencible of, for many to whome we gave Cloth &c^a to, left it carlessly upon the Sea beach and in the woods as a thing they had no manner of use for. In short they seem'd to set no Value upon any thing we gave them, nor would they ever part with any thing of their own for any one article we could offer them; this in my opinion argues that they think themselves provided with all the necessarys of Life and that they have no superfluities.

* Here followed a list of words.

It is not an encouraging account. There were some good things to be said for the new land and the fair-minded Cook made these points. But the country seemed to offer Europe very little. There was nothing to trade and almost no inducement to settle, though settlers, if they did come, might make something of the land, at least in the more southern parts of 'New South Wales'. Moreover, the kindly Cook (he was a sea-captain – colonization was no part of his business) added a timely warning against the cruelty and tyranny that a European presence would surely visit upon the natives.

If there was no trade and little hope for colonists, if justice demanded that the aboriginals be left alone, what possible reason could there be for men to go to Australia?

CHAPTER TWO

THE POLICY OF TRANSPORTATION

Many respectable historians would have us believe that the eighteenth century, in England, was a time of wonders. The country was at last rid of the bad Stuarts and Parliament ruled supreme. The constitutional crisis had been weathered and the new Hanoverian dynasty, imported from Germany in 1714, was too alien and too slothful to try to reimpose the royal prerogative. Foreign policy, it is true, remained something of a mess throughout the century, but trade and manufacture were booming. Invention and enterprise were in the air. England was growing richer by the day and making more and more noise in the world.

An Age of Reason had arrived. Old tyrannies and superstitions were being swept away. Rational order would overcome the chaos of the old despotism. The decent country gentlemen and great-hearted merchants of Parliament could be expected to have the well-being of the nation perpetually in mind. The crown was shackled, freedom secure and property safeguarded. It was, as the cynical Frenchman Voltaire said with bitter irony, 'the best of all possible worlds'. Things were going marvellously well.

But this picture, had it ever been put to the large army of the poor, would have been rejected in anger and disbelief. For it was their experience that despair, not reason, governed the lower reaches of English society. These people in the depths had, naturally, no voice in the conduct of affairs, but even the deaf and the blind could not help noticing, as the century went on, that things were seriously wrong.

Some of the reasons for this desperation were not hard to find. A country with a fast-growing population, once agrarian but now moving at speed from a rural to a mercantile urban economy, cast all labouring life into turmoil. And the new

23

opportunities to make money, by speculation in land and property or through the unregulated manufacturing process, ensured that a rootless and defenceless poor would be exploited. Out of the debasement of the many came the prosperity of the few; and though the men of property, who alone sat in Parliament, could find no inducement in their respectable Protestant hearts to put right the evils that made them rich, at least they could not escape the evidence of the misery they had sown.

Suffering, degradation and want stalked town and country alike. Here is a country parson on the state of his parish:

In visiting the labouring families of my parish as my duty led me, I could not but observe with concern their mean and distressed condition. I found them in general but indifferently fed; badly clothed; some children without shoes and stocking; very few put to school; and most families in debt to little shopkeepers. In short, there was scarcely any appearance of comfort about their dwellings, except that the children looked tolerably healthy. Yet I could not impute the wretchedness I saw either to sloth or wastefulness. For I knew that the farmers were careful that the men should not want employment: and had they been given to drinking, I am sure I should have heard of it.

These poor people, in assigning the cause of their misery, agree in ascribing it to the high prices of the necessaries of life. 'Everything (said they) is so dear, that we can hardly live'.

I have read somewhere, that about the beginning of this century, the poor of this country receiving relief were computed to be about 600,000. I think it probable that their number is now [1787] almost tripled. In this parish the poor-rate is somewhat lower than in any of the contiguous parishes. ... The number of poor receiving relief, either individually or by families, (including those in the poor-house) is about forty, besides others assisted occasionally in sickness: that is, the number of individuals assisted by the rate is about *one-fifth* of the whole. Supposing this proportion to hold throughout the Kingdom, and our population to be 8,000,000, the number of paupers comes out 1,600,000.

Such being the unhappy condition of poor people, particularly of day-labourers: left, for the most part, destitute of instruction in their early years, and copying as they grow up the example of vicious parents; being, in consequence of this, thoughtless, improvident, and irreligious in youth; unable, when married, by incessant labour, to provide for the necessities of even a moderate family; their spirits sinking, as children come on, under a growing weight of wretchedness and woe; their applications for assistance often treated by contempt by the persons appointed to relieve them; can we wonder, if thus circumstanced, they receive occasional favours without gratitude and brood over their miseries in sulky silence? Can we wonder at that wide-spread dishonesty, and profligacy of manners, the fatal effects of which we are daily lamenting? Our astonishment will assuredly ease, if we do but reflect that the very best education will scarcely keep a man honest and virtuous, whose family is perishing for want of necessaries.

And the same observer found conditions in the new manufacturing industries to be, if anything, even worse:

Whatever opinion we may adopt as to the general population of the kingdom, all will acknowledge that *this* class of people is multiplied exceedingly. And depending upon their employers for their daily subsistance, they are in much the same situation with reduced farmers and impoverished labourers; that is, they are very liable to come to want. The caprice of fashion causes by fits and starts a great demand for one species of goods, and a cessation of demand for another; and thus workmen, who to-day are fully employed, may be tomorrow in the streets begging their bread. By living in towns, and associating at publick-houses, they are habitually improvident, and mind nothing but present enjoyment; and when flung out of work, they are immediately in want. They are also, from their sedentary occupations and habitual intemperance, more short-lived than day-labourers; and leaving families behind them unable wholly to maintain themselves, these, as the men die off, fall on the parishes. All this will account for the misery visible in manufacturing towns, in most of which the poor are numerous, and the rates higher than in other places. Manufacturers enjoy, however, one advantage over day-labourers, though they seldom make a right use of it. Several manufactures employ women and children, as well as men: and wherever this is the case, these families might earn a great deal more money, and live better, than labouring families do; but by contracting early the vices of towns, they commonly misspend their earnings, which if used with frugality, would render their condition comfortable and themselves happy.

Peasant farmers, dispossessed and thrown out of their livelihood by agricultural enclosures and land speculation, drifted into the towns where a variety of avaricious sharks waited to consume them. Henry Fielding, the famous novelist who was also a reforming London magistrate, had this account from the high-constable in Holborn:

In the parish of St. Giles's there are great numbers of houses set apart for the reception of idle persons and vagabonds, who have their lodgings there for twopence a night; that in the above parish, and in St. George, Bloomsbury, one woman alone occupies seven of these houses, all properly accommodated with miserable beds from the cellar to the garret, for such twopenny lodgers: that in these beds, several of which are in the same room, men and women, often strangers to each other, lie promiscuously; the price of a double bed being no more than three-pence, as an encouragement to them to lie together; but as these places are thus adapted to whoredom, so are they no less provided for drunkenness, gin being sold in them all at a penny a quartern; so that the smallest sum of money serves for intoxication; that in the execution of search-warrants Mr. Welch rarely finds less than twenty of these houses open for the receipt of all comers at the latest hours; that in one of these houses, and that not a large one, he hath numbered fifty-eight persons of both sexes, the stench of whom was so intolerble that it compelled him in a short time to quit the place.

And Fielding did not know whether these unlucky devils were 'more the objects of detestation or compassion':

For such is the poverty of these wretches, that, upon searching all the above number, the money found upon all of them did not amount to one shilling; and I have been credibly informed, that a single loaf hath suuplied a whole family with their provisions for a week. Lastly, if any of these miserable creatures fall sick (and it is almost a miracle that stench, vermin, and want, should ever suffer them to be well) they are turned out in the streets by their merciless host or hostess, where, unless some parish office of extraordinary charity relieves them, they are sure miserably to perish, with the addition of hunger and cold to their disease.

Desperate lives erupted into desperate acts. The natural consequence of the increase in poverty and misery was an increase in crime. Henry Fielding, who was an experienced magistrate and no alarmist, in 1751 warned his fellow citizens what to expect:

The great increase of robberies within these few years is an evil which to me appears to deserve some attention; and the rather as it seems (though already become so flagrant) not yet to have arrived to that height of which it is capable, and which it is likely to attain. In fact, I make no doubt, but that the streets of this town, and the roads leading to it, will shortly be impassable without the utmost hazard; surely there are few matters of more general concern than to put an immediate end to these outrages, which are already become so notorious, and which, as I have observed, seem to threaten us with such a dangerous increase.

These facts were no secret to those who cared to look. But since the authorities, for reasons of self-interest, refused to remedy the root causes of social disorder, the only way left to deal with the consequences of unrest was by repression. The respectable howl was for law and order. But here the authorities ran up against a problem. England had a highly developed system of law and punishment, but almost no penal policy. It was enough that wrong-doers were judged and sentenced; what happened to them afterwards was left largely to chance and private enterprise. Moreover, society was already armed with a body of laws of such startling ferocity that new penalties were superfluous, if not ridiculous. There were, according to one authority, 222 offences warranting the death penalty. These included: picking pockets above one shilling; shoplifting above five shillings; maiming cattle; stealing sheep; cutting down garden trees; breaking open a fishpond; cutting hop binds; concealing the death of a bastard; sending threatening letters; challenging more than twenty jurors; rioting with twelve or more persons; breaking out of prison; desertion; enlisting in foreign armies. There was almost nothing left to proscribe but breathing, eating and sleeping.

So savage were the laws that juries (then as now the best safeguard against legislative and judicial tyranny) were reluctant to convict. The lawyer Blackstone, in his famous *Commentaries*, lamented this state of affairs:

> It is a melancholy truth, that among the variety of actions which men are daily liable to commit, no less than an hundred and sixty have been declared by act of parliament to be felonies without benefit of clergy; or, in other words, to be worthy of instant death. So dreadful a list, instead of diminishing, increases the number of offenders. The injured, through compassion, will often forbear to prosecute: juries, through compassion, will sometimes forget their oaths, and either acquit the guilty or mitigate the nature of the offence: and judges, through compassion, will respite one half of the convicts, and recommend them to the royal mercy. Among so many chances of escaping, the needy and hardened offender overlooks the multitude that suffer: he boldly engages in some desperate attempt, to relieve his wants or supply his vices; and, if unexpectedly the hand of justice overtakes him, he deems himself peculiarly unfortunate, in falling at last to those laws, which long impunity has taught him to contemn.

Judicial murder, as the eighteenth century authorities learnt to their cost, was no answer. 'All the social problems of all countries,' wrote the mischievous Bernard Shaw, 'can be got rid of by extirpating the inhabitants; but to get rid of a problem is not to solve it.' Something else had to be done. England was awash with rogues and malefactors. They were caught and judged, and then nothing much could be done with them except to throw them back into the cesspools where they had learnt their criminality in the first place. The prisons were no answer either. They were wholly inadequate to receive the great numbers liable to sentence under the laws. They were utterly corrupt under the administration of private enterprise, and they taught more crime than ever they punished.

Only one policy seemed to have some chance of success, and that was the policy of transportation. This policy, which was by no means new, had a double appeal to those in authority since it satisfied the old principle that what was out of sight was out of mind and also transferred the problem of repeated criminal behaviour elsewhere.

The settlement of North America, after the landing of the Pilgrim Fathers, became a boon to the English system of criminal justice. From the beginning of the eighteenth century, no less than seventeen Acts of Parliament hustled wrong-doers away to confront the Red Indians and the wilderness. Among the actions that made a person liable for transportation were the following:

Grand Larceny, which comprehends every species of Theft above the value of One Shilling, not otherwise distinguished

Receiving or buying Stolen Goods, Jewels and Plate

Ripping and stealing Lead, Iron, Copper, &c. or buying or receiving

Stealing (or receiving when stolen) Ore from Black Lead Mines

Stealing from Furnished Lodgings

Setting fire to Underwood

Stealing Letters, or destroying a Letter or Packet, advancing the Postage, and secreting the Money

Embezzling Naval Stores, in certain cases

Petty Larcenies, or Thefts under One Shilling

Assaulting with an intent to Rob

Aliens returning after being ordered out of the kingdom

Stealing Fish from a Pond or River – Fishing in inclosed Ponds, and buying stolen Fish

Stealing Roots, Trees, or Plants, of the value of 5s. or destroying them

Stealing Children with their apparel

Bigamy, or Marrying more Wives or Husbands than one (now punishable with transportation)

Assaulting and Cutting, or Burning Clothes

Counterfeiting the Copper Coin, &c.
Marriage, solemnizing clandestinely
Manslaughter, or killing another without Malice, &c.
Cutting or Stealing Timber Trees, &c. &c. &c.
Stealing a Shroud out of a Grave
Watermen carrying too many passengers in the Thames, if
    any drowned

By the middle years of the century, transportation had
become not only a penal policy but also a commercial operation
that was making handsome profits. Private contractors transported the felons and sold them on the American market as
cheap labour. The price varied, according to age, sex, health
and skill, but a good craftsman might fetch as much as £25. As
the number of convicts sent to America in the mid-eighteenth
century amounted to 100,000 or more, it was by any estimate a
considerable business. Looking back on this business in 1785,
a select committee of Parliament regarded it with satisfaction,
as a system that reconciled all interests, even those of the
convicts:

> The old system of transportation to America answered every
> good purpose that could be expected of it; it tended directly
> to reclaim the convicts and make them good citizens; the
> climate was good and the means of gaining a livelihood easy,
> so that country magistrates could safely be entrusted with the
> power of inflicting it; it applied to the whole country and not
> only to London; it was cheap, the men being taken out in
> Jamaica or tobacco ships; the colonies seem to have apprec-
> iated the benefits of the practice; the convicts were usually
> removed to the backwoods, away from the temptations of the
> cities, and the public order does not seem to have suffered.

No wonder that same Committee lamented the loss of the
American colonies in 1776, an event that brought to an end this
profitable and expedient solution to English lawlessness.

But the idea of transportation, despite the loss of America,
was too convenient to be abandoned wholly. As a temporary
solution, and to overcome the inadequacies of English prisons,

a number of hulks were placed around the coast in which criminals could be held ready for transportation to foreign parts at a later date.

In the meantime, the search for foreign parts continued. America was out. Canada would not accept the convicts. In the West Indies, the plantation owners were already the happy beneficiaries of the slave-trade. Africa was suggested, but those who knew Africa reported that the only result of transportation to the Gambia and Senegal would be a quick and unpleasant death for convicts, guards and settlers alike. At last, the discoveries of Captain Cook in New South Wales were recalled.

The suitability of Australia was first raised in 1779 when a committee of the House of Commons, still anxiously casting about for some foreign land to replace America, began to question Joseph (later Sir Joseph) Banks, the scientist of Cook's expedition:

Joseph Banks, Esquire, being requested, in case it should be thought expedient to establish a Colony of convicted Felons in any distant Parts of the Globe, from whence their Escape might be difficult, and where, from the Fertility of the Soil, they might be enabled to maintain themselves, after the First Year, with little or no Aid from the Mother Country, to give his Opinion what Place would be most eligible for such Settlement? informed your Committee, That the Place which appeared to him best adapted for such a Purpose, was *Botany Bay*, on the coast of *New Holland*, in the *Indian* Ocean, which was about Seven Months Voyage from *England*; that he apprehended there would be little Probability of any Opposition from the Natives, as, during his Stay there, in the Year 1770, he saw very few, and did not think there were above Fifty in all the Neighbourhood, and had Reason to believe the Country was very thinly peopled; those he saw were naked, treacherous, and armed with Lances, but extremely cowardly, and constantly retired from our People when they made the least Appearance of Resistance: He was in this Bay in the End of APRIL and Beginning of MAY 1770, when the Weather was mild and moderate; that the Climate, he apprehended, was similar to that about TOULOUSE, in the South of FRANCE, having found the Southern Hemisphere colder than the Northern, in such Proportion, that any given Climate in the Southern answered to one in the Northern about Ten Degrees nearer to the Pole; the Proportion of rich Soil was small in Comparison to the barren, but sufficient to support a very large Number of People; there were no tame Animals, and he saw no wild Ones during his Stay of Ten Days, but he observed the Dung of what were called KANGOUROUS, which were almost the Size of a middling Sheep, but very swift, and difficult to catch; some of those Animals he saw in another Part of the Bay, upon the same Continent; there were no Beasts of Prey, and he did not doubt but our Oxen and Sheep, if carried there, would thrive and increase; there was great Plenty of Fish, he took a large Quantity by hauling the Seine, and struck several Stingrays, a kind of Skate, all very large; one weighed 336 Pounds. The Grass was long and luxuriant, and there were some eatable Vegetables, particularly a Sort of wild Spinage; the Country was well supplied with Water; there was Abundance of Timber and Fuel, sufficient for any Number of Buildings, which might be found necessary. Being asked How a Colony of that Nature could be subsisted in the Beginning of their Establishment? he answered, They must certainly be furnished, at landing, with a full Year's Allowance of Victuals, Raiment, and Drink; with all Kinds of Tools for labouring the Earth, and building Houses: with Black Cattle, Sheep, Hogs, and Poultry; with Seeds of all Kinds of EUROPEAN Corn and Pulse; with Garden Seeds; with Arms and Ammunition for their Defence; and they should likewise have small Boats, Nets, and Fishing-tackle; all of which, except Arms and Ammunition, might be purchased at the CAPE OF GOOD HOPE; and that afterwards, with a moderate Portion of Industry, they might, undoubtedly, maintain themselves without any Assistance from *England*. He recommended sending a large Number of Persons, Two or Three Hundred at least; their Escape would be difficult, as the Country was far distant from any Part of the Globe inhabited by EUROPEANS. . . . And being asked, Whether he conceived the Mother Country was likely to reap any Benefit from a Colony established in BOTANY BAY? he replied, If the People formed among themselves a Civil Government, they would necessarily increase and find Occasion for many EUROPEAN Commodities; and it was not to be doubted, that a Tract of Land such as *New Holland*, which was larger than the Whole of EUROPE, would furnish Matter of advantageous Return.

Was this the place the committee had been seeking? 'New Holland', a land sufficiently far away, untamed but potentially luxuriant, occupied only by miserable tribesmen, a place almost impossible to escape from? Banks had not been quite candid with the committee (elsewhere he had written of New South Wales, 'a soil so barren could not be supposed to yield much to the support of man'), but his words fired the committee with cautious enthusiasm. It reported to Parliament in these terms:

It is not in the power of the Government now to dispose of convicts in North America, and every other plan of transportation hitherto suggested appears to be fraught with difficulties. Sending atrocious criminals to unhealthy places where their labour may be used, and their lives hazarded in the place of better citizens, may in some cases be advisable, and in the case of capital respites is indisputably just.

The plan of establishing a colony or colonies of young convicts in some distant part of the globe, and in new-discovered countries, where the climate is healthy and the means of support attainable, is equally agreeable to the dictates of humanity and sound policy, and might prove in the result advantageous both to navigation and commerce.

It might be of public utility if the laws which now direct and authorise the transportation of certain convicts to His Majesty's colonies and plantations in North America were made to authorise transportation to any other part of the globe that may be found expedient.

The implication, clearly, was that New South Wales might be just the place.

Sir Joseph Banks, on account of his testimony, has been called the 'Father of Australia'. But for a long time, in the manner of stately conservative bureaucracies, nothing happened. The government realized that transportation to an unknown land was a different matter from selling convicts on the American market as cheap labour. A convict colony in New South Wales would have to be founded and supported for some years. That meant considerable expense. But by 1784, with the penal system groaning and the hulks bursting, something had to be done. Late in that year, an Act 'for the effectual transportation of felons and other offenders' legally re-established the policy of transportation, though the destination was still unspecified.

Once again, Africa was considered. But the Africa Company refused the gift of convicts and even Edmund Burke, no friend to crime and disorder, declared that he 'could not reconcile it with justice that persons respited from death should, after a mock display of mercy, be compelled to undergo it, by being sent to a country where they could not live'. There was nothing for it, if transportation was to work, but to take Banks' recommendation, choose New South Wales, and damn the expense. Accordingly, in August 1786 the Home Secretary, Lord Sydney, conveyed to the Treasury the decision of the Pitt government:

The several gaols and places for the confinement of felons in this kingdom being in so crowded a state that the greatest danger is to be apprehended, not only from their escape, but from infectious distempers, which may hourly be expected to break out amongst them, his Majesty, desirous of preventing by every possible means the ill consequences which might happen from either of these causes, has been pleased to signify to me his royal commands that measures should immediately be pursued for sending out of this kingdom such of the convicts as are under sentence or order of transportation.

The Nautilus sloop, which, upon the recommendation of a committee of the House of Commons, had been sent to explore the southern coast of Africa, in order to find out an eligible situation for the reception of the said convicts, where from their industry they might soon be likely to obtain means of subsistence, having lately returned, and it appearing by the reports of her officers that the several parts of the coast which they examined between 15°50' south and the latitude of 33°00' are sandy and barren, and from other causes unfit for a settlement of that description, his Majesty has thought it advisable to fix upon Botany Bay, situated on the coast of New South Wales, the latitude of about 33 degrees south, which, according to the accounts given by the late Captain

Cook, as well as the representatives of persons who accompanied him during his last voyage, and who have been consulted upon the subject, is looked upon as a place likely to answer the above purposes.

I am, therefore, commanded to signify to your Lordships his Majesty's pleasure that you do forthwith take such measures as may be necessary for providing a proper number of vessels for the conveyance of 750 convicts to Botany Bay, together with such provisions, necessaries, and implements for agriculture as may be necessary for their use after their arrival.

According to the best opinions that can be obtained, it is supposed that a quantity of provisions equal to two years' consumption should be provided, which must be issued from time to time, according to the discretion of the superintendent, in the expenditure of which he will, of course, be guided by the proportion of food which the country and the labour of the new settlers may produce.

In the meantime, I have only to recommend it to your Lordships to cause every possible expedition to be used in preparing the shipping for the reception of the said convicts, and for transporting the supplies of provisions and necessaries for their use to the place of their destination.

Once the decision was made the details followed quickly and Sydney was able to give the Treasury a full plan of action:

HEADS OF A PLAN

Heads of a plan for effectually disposing of convicts, and rendering their transportation reciprocally beneficial both to themselves and to the State, by the establishment of a colony in New South Wales, a country which, by the fertility and salubrity of the climate, connected with the remoteness of its situation (from whence it is hardly possible for persons to return without permission), seems peculiarly adapted to answer the views of Government with respect to the providing a remedy for the evils likely to result from the late alarming and numerous increase of felons in this country, and more particularly in the metropolis.

It is proposed that a ship of war of a proper class, with a part of her guns mounted, and a sufficient number of men on board for her navigation, and a tender of about 200 tons burthen, commanded by discreet officers, should be got ready as soon as possible to serve as an escort to the convict ships, and for other purposes hereinafter mentioned.

That, in addition to their crews, they should take on board two companies of marines to form a military establishment on shore (not only for the protection of the settlement, if requisite, against the natives, but for the preservation of good order), together with an assortment of stores, utensils, and implements, necessary for erecting habitations and for agriculture, and such quantities of provisions as may be proper for the use of the crews.

As many of the marines as possible should be artificers, such as carpenters, sawyers, smiths, potters (if possible), and some husband-men. To have a chaplain on board, with a surgeon, and one mate at least; the former to remain at the settlement.

That these vessels should touch at the Cape of Good Hope, or any other places that may be convenient, for any seed that may be requisite to be taken from thence, and for such live stock as they can possibly contain, which, it is supposed, can be procured there without any sort of difficulty, and at the most reasonable rates, for the use of the settlement at large.

That Government should immediately provide a certain number of ships of a proper burthen to receive on board at least seven or eight hundred convicts, and that one of them should be properly fitted for the accommodation of the women, to prevent their intercourse with the men.

That these ships should take on board as much provisions as they can possibly stow, or at least a sufficient quantity for two years' consumption; supposing one year to be issued at whole allowance, and the other year's provisions at half allowance, which will last two years longer, by which time, it is presumed, the colony, with the livestock and grain which may be raised by a common industry on the part of the new settlers, will be fully sufficient for their maintenance and support.

That, in addition to the crews of the ships appointed to contain the convicts, a company of marines should be divided between them, to be employed as guards for preventing ill consequences that might arise from dissatisfaction amongst the convicts, and for the protection of the crew in the navigation of the ship from insults that might be offered by the convicts.

That each of the ships should have on board at least two surgeons' mates, to attend to the wants of the sick, and should be supplied with a proper assortment of medicines and instruments, and that two of them should remain with the settlement.

After the arrival of the ships which are intended to convey the convicts, the ship of war and tender may be employed in obtaining livestock from the Cape, or from the Molucca Islands, a sufficient quantity of which may be brought from either of those places to the new settlement in two or three trips; or the tender, if it should be thought most adviseable, may be employed in conveying to the new settlement a further number of women from the Friendly Islands, New Caledonia, Etc., which are contiguous thereto, and from whence any number may be procured without difficulty; and without a sufficient proportion of that sex it is well-known that it would be impossible to preserve the settlement from gross irregularities and disorders.

The whole regulation and management of the settlement should be committed to the care of a discreet officer, and provision should be made in all cases, both civil and military, by special instructions under the Great Seal or otherwise, as may be thought proper.

Upon the whole, it may be observed with great force and truth that the difference of expence (whatever method of carrying the convicts thither may be adopted) that this mode of disposing of them and that of the usual ineffectual one is too trivial to be a consideration with Government, at least in comparison with the great object to be obtained by it, especially now the evil is increased to such an alarming degree, from the inadequacy of all other expedients that have hitherto been tried or suggested.

With this, some estimates of yearly cost were sent to the nervous Treasury, and these included £1,497. 10s. for the salary of officials, £1,268. 10s. for implements, and £2. 19s. 6d. to clothe each convict.

After so much dithering and delay, matters now began to move fast. Captain Arthur Phillip was given his Commission in

October, to be Governor of the new colony. Orders in council were issued promptly for the gathering of the fleet and for the disposition of the convicts. Officials were chosen, supplies were arranged. By May 1787 the fleet was ready to sail. An experiment in living was about to begin in a new land.

*

The motive of the British government in all these dealings was quite clear. Transportation to New South Wales was an attempt to export criminality by an administration which was frightened by the rotten underlayer of English (and Irish) society yet resolutely refused to tackle the problem at source. It was, the House of Commons declared, 'a measure of absolute necessity, in order to remove the inconvenience which arose from the crowded state of the gaols in the different parts of the kingdom.' As to the nature of this far-flung settlement, whether it was to be a colony or a prison was not the main question; no doubt it would develop in unforeseen ways, following a pattern of evolution that was peculiar to itself. In the meantime, the chief aim was to remove the convicts as quickly as possible, for transportation was 'the only remedy for an evil that required immediate redress'.

The policy, even at the time, had its opponents who attacked it on the grounds of justice and practicality. The sharpest and angriest critic was Alexander Dalrymple, the Hydrographer to the East India Company, who put together a formidable list of objections on behalf of his Company employers:

> We often see men grow giddy, and lose their senses, by being carried to a great elevation: This happens, not less frequently in the Political, than in the Natural, World: To what other cause can we ascribe the Plan of the present Ministry? to send the *Convicts* [to] *Botany Bay*, on the East-Side of NEW HOLLAND, whilst this country is still smarting for a war with the old Colonies, whom she found herself unable to keep in dependence.
>
> The Plan the Ministry propose, must rather be considered as *encouraging* than *detering Felons*; for, What is the Punishment intended to be inflicted? *Not* to make the Felons

undergo *servitude* for the *benefit of others*, as was the Case in America: but to place them, as Their own Masters, in a temperate Climate, where they have *every object of comfort* or *Ambition* before them! and although it might be going too far to suppose, This will *incite* men to become *Convicts*, that they may be *comfortably* provided for; yet sure it cannot *deter* men, inclined to commit Theft and Robbery, to know that, in case they are detected and convicted, *all* that will happen to them is, That they will be sent, at the Publick Expense, to a good Country and temperate Climate, where they will be their own Masters!

If this be considered, it cannot be doubted that an intercourse kept with *New Holland*, would act as a two edged weapon, to promote smuggling at home, and to cover that worst of all kinds of illicit *Trade*, The increase of the Trade of Foreigners, carried out by Englishmen, The English Property, under false colours: which though most *injurious* to THIS COUNTRY, is less the Object of Ministerial Attention, as its *effect* on their Darling, the *Revenue*, being *not immediate*, is *not* obvious, to their narrow-sighted Policy.

If we had *nothing* to *lose* in the EAST, it might be a curious subject of *Political Speculation*, to see what kind of Government, a Set of lawless Ragamuffins would constitute. . . . But *We* having so much at Stake, It is, surely Madness, or Folly, to expose our possessions and Commerce in the East Indies, to so much hazard, without some great and important Motive.

The *Security* of the *Individual* is the FIRST OBJECT, for which men submitted to be *governed*; and that Government which does not *secure* the *Individual*, is weak or prostituted: but what Man is there, in London, who can go to bed in safety without a House full of Servants?

The alarming Number of Convicts, and the great difficulty of keeping them in England, without danger to Society, and the many civil consequences of the Hulks, not to mention the very great expense, are *Facts*, too well known, to be doubted or denied, but *reverse* of wrong, is *not right*: and although I am an Enemy to the proposed Scheme, I am no Advocate for continuing the present abominable practice.

If this mad Scheme must go on, I hope we shall not hear of any *Grants* of *Land* to *Ministers*, or their Friends, whereby this Country may be linked to that *Land* of *Thieves*.

At every point, Dalrymple's objections struck the chord of contemporary prejudice, and no doubt Pitt's ministry received these admonitions with blushes. The government certainly had no desire to make things easy for criminals, to infringe trading charters, or to deny commerce the use of sweated labour. But to try to solve the intractable problem of English lawlessness, the government swept away the objections and instituted, quite unintentionally, a programme of penal experiment in which the idea of redemption through useful work had as much place as the infliction of pain and vindictive punishment. It was a secret acknowledgement that a youth who stole a shilling out of desperate hunger might, under more fortunate circumstances, become a pioneer, a town-father and a patriarch.

CHAPTER THREE

THE FIRST FLEET

The land to which Captain Arthur Phillip was appointed Governor, a land designated in the official documents as 'our territory called New South Wales', was nothing but a vast unknown. Claimed by the English as a result of the 'discovery' and 'possession' by Captain Cook, it lay between 10°37' south and 43°39' south. But its coast was only a sketch in Cook's Journal, its interior a mystery, and its geography largely a blank. A description of flora and fauna, such as it was, existed only in a few scant passages among the writings of Cook and Banks. For the Europeans, its native inhabitants were as alien as the man in the moon.

Yet within the profundity of this ignorance, William Pitt and his ministers discovered one consoling fact. Their only certainty (and perhaps their only care) was that they had at last found a 'place to which offenders shall be transported for the term or terms of their several sentences'.

By the spring of 1787, the government had prepared a final Commission, investing Phillip with his titles and responsibilities, and a set of Instructions for the carrying out of his tasks:

With these our Instructions you will receive our Commission under our Great Seal constituting and appointing you to be our Captain-General and Governor-in-Chief of our territory called New South Wales, extending from the northern cape or extremity of the coast, called Cape York, in the latitude of 10°37' south, to the southern extremity of the said territory of New South Wales, or South Cape, in the latitude of 43°39' south, and of all the country inland to the westward as far as the 135° of east longitude, reckoning from the meridian of Greenwich, including all the islands adjacent in the Pacific Ocean within the latitudes aforesaid – 10°37' south and 43°39' south – and of all towns, garrisons, castles, forts, and all other fortifications or other military works which may be hereafter erected upon the said territory or any of the said islands, with directions to obey such orders and instructions as shall from time to time be given to you, under our signet and sign manual, or by our Orders in our Privy Council.

The Instructions, trying to foresee unknown eventualities from a distance of half the globe, were a hotch-potch of exhortation and cautious practical advice. They imposed a heavy weight on the capable shoulders of Captain Phillip:

And whereas we have ordered that about 600 male and about 180 female convicts now under sentence or order of trans-portation, whose names are contained in the list hereunto annexed, should be removed out of the gaols and other places of confinement in this our kingdom, and be put on board the several transport ships which have been taken up for their reception: It is our royal will and pleasure that as soon as the said convicts, the several persons composing the civil establishments, and the stores, provisions, &c., provided for their use shall be embarked on board the Supply tender and the transport ships named in the margin [Alexander Scarborough, Lady Penhryn, Friendship, Charlotte, Prince of Wales, Golden Grove, Fishbourn], and be in readiness to depart, that you do take them under your protection and proceed in the Sirius with the said tender and transports to the port on the coast of New South Wales situated in the latitude of 33°41', called by the name of Botany Bay, agree-ably to the instructions you will be furnished with by the Commissioners of our Admiralty, in pursuance of our Royal commands already signified to them.

According to the best information which We have ob-tained, Botany Bay appears to be the most eligible situation upon the said coast for the first establishment, possessing a commodious harbour and other advantages which no part of the coast hitherto discovered affords. It is therefore our will and pleasure that you do, immediately upon your landing, after taking measures for securing yourself and the people who accompany you as much as possible from any attacks or interruptions of the natives of that country, as well as for the preservation and safety of the public stores, proceed to the cultivation of the land, distributing the convicts for that purpose in such manner, and under such inspectors or overseers, and under such regulations as may appear to you to be necessary and best calculated for procuring supplies of grain and ground provisions. The assortment of tools and utensils which have been provided for the use of the convicts and other persons who are to compose the intended settlement are to be distributed according to your discretion, and according to the employment assigned to the several persons. In the distribution, however, you will use every proper degree of economy, and be careful that the Commissary do transmit an account of the issues from time to time to the Commissioners of our Treasury, to enable them to judge of the propriety or expediency of granting further supplies. The clothing of the convicts, and the provisions issued to them and the civil and military establishments, must be accounted for in the same manner.

The increase of the stock of animals must depend entirely upon the measures you may adopt on the outset for their preservation, and as the settlement will be amply supplied with vegetable productions, and most likely with fish, fresh provisions, excepting for the sick and convalescents, may in a great degree be dispensed with. For these reasons it will become you to be extremely cautious in permitting any cattle, sheep, hogs, &c., intended for propagating the breed of such animals to be slaughtered, until a competent stock may be acquired to admit of your supplying the settlement from it with animal food, without having further recourse to the places from whence such stock may have originally been obtained.

It is our will and pleasure that the productions of all descriptions, acquired by the labour of the convicts, should be considered as a public stock, which we so far leave to your disposal that such parts thereof as may be requisite for the subsistence of the said convicts and their families, or the subsistence of the civil and military establishments of the settlement, may be applied by you to that use. The remainder of such productions you will reserve as a provision for a further number of convicts, which you may expect will shortly follow you from hence, to be employed under your direction in the manner pointed out in these our instructions to you.

You are to endeavour, by every possible means, to open an intercourse with the natives, and to conciliate their affections, enjoining all our subjects to live in amity and kindness with them. And if any of our subjects shall wantonly destroy them, or give them any unnecessary interruption in the exercise of their several occupations, it is our will and pleasure that you do cause such offenders to be brought to punishment according to the degree of the offence. You will endeavour to procure an account of the numbers inhabiting the neighbourhood of the intended settlement, and report your opinion to one of our Secretaries of State in what manner our intercourse with these people may be turned to the advantage of this colony.

And whereas, as from the great disproportion of female convicts to those of the males who are put under your superintendence, it appears advisable that a further number of the former should be introduced into the new intended settlement, you are, whenever the Sirius or the tender shall touch at any of the islands in those seas, to instruct their commanders to take on board any of the women who may be disposed to accompany them to the said settlement. You will, however, take especial care that the officers who may happen to be employed upon this service do not on any account exercise any compulsive measures or make use of fallacious pretences for bringing away any of the said women from the places of their present residence.

And whereas We have by our Commission bearing date [2 April, 1787] given and granted unto you full power and authority to emancipate and discharge from their servitude any of the convicts under your superintendence who shall for their good conduct and a disposition to industry be deserving of favour: It is our will and pleasure that in every such case you do issue your warrant to the Surveyor of Lands to make surveys of and mark out in lots such lands upon the said territory as may be necessary for their use, and when that shall be done, that you do pass grants thereof with all convenient speed to any of the said convicts so emancipated, in such proportions and under such conditions and acknowledgements as shall hereafter be specified, viz., To every male shall be granted thirty acres of land, and in case he shall be married twenty acres more, and for every child who may

44

be with them at the settlement at the time of making the said grant a further quantity of ten acres, free of all fees, taxes, quit-rents or other acknowledgements whatsoever, for the space of ten years, Provided that the person to whom the said land shall have been granted shall reside within the same and proceed to the cultivation and improvement thereof, reserving only to us such timber as may be growing or to grow hereafter upon the said land which may be fit for naval purposes and an annual quit-rent of . . . after the expiration of the term or time before mentioned. You will cause copies of such grants as may be passed to be preserved, and make a regular return of the said grants to the Commissioners of our Treasury and the Lords of the Committee of our Privy Council for trade and plantations.

And whereas it is likely to happen that the convicts who may after their emancipation, in consequence of this instruction, be put in possession of lands will not have the means of proceeding to their cultivation without public aid: It is our will and pleasure that you do cause every such person you may so emancipate to be supplied with such a quantity of provisions as may be sufficient for the subsistence of himself and also of his family for twelve months, together with an assortment of tools, &c., utensils and such a proportion of seed, grain, cattle, sheep, hogs, &c., as may be proper and can be spared from the general stock of the settlement.

And whereas many of our subjects employed upon military service at the said settlement, and others who may resort thither upon their private occupations, may hereafter be desirous of proceeding to the cultivation and improvement of the land, and as we are disposed to afford them every reasonable encouragement in such an undertaking, it is our will and pleasure that you do, with all convenient speed, transmit a report of the actual state and quality of the soil at and near the said intended settlement, the probable and most effectual means of improving and cultivating the same, and of the mode and upon what terms and conditions, according to the best of your judgment, the said lands should be granted, that proper instructions and authorities may be given to you for that purpose.

And whereas it is our Royal intention that every sort of intercourse between the intended settlement at Botany Bay, or other place which may be hereafter established on the coast of New South Wales and its dependencies, and the settlements of our East India Company, as well as the coasts of China, and the islands situated in that part of the world to which any intercourse has been established by any European nation, should be prevented by every possible means: It is our royal will and pleasure that you do not, on any account, allow craft of any sort to be built for the use of private individuals which might enable them to effect such intercourse, and that you do prevent any vessesl which may at any time hereafter arrive at the said settlement from any of the ports before-mentioned from having communication with any of the inhabitants residing within your government, without first receiving especial permission from you for that purpose.

Although there was much in these Instructions to please the liberal and far-sighted Governor Phillip, specially the hints as to future colonization by free settlers, he was also only too well aware that the members of his expedition were not a dedicated group of pioneers and craftsmen but rather a bunch of criminal ruffians.

For the sentence of transportation was not supposed to be an easy option. It was the second most severe punishment in the English penal code and was regarded with such horror that many prisoners, offered according to custom the choice between transportation and death, willingly chose death. There were always those, said a contemporary record, 'who preferred hanging and were immediately gratified with the object of their choice.' Nor was the policy to choose the most docile or useful from among the prisoners waiting in the hulks. The first candidates for transportation were the incorrigible and the trouble-makers:

When the hulks are full up to their establishment, and the convicted offenders in the different counties are beginning to accumulate, a vessel is taken up for the purpose of conveying a part of them to New South Wales. As selection is in the first instance made of all the male convicts under the age of 50, who are sentenced to transportation for life and for 14 years; and the number is filled up with such from among those sentenced to transportation for 7 years, as are the most unruly in the hulks, or are convicted of the most atrocious crimes; with respect to female convicts, it has been customary to send, without exception, all whose state of health will admit of it, and whose age does not exceed 45 years.

This was the raw material with which Governor Phillip was expected to work.

Six transports – the *Alexander, Scarborough, Prince of Wales, Charlotte, Lady Penrhyn* and *Friendship* – were chartered to carry the convicts; and they were to be accompanied by the small naval vessels *Sirius* and *Supply*, and by three store-ships – the *Fishburn, Golden Grove* and *Borrowdale*. The chartering of the ships and the victualling and preparation of the fleet were, as usual, put out to private contract:

The terms of contract with the owners of the above ships are 10 shillings p. ton. p. month till their arrival at Deptford. The transports are fitted up for the convicts the same as for carrying troops, except the security, which consists in very strong and thick bulkheads, filled with nails and run across from side to side 'tween decks abaft the mainmast, and with loop-holes to fire between decks in case of irregularities. The hatches are well secured down by cross-bars, bolts, and locks, and are likewise rail'd round from deck to deck with oak stanchions. There is also a barricadoe of plank about 3 feet high, armed with pointed prongs of iron, on the upper deck abaft the mainmast, to prevent any connection between the marines and the ship's company with the convicts. Centinels are placed at the different hatchways, and a guard always under arms on the quarter-deck of each transport, in order to prevent any improper behaviour of the convicts, as well as to guard ag't any surprise. Each transport has on board a certain quantity of each kind of utensils proper for agriculture, as well as a distribution of other stores for the use of the colony, so distributed that an accident happening to one ship would not have those disagreeable consequences which must be the case if ye whole of one species of stores was on board each ship. The victuallers are loaded with two years' provisions of all species for the marines, convicts, &c., for two years from the time of their landing in New South Wales.

Ships for the transport of convicts were chosen primarily for cheapness and were in most other respects less than perfect. Very often they were cramped, leaky and had poor sailing qualities. The tonnage of the First Fleet was a mere 3,892 tons, which was expcted to carry 1,400 people (including 586 male convicts and 192 female among whom were also thirteen children) some 15,000 miles to Botany Bay by way of Rio de Janeiro and the Cape of Good Hope.

The same principles of economy and penny-pinching that went into the choice of ships were, in general, applied also to the preparation of the fleet, so much so that the conscientious Phillip was forced to complain often and vehemently. He found many things to worry him in the early months of 1787. The convicts already gathered into the transports were over-crowded. Many were disabled and too many were sick. The clothing was miserably insufficient. He needed more tools and implements, and more medical supplies. The anti-scorbutics would not last the journey. He harried Lord Sydney's office with a voluminous correspondence for which he saw no reason to apologize. On 18 March he wrote:

> These complaints, my dear sir, do not come unexpected, nor were they unavoidable. I foresaw them from the beginning, and repeatedly pointed them out when they might have been so easily prevented at a very small expense, and with little trouble to those who have had the conducting of this business. At present the evils complained of may be redressed, and the intentions of the Government by this expedition answered. But if now neglected it may be too late hereafter, and we may expect to see the seamen belonging to the transports run from the ships to avoid a jail distemper, and may be refused entrance into a foreign port.
>
> The situation in which the magistrates sent the women on board the Lady Penrhyn stamps them with infamy; though almost naked and so very filthy that nothing but cloathing them could have prevented them from perishing, and which could not be done in time to prevent a fever, which is still on board that ship, and where there are many with veneral complaints that must spread in spite of every precaution I may take hereafter, and will be fatal to thousands.
>
> There is a necessity for doing something for the young

man who is on board the ship as surgeon, or I fear that we shall lose him, and then a hundred women will be left without any assistance, several of them with child. Let me repeat my desire that orders immediately may be given to increase the convict allowance of bread – 16 lb. of bread for forty-two days is very little; to supply all the convicts with fresh meat while they remain at Portsmouth, the sick with some small quantity of wine; lighters to be ordered to attend the Alexander while that ship is smoaked, &c.; to wash and cloathe the convicts that are still to be sent down before they are put on board the transports; and to have one of the transports ordered to serve as a hospital ship.

This is a long letter, but it is my duty to repeat complaints that may be redressed, and which I am certain you desire equally with myself.

Surrounded by negligence and shortcomings Governor Phillip, perhaps in self-defence, penned an undated memorandum in which he considered his responsibilities and reflected on the best way to meet them. The document, particularly in its vision of a colony allowed to develop in freedom under the law, is a testament to the Governor's sound judgment and humanity:

By arriving at the settlement two or three months before the transports, many and very great advantages would be gained. Huts would be ready to receive the convicts who are sick, and they would find vegetables, of which it may naturally be supposed they will stand in great need, as the scurvy must make a great ravage amongst people naturally indolent and not cleanly.

Huts would be ready for the women; the stores would be properly lodged and defended from the convicts, in such manner as to prevent their making any attempt on them. The cattle and stock would be likewise properly secured, and the ground marked out for the convicts; for lists of those intended to be sent being given to the commanding officers, mentioning their age, crimes, trades, and character, they might be so divided as to render few changes necessary, and the provisions would be ready for issuing without any waste. But if convicts, provisions, &c., must be landed a few days after the ships' arrival, and consequently nearly at the same time, great inconvenience will arise, and to keep the convicts more than a few days on board, after they get into a port, considering the length of time which they must inevitably be confined, may be attended with consequences easier to conceive than to point out in a letter. Add to this, fevers of a malignant kind may make it necessary to have a second hospital.

The confining the convicts on board the ships requires some consideration. Sickness must be the consequence in so long a voyage (six months may be allowed for the voyage – that is, from the time of leaving England to the arrival in Botany Bay), and disagreeable consequences may be feared if they have the liberty of the deck. The sooner the crimes and behaviour of these people are known the better, as they may be divided, and the greatest villains particularly guarded against in one transport.

The women in general, I should suppose, possess neither virtue nor honesty. But there may be some for theft who still retain some degree of virtue, and these should be permitted to keep together, and strict orders to the master of the transport be given that they are not abused and insulted by the ship's company – which is said to have been the case too often when they were sent to America.

The greatest care will be necessary to prevent any of the convicts from being sent that have any veneral complaints. During the passage, when light airs or calms permit it, I shall visit the transports to see that they are kept clean, and receive the allowance ordered by Government; and at these times shall endeavour to make them sensible of their situation, and that their happiness and misery is in their own hands; that those who behave well will be rewarded by being allowed to work occasionally on the small lots of land set apart for them, and which they will be put in possession of at the expiration of the time for which they are transported.

On landing in Botany Bay, it will be necessary to throw up a slight work as a defence against the natives – who, though only seen in small numbers by Captain Cook, may be very numerous on other parts of the coast – and against the convicts; for this, my own little knowledge as a field engineer will be sufficient, and will be the work of a few days only; but some small cannon for a redoubt will be necessary. Within the lines the stores and provisions will be secured, and I should hope that the situation I should be able to take may admit of having the small rivers between the garrison and the convicts so situated that I may be able to prevent their having any intercourse with the natives.

I shall think it a great point gained if I can proceed in this business without having any dispute with the natives, a few of which I shall endeavour to persuade to settle near us, and who I mean to furnish with everything that can tend to civilise them, and to give them a high opinion of their new guests; for which purpose it will be necessary to prevent the transports' crews from having any intercourse with the natives, if possible. The convicts must have none, for if they have, the arms of the natives will be very formidable in their hands, the women abused, and the natives disgusted.

The keeping of the women apart merits great considera-tion, and I don't know but it may be best if the most abandoned are permitted to receive the visits of the convicts in the limits allotted them at certain hours, and under certain restrictions. Something of this kind was the case on Mill Bank formerly. The rest of the women I should keep apart, and by permitting the men to be in their company when not at work they will, I should suppose, marry, in which case they should be encouraged, if they are industrious, by being allowed to work one day in the week more than the unmarried on their own lots of ground.

The natives may, it is probable, permit their women to marry and live with the men after a certain time, in which case I should think it necessary to punish with severity the man who used the woman ill; and I know of no punishment likely to answer the purpose of deterring others so well as exiling them to a distant spot, or to an island, where they would be obliged to work hard to gain their daily subsistence, and for which they would have the necessary tools; but no two to be together, if it could be avoided.

Rewarding and punishing the convicts must be left to the Governor; he will likely be answerable for his conduct, and death, I should think, will never be necessary. In fact, I doubt if the fear of death ever prevented a man of no principle from committing a bad action. There are two crimes that would merit death – murder and sodomy; for either of these crimes I should wish to confine the criminal till an opportunity offered of delivering him as a prisoner to the natives of New Zealand, and let them eat him. The dread of this will operate much stronger than the fear of death.

As the getting a large quantity of stock together will be my first great object, till that is obtained the garrison should, as in Gibraltar, not be allowed to kill any animal without first reporting his stock and receiving permission.

Women may be brought from the Friendly and other islands, a proper place prepared to receive them, and where they will be supported for a time, and lots of land assigned to such as marry with the soldiers of the garrison.

As I would not wish convicts to lay the foundations of an Empire, I think they should ever remain separated from the garrison and other settlers that may come from Europe, and not be allowed to mix with them, even after the seven or fourteen years for which they are transported may be expired.

The laws of this country will, of course, be introduced in New South Wales, and there is one that I would wish to take place from the moment his Majesty's forces take possession of the country – that there can be no slavery in a free land, and consequently no slaves.

The cloathing for the convicts will last for a certain time, after which, what means should I have of furnishing them with materials for their making their own cloathes?

It will be necessary to know how far I may permit the seamen and marines of the garrison to cultivate spots of land when the duty of the day is over; and how far I can give them hopes that the grounds they cultivate will be secured to them hereafter; likewise, how far I may permit any of the garrison to remain, when they are ordered home in consequence of relief.

By what I am informed, hatchets and beads are the articles for barter, with a few small grindstones for the Chiefs; and as when they use a light they hold it in their hands, small tin lamps on a very simple construction must be very acceptable.

The saddles I mentioned will be absolutely necessary for two or three horsemen, who will examine the country to a certain distance, when it might be dangerous to attempt it with half the garrison; for I am not of the general opinion that there are very few inhabitants in this country, at least so few as have been represented; but this article I take upon myself, as likewise the knives, &c., that I mentioned.

Such fruit trees and cuttings that will bear removing should be added to the seeds carried from England, as likewise roots that will bear keeping that length of time out of the ground.

A certain quantity of the articles of husbandry, stores, corn, seeds, and of the articles for traffick, should be put on board the Berwick [*Sirius*], that in case of an accident we may not be in immediate want of those things, and the same on board the store-ship in which the Lieutenant-Governor goes.

Thanks largely to Phillip's vigilance, the fleet was ready to sail in the early part of May 1787. The transports had been fumigated and the health of the convicts improved. Regulation clothing was issued – light garments only, quite unsuitable for exposed voyages, since the Admiralty objected to wool and flannel as unhygienic carriers of bugs and infection. The food, both for this First Fleet and for the convict fleets that followed, was surprisingly good. A ship's surgeon, writing some years later, commented:

The rations are both good and abundant – three-quarters of a pound of biscuit being the daily allowance of bread, while each day the convict sits down to dinner of either beef, pork or plum-pudding, having pea soup four times a week, and a pot of gruel every morning, with sugar or butter in it. Vinegar is issued to the messes weekly; and as soon as the ship has been three weeks at sea, each man is served with an ounce of lime-juice and the same of sugar daily, to guard against scurvy, while two gallons of good Spanish red wine and 140 gallons of water are put on board for issuing to each likewise – three to four gills of wine weekly, and three quarts of water daily, being the general allowance.

Strangely, the ration was better than the one allowed for soldiers and sailors; but whether the convicts received their ration was in the hands of the ship's master who, on many transports, saw to it that his prisoners were cheated out of at least half their allowance.

On Sunday, 13 May 1787, the fleet sailed from Spithead, a motley collection of small vessels liable to make heavy weather of such a long ocean voyage. To keep the ill-suited, labouring fleet together required Governor Phillip's sharp eye and determination. The *Charlotte* and *Lady Penrhyn*, the Governor admitted, 'sail very badly'. The *Alexander* was a particularly wet ship. The accommodation for the convicts was foul and dark:

> Two rows of sleeping-berths, one above the other extend on each side of the between-decks, each berth being 6 feet square, and calculated to hold four convicts, every one thus possessing 18 inches space to sleep in – and ample space, too! The hospital is in the fore-part of the ship, with a bulkhead across, separating it from the prison, having two doors with locks to keep out intruders; while a separate prison is built for the boys, to cut off all intercourse between them and the men. Strong wooden stanchions, thickly studded with nails, are fixed round the fore and main hatchways, between decks, in each of which is a door with three padlocks, to let the convicts out and in, and secure them at night. The convicts by these means have no access to the hold through the prison, a ladder being placed in each hatchway for them to go up and down by, which is pulled on deck at night.

The suffering of the convicts between decks, even on such a well-conducted voyage as that of the First Fleet, was always considerable and sometimes unbearable. An Irish political convict on a later voyage gave an account of typically bad times:

> When the ship was becalmed in the tropics, the suffering of the imprisoned wretches in the steaming and crowded hold was piteous to see. They were so packed that free movement was impossible. The best thing to do was to sit each on his or her berth, and suffer in patience. The air was stifling and oppressive. There was no draught through the barred hatches. The deck above them was blazing hot. The pitch dropped from the seams, and burned their flesh as it fell. There was only one word spoken or thought – one yearning idea in every mind – water, cool water to slake the parching thirst. Two pints of water a day were served out to each convict – a quart of half-putrid and blood-warm liquid. It was a woeful sight to see the thirsty souls devour this allowance as soon as their hot hands seized the vessel. Day in and day out, the terrible calm held the ship, and the

consuming heat sapped the lives of the pent-up convicts. Hideous incidents filled the days and nights as the convict ship sailed southward with her burden of disease and death. The mortality among the convicts was frightful. Weakened and depressed by the long drought, the continuous heat, and the poisonous atmosphere, they succumbed to the fever in its first stages.

Another sad account, written in 1790, expresses the full range of misery endured by prisoners on a convict ship:

Would I could draw an eternal shade over the remembrance of this miserable part of our voyage – miserable, not so much in itself, as rendered so by the villany, oppression, and shameful peculation of the masters of two of the transports. The bark I was on board of was, indeed, unfit, from her make and size, to be sent so great a distance; if it blew but the most trifling gale she was lost in the waters, of which she shipped so much; that, from the Cape, the unhappy wretches, the convicts, were considerably above their waists in water, and the men of my company, whose berths were not so far forward, were nearly up to the middles. In this situation they were obliged, for the safety of the ship, to be pen'd down; but when the gales abated no means were used to purify the air by fumigations, no vinegar was applied to rectify the nauseous steams issuing from their miserable dungeon. Humanity shudders to think that of nine hundred male convicts embarked in this fleet, three hundred and seventy are already dead, and four hundred and fifty are landed sick and so emaciated and helpless that very few, if any of them, can be saved by care or medicine, so that the sooner it pleases God to remove them the better it will be for this colony.

The irons used upon these unhappy wretches were barbarous. The contractors had been in the Guinea trade, and had put on board the same shackles used by them in that trade, which are made with a short bolt, instead of chains that drop between the legs and fasten with a bandage about the waist, like those at the different gaols: these bolts were not more than three-quarters of a foot in length, so that they could not extend either leg from the other more than an inch or two at most; thus fettered, it was impossible for them to move but at the risk of both their legs being broken. Inactivity at sea is a sure bane, as it invites the scurvy equal to, if not more than, salt provisions; to this they were consigned, as well as a miserable pittance of provisions, altho' the allowance by Government is ample; even when attacked by disease their situations were not altered, neither had they any comforts administered. The slave trade is merciful compared with what I have seen in this fleet; in that it is the interests of the masters to preserve the healths and lives of their captives, they having a joint benefit with the owners; in this, the more they can withhold from the unhappy wretches the more provisions they have to dispose of at a foreign market, and the earlier in the voyage they die the longer they can draw the deceased's allowance to themselves; for I fear few of them are honest enough to make a just return of the dates of their deaths to their employers. It, therefore, highly concerns Government to lodge, in future, a controlling power in each ship over these low-lifed, barbarous masters, to keep them honest, instead of giving it to one man (an agent) who can only see what is going forward in his ship.

My feelings never have been so wounded as in this voyage, so much so, that I never shall recover my accustomed vivacity and spirits; and had I been empowered, it would have been the most grateful task in my life to have prevented so many of my fellow-creatures so much misery and death.

But there was something about the departure of the First Fleet that was not wholly sad. There was an air of expectation, even among the convicts, a realization perhaps that here was a moment worthy of historical record. Captain Watkin Tench caught a glimpse of this mood in his narrative of the voyage:

By ten o'clock 13th May, 1787 we had got clear of the Isle of Wight, at which time, having little pleasure in conversing with my own thoughts, I strolled down among the convicts, to observe their sentiments at this juncture. A very few excepted their countenances indicated a high degree of satisfaction though in some, the pang of being severed, perhaps for ever, from their native land, could not be wholly suppressed; in general, marks of distress were more perceptible among the men than the women; for I recollect to have seen but one of those affected on the occasion, 'Some natural tears she dropp'd, but wip'd them soon.' After this the accent of sorrow was no longer heard; more genial skies and change of scene banished repining and discontent, and introduced in their stead cheerfulness and acquiescence in a lot, now not to be altered.

Once the fleet had cleared the Channel, Governor Phillip was in a cheerful frame of mind and spoke of 'our difficulty as ended'. On the run down to Tenerife, the master of the *Scarborough* thought he detected a plot among the convicts and transferred the two ring-leaders to the *Sirius* to be given twenty-four lashes each. Reaching Tenerife on 3 June, the ships replenished their stores of fresh food and Phillip took stock of the state of the fleet. Health had improved since leaving Portsmouth, though eighty-one convicts were still sick, including ten with venereal disease. Nine convicts had died at sea, most of them on board the fetid and leaky *Alexander*.

They departed from Tenerife on 10 June and began the long, sweltering ocean passage to Rio de Janeiro. The extraordinary circuitous route, across the Atlantic and back, had been chosen to avoid the summer calms off the African coast, but the great distance to be covered in hot weather put an extra stress on the already cramped prisoners. The women convicts, in particular, were troublesome. Foolishly, both men and women were imprisoned in the same ship and this gave the shipboard authorities some lively and difficult moments. John White, the surgeon of the *Charlotte*, related that the women had to be battened down at night:

The hatches over the place where they were confined could not be suffered to lay off, during the night, without a promiscuous intercourse immediately taking place between them and the seamen and marines. In some ships the desire of the women to be with the men was so uncontrollable that neither shame nor the fear of punishment could deter them from making their way through the bulk heads to the apartments assigned to the seamen.

'These damned troublesome whores,' as Lieutenant Clark of the *Friendship* called some of his female convicts, continued to be a turbulent nuisance, despite the floggings and punishment in irons. The sailors and the marines also had to be watched. One marine was given 100 lashes for immoral intercourse with a convict.

After a slow passage, with the fleet being continually held up by the slowness of the *Lady Penrhyn*, the ships entered Rio on 5 August. Despite a further six deaths at sea, Governor Phillip was pleased by the steady progress and found morale satisfactory. His worst problem was the light clothing, which soon disintegrated, and had to be replaced with sacking to cover the many convicts who were 'nearly naked'.

A month was spent recuperating in Rio, then the fleet ran for the Cape of Good Hope under boisterous winds so that even the deeply laden transports made good time. On 13 October they anchored in Table Bay. The sick list now numbered ninety-three convicts and twenty marines. Governor Phillip had some difficulty finding fresh provisions but managed to buy fodder and livestock. Having transferred the women convicts from the *Friendship*, he moved the sheep in. This seemed a great improvement to Lieutenant Clark, who welcomed the sheep because 'we will find them much more agreeable shipmates than the women'.

On 13 November they left Table Bay and began the final and worst leg of the journey. Winds were hard, up to gale force, though sometimes interspersed with fogs and sudden calms. Sails were often carried away. The transports wallowed and dipped their rails below the waves. Conditions in the prison-holds were atrocious. At the end of the year came more storms, with hail and snow. 'The convict women,' wrote Surgeon Bowes of the *Lady Penrhyn*, 'were so terrified that most of them were down on their knees at prayers, and in less than one hour after it had abated they were uttering the most horrid oaths and imprecations that could proceed out of the mouths of such abandoned prostitutes as they are.'

On 5 January 1788, the coast of Van Diemen's Land was sighted through the gale. The Governor had already transferred from the flagship *Sirius* into the swift little *Supply*, to make the landfall first and to prepare the way for the rest of the fleet. On 18 January, the *Supply* was safely within Botany Bay and two days later the rest of the fleet were at anchor also. Captain Watkin Tench gave vent to the general sense of relief and achievement:

> The wind was now [19 January] fair, the sky serene, though a little hazy, and the temperature of the air delightfully pleasant: joy sparkled in every countenance, and congratulations issued from every mouth. Ithaca itself was scarcely more longed for by Ulysses, than Botany Bay by the adventurers who had travelled so many thousand miles to take possession of it.
>
> 'Heavily in clouds came on the day' which ushered in our arrival. To us it was 'a great, an important day,' though I hope the foundation, not the fall, of an empire will be dated from it.
>
> Thus, after a passage of exactly thirty-six weeks from Portsmouth, we happily effected our arduous undertaking, with such a train of unexampled blessings, as hardly ever attended a fleet in a like predicament. To what cause are we to attribute this unhoped for success? I wish I could answer to the liberal manner in which Government supplied the expedition. But when the reader is told, that some of the necessary articles allowed to ships on a common passage to the West Indies, were with-held from us; that portable soup, wheat, and pickled vegetables were not allowed; and that an inadequate quantity of essence of malt was the only antiscorbutic supplied, his surprise will redouble at the result of the voyage. For it must be remembered, that the people thus sent out were not a ship's company with every advantage of health and good living, which a state of freedom produces; but the major part a miserable set of convicts, emaciated from confinement, and in want of cloaths, and almost every convenience to render so long a passage tolerable.

The members of the First Fleet were right to congratulate themselves. They had accomplished a remarkable feat of navigation. Eleven ill-assorted vessels had kept together through storm and calm for 15,000 miles, a distance which they covered in 184 sailing days. And in the whole voyage only thirty-two people had died (two of them in accidents) which was the more impressive because the majority of the fleet consisted not of healthy, eager emigrants, but of disease-ridden and undisciplined convicts cramped into intolerable quarters. Surgeon Bowes had this view of his charges on the *Lady Penrhyn*:

> I believe I may venture to say there was never a more abandoned set of wretches collected in one place at any period than are now to be met with in this ship in particular, and I am credibly informed the comparison holds with regard to all convicts in the fleet. The greater part of them are so totally abandoned and calloused to all sense of shame and even common decency that it frequently becomes indispensably necessary to inflict corporal punishment upon them, and sorry I am to say that this rigid mode of proceeding has not the desired effect, since every day furnishes proofs of their being more hardened in their wickedness, nor do I conceive it possible in their present situation to adopt any plan to induce them to behave like rational or even human beings. Perpetually thieving the clothes from each other, nay almost from their backs, may be ranked amongst the least of their crimes. The oaths and imprecations they daily make use of in their common conversation and little disputes with each other far exceed anything of the kind to be met with amongst the most profligate wretches in London. Nor can their matchless hypocrisy be equalled except by their base ingratitude, many of them plundering the sailors (who have at every port they arrived at spent almost the whole of the wages due to them in purchasing different articles of wearing apparel and other things for their accommodation) of their necessary clothes and cutting them up for some purpose of their own.

The comparatively few deaths in the First Fleet, especially when compared to the painful voyage of the Second Fleet during which over a third of the convicts perished amid scenes of dreadful brutality, resulted, as all the narratives agreed, from the care taken by the officers of the fleet under the keen supervision of Governor Phillip. David Collins, appointed to be Judge-Advocate of the new colony, expressed their satisfaction in this way:

Thus, under the blessing of God, was happily completed, in eight months and one week, a voyage which, before it was undertaken, the mind hardly dared venture to contemplate, and on which it was impossible to reflect without some apprehension as to its termination. This fortunate completion of it, however, afforded even to ourselves as much matter of surprise as of general satisfaction; for in the above space of time we had sailed five thousand and twenty-one leagues; had touched at the American and African continents; and had at last rested within a few days sail of the antipodes of our native country, without meeting any accident in a fleet of eleven sail, nine of which were merchantmen that had never before sailed in that distant and imperfectly explored ocean: and when it is considered, that there was on board a large body of convicts, many of whom were embarked in a very sickly state, we might be deemed peculiarly fortunate, that of the whole number of all descriptions of persons coming to form the new settlement, only thirty-two had died since their leaving England, among whom were to be included one or two deaths by accidents; although previous to our departure it was generally conjectured, that before we should have been a month at sea one of the transports would have been converted into an hospital ship. But it fortunately happened otherwise; and the spirits visible in every eye were to be ascribed to the general joy and satisfaction which immediately took place on finding ourselves arrived at that port which had been so much and so long the subject of our most serious reflections, the constant theme of our conversations.

The tender colony on the shores of New South Wales, born in such infamous circumstances, had at least made a responsible first step which promised something better for the future.

CHAPTER FOUR

18 JANUARY 1788: BOTANY BAY AND BEYOND

They had endured 15,000 miles of tedium, misery and privation. At 2.15 p.m. on 18 January 1788, a pleasant day of summer in the southern hemisphere, the little *Supply* slipped past the point into Botany Bay. From the deck, anxious faces saw before them a calm landscape, strange but not unfriendly, which they gazed on with a feeling of heartfelt relief:

At 3, the boats were hoisted out and Governor Phillip & some officers belonging to the *Supply*, with Lieutenant Dawes and Myself, landed on the north side of the Bay and just looked at the face of the Country which is, as Mr. Cook remarks, very much like the Moors in England, except that there is a great deal of very good grass & some small timber trees. We went a little way up the bay to look for water but finding none, we returned abreast of the *Supply*, where we observed a group of the Natives. We put the boats onshore near where we observed two of their canoes lying. They immediately got up & called to us in a menacing tone and at the same time brandishing their spears or lances. However, the Governor shewed them some beads and ordered a man to fasten them to the stern of the canoe. We then made signs that we wanted water, when they pointed round the point on which they stood and invited us to land there; on landing, they directed us by pointing to a very fine stream of fresh water. Governor Phillip then advanced toward them alone & unarmed, on which one of them advanced towards him but would not come near enough to receive the beads which the Governor held out for him, but seemed very desirous of having them & made signs for them to be lain on the ground, which was done. He (the Native) came on with fear & trembling and took them up, & by degrees came so near as to receive looking glasses, etc., & seemed quite astonished at the figure we cut in being cloathed. I think it is very easy to conceive the ridiculous figure we must appear to these poor creatures, who were perfectly naked. We soon after took leave of them & returned on board.

Here, at least, were no extraordinary dangers, no horror came stalking out of the bush.

But after the first thanksgiving came, as so often, the first disappointment. Within two days the whole fleet had arrived and cautious feelers were extended into the unknown land. They had expected some trouble from the native inhabitants but soon their fears were at rest. Naturally suspicious and armed to resist force, the inhabitants were instead greeted by Governor Phillip's peaceful overtures. To these, the natives responded almost immediately with disarming trust and curiosity. Lieutenant King, prepared to view the indigenous peoples as biological specimens, found himself the subject of a keener amazement:

They wanted to know of what sex we were, which they explained by pointing where it was distinguishable. As they took us for women, not having our beard grown, I ordered one of the people to undeceive them in this particular, when they made a great shout of admiration, and pointing to the shore, which was but ten yards from us, we saw a great number of Women & Girls, with infant children on their shoulders, make their appearance on the beach – all in *puris naturalibus, pas même la feuille de figueur*. Those natives who were round the boats made signs for us to go to them & made us understand their persons were at our service. However, I declined this mark of their hospitality but shewed a handkerchief, which I offered to one of the women, pointing her out. She immediately put her child down & came alongside the boat and suffered me to apply the handkerchief where Eve did the Fig leaf; the natives then set up another very great shout & my female visiter returned on shore. As the evening

Overleaf. An early map of Port Jackson and Botany Bay. From Watkin Tench, *Complete Account of the Settlement at Port Jackson*, 1793

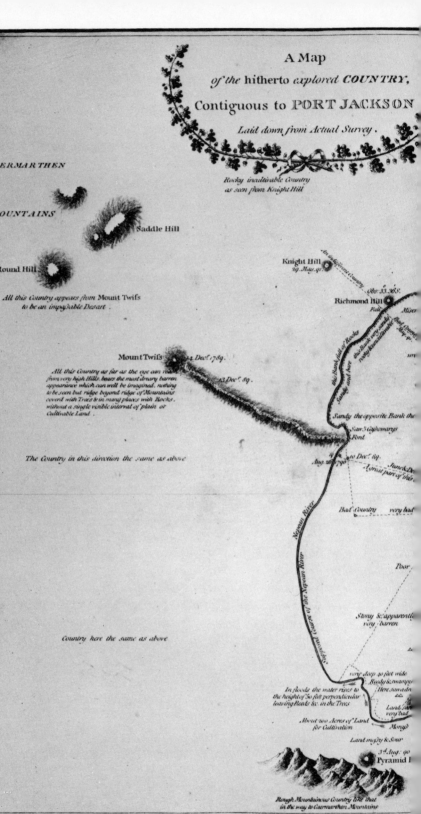

A Map

of the hitherto *explored* COUNTRY,

Contiguous to PORT JACKSON

Laid down from Actual Survey .

Rocky incultivable Country
as seen from Knight Hill

CAERMARTHEN

MOUNTAINS

Saddle Hill

Round Hill

Knight Hill
29. May. 91.

Obs. 33.36 S.

Richmond Hill

All this Country appears from Mount Twiss
to be an impassable Desart .

Mount Twiss *14 Dec.r 1789*

13 Dec.r 89 .

All this Country as far as the eye can reach
from very high Hills, bears the most dreary barren
appearance which can well be imagined, nothing
to be seen but ridge beyond ridge of Mountains
cover'd with Trees & in many places with Rocks,
without a single visible interval of plain or
Cultivable Land .

Sandy the opposite Bank the

Sir S. Gibsonarys
Font

Aug. w.th 90 *10 Dec.r 89.*

The Country in this direction the same as above

Bad Country   very bad

Nepean River

Poor

Stony & apparently
very barren

Country here the same as above

very deep 30 feet wide
Reedy & swampy
Here some ad n

In floods the water rises to
the height of 80 feet perpendicular
leaving Reeds &c. in the Trees

Land Sur
very bad

About 200 Acres of Land
for Cultivation

Land mossy & Sour

3.d Aug. 90
Pyramid I

Rough Mountainous Country like that
in the way to Caermarthen Mountains

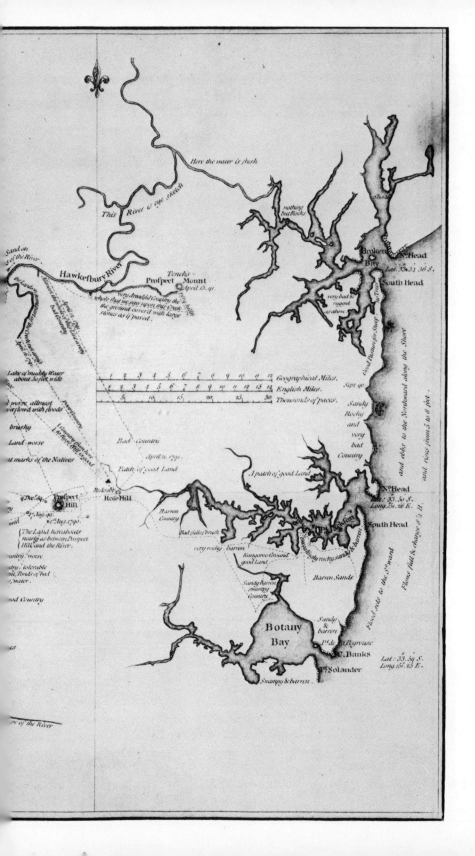

was coming on fast and we were twelve miles from the fleet, it was time to return. We wished the natives good be wi' ye, which they repeated. We got on board about midnight.

No, the trouble was not likely to be with the natives but with the land. Perhaps Cook had misled them. Surgeon Bowes was not impressed by Botany Bay:

> Upon first sight, one would be induced to think this a most fertile spot, as there are great numbers of very large and lofty trees reaching almost to the water's edge and every vacant spot between the trees appears to be covered with verdure. But upon a nearer inspection, the grass is found long and coarse, the trees very large and in general hollow, and the wood itself fit for no purposes of building or anything but the fire. The soil to a great depth is nothing but a black sand. Add to this, that every part of the grown is in a manner covered with black and red ants of a most enormous size.

Quickly deciding that Botany Bay was unsuitable for his colony, Phillip explored to the north with three boats. He returned on 23 January having found what he wanted. He reported his discovery to Lord Sydney in England:

> We got into Port Jackson early in the afternoon, and had the satisfaction of finding the finest harbour in the world, in which a thousand sail of the line may ride in the most perfect security.
>
> The different coves were examined with all possible expedition. I fixed on the one that had the best spring of water and in which the ships can anchor so close to the shore that at a very small expence quays may be made at which the largest ships may unload.
>
> This cove, which I honoured with the name of Sydney, is about a quarter of a mile across at the entrance, and half a mile in length.

Port Jackson and Sydney Cove, though not ideal in every respect (apart from the magnificent harbour), were good ground on which to plant a colony. Captain Watkin Tench of the Marines, writing after the passage of the seasons, gave the country high marks in general for productivity, convenience and health:

> The general face of the country is certainly pleasing, being diversified with gentle ascents, and little winding vallies, covered for the most part with large spreading trees, which afford a succession of leaves in all seasons. In those places where trees are scarce, a variety of flowering shrubs abound, most of them entirely new to an European, and surpassing in beauty, fragrance, and number, all I ever saw in an uncultivated state: among these, a tall shrub, bearing an elegant white flower, which smells like English May, is particularly delightful, and perfumes the air around to a great distance. The species of trees are few, and, I am concerned to add, the wood universally of so bad a grain, as almost to preclude a possibility of using it: the increase of labour occasioned by this in our buildings has been such, as nearly to exceed belief.
>
> Fresh water is found but in inconsiderable quantities. For the common purposes of life there is generally enough, but we know of no stream in the country capable of turning a mill: and the remark made by Mr Anderson, of the dryness of the country round Adventure Bay, extends without exception to every part of it which we have penetrated.
>
> Fish, which our sanguine hopes led us to expect in great quantities, do not abound. In summer they are tolerably plentiful, but for some months past very few have been taken.
>
> The climate is undoubtedly very desirable to live in. In summer the heats are usually moderated by the sea breeze, which sets in early; and in winter the degree of cold is so slight as to occasion no inconvenience; once or twice we have had hoar frosts and hail, but no appearance of snow. The thermometer has never risen beyond 84, nor fallen lower than 35, in general it stood in the beginning of February at between 78 and 74 at noon. Nor is the temperature of the air less healthy than pleasant. Those dreadful putrid fevers by which new countries are so often ravaged, are unknown to us; and excepting a slight diarrhoea, which prevailed soon after we had landed, and was fatal in very few instances, we are strangers to epidemic diseases.

Immediately, the fleet sailed up the coast to the new territory at Port Jackson. On the 26th, in an informal act of possession, a pole was erected at the landing place and the Union Jack run up amid volleys from the marines. 'At sunset the Governor, the principal officers of the settlement and many of the private soldiers drank His Majesty's health and Success to the new Colony.'

But the health of the colony was precarious, since the convicts had landed with a variety of shipboard diseases, and success for the venture was far from certain. Governor Phillip had been dealt a poor hand which he must play as best he could. He had over a thousand souls to feed from uncleared, virgin ground, and of these 736 were convicts among whom too many were idle, sick, work-shy and incompetent. They were 'helpless and a deadweight on the settlement.' The provisions the fleet had brought were supposed to last two years, but much had been spoiled on the long voyage, the breeding stock died, the tools and implements were of the poorest quality so that they soon broke or became unserviceable. There was not even a plough.

There was no remedy but work and Governor Phillip set to with speed and decision. Lieutenant King was despatched to found the subsidiary colony on Norfolk Island. Male convicts were put in tents on shore from where several escaped to the French fleet that had recently arrived in Botany Bay. But the commander, La Pérouse, refused to accept them and they returned for punishment. On 6 February the women convicts, segregated in the transports until now, were landed amid scenes of spectacular debauch:

At five o'clock this morning, all things were got in order for landing the whole of the women, and 3 of the ships long-boats came alongside us to receive them; previous to their quitting the ship, a strict search was made to try if any of the many things which they had stolen on board could be found, but their artifice eluded the most strict search, and at six o'clock p.m. we had the long wished for pleasure of seeing the last of them leave the ship. They were dressed in general very clean, and some few amongst them might be said to be well dressed. The men convicts got to them very soon after they landed, and it is beyond my abilities to give a just description of the scene of debauchery and riot that ensued during the night.

On the next day, the 7th, Phillip formally instituted the government of the colony. The marines paraded, the convicts were drawn up, the Governor read out his Commission and then addressed his charges, letting them know what wretches they were and what misery they could expect unless they mended their ways:

> The Governor harangued the convicts, telling them that he had tried them hitherto to see how they were disposed. That he was now thoroughly convinced there were many amongst them incorrigable, and that he was persuaded nothing but severity would have any effect upon them, to induce them to behave properly in future. He also assured them that if they attempted to get into the women's tents of a night there were positive orders for firing upon them. That they were very idle – not more than 200 out of 600 were at work, that the industrious should not labour for the idle. If they did not work, they should not eat. In England, theiving poultry was not punished with death; but here where a loss of that kind could not be supplied, it was of the utmost consequence to the settlement, as well as every other species of stock, as they were preserved for breeding. Therefore stealing the most trifling article of stock or provisions should be punished with Death. That, however such severity might militate against his humanity and feelings towards his fellow creatures, yet that Justice demanded such rigid execution of the Laws and they might implicitly relye upon justice taking place. Their labour would not be equal to that of an husbandman in England, who has a wife and family to provide for. They would never be worked beyond their abilities, but every individual should contribute his share to render himself and Comunity at large happy and comfortable as soon as the nature of the settlement will admit of. That they should be employed erecting houses for the different officers, next for the marines, and lastly for themselves.

The one certainty was that they were alone in their efforts and could expect help from no one. The Instructions which Phillip carried from England cast them off from the world. 'Every sort of intercourse,' said the Instructions, 'between the intended settlement at Botany Bay and the settlements of our

East India Company should be prevented by every possible means: It is our Royal will and pleasure that you do not on any account allow craft of any sort to be built for the use of private individuals, which might enable them to effect such intercourse.' Life or death was in their own hands.

By early February work was well under way but it was hard going. The Governor reported to England:

The clearing the ground for the people, and for erecting storehouses, was begun as soon as the ships got round, a labour of which it will be hardly possible to give your lordship a just idea.

The necks of land that form the different coves, and near the water for some distance, are in general so rocky that it is surprising such large trees should find sufficient nourishment; but the soil between the rocks is good, and the summits of the rocks, as well as the whole country round us, with few exceptions, are covered with trees, most of which are so large that the removing them off the ground, after they are cut down, is the greatest part of the labour; and the convicts, naturally indolent, having none to attend them but overseers drawn from amongst themselves, and who fear to exert any authority, makes this work go on very slowly.

Your lordship will permit me to observe that our situation, though so very different from what might be expected, is nevertheless the best that offered. My instructions did not permit me to detain the transports a sufficient length of time to examine the coast to any considerable distance. It was absolutely necessary to be certain of a sufficient quantity of fresh water, in a situation that was healthy, and which the ships might approach within a reasonable distance for the conveniency of landing the stores and provisions; and I am fully persuaded that we should never have succeeded had it been attempted to move them only one mile from where they were landed. There are some parts of this harbour where the trees stand at a considerable distance from each other, and where there are small runs of water, which shall be cultivated when our numbers permit; and when the country can be examined, I make no doubt but some good situations will be found that have water, which I have never yet been able to find either in Botany Bay, or in this harbour, but in very small streams.

Some land that is near, and where the trees stand at a considerable distance from each other, will, as soon as convicts can be spared, be cultivated by the officers for raising a little corn for their stock, and this I have endeavoured to promote as much as possible, for I fear the consequences if a ship should be lost in her passage out with provisions.

From the first, the convicts gave trouble. They were never the disciplined workforce that the raw situation required. Those who had been feckless rogues in England were not changed by a journey of 15,000 miles. In particular, the presence of the women, who had little to do, was a constant provocation to disorder, both among the male convicts and among the members of the staff. Lieutenant Clark called the women's tents 'the whore's camp. I would call it by the name of sodom, for there is more sin commited in it than in any other part of the world.' And Arthur Bowes gave a description of some typical misconduct:

> This day our carpenter, one of our sailors, and a Boy belonging to the *Prince of Wales* were caught in the women's tents. They were drummed out of the camp with the Rogue's March playing before them, and the boy had petticoats put upon him. They had all of them their hands tyed behind 'em. The anarchy and confusion which prevails throughout the camp and the audacity of the Convicts, both men and women, is arrived to such a pitch as is not to be equalled, I believe, by any set of villains in any other spot upon the Globe. The men seize upon any sailors on shore who are walking near the women's camp, beat them most unmercifully, and desire them to go on board.

In the face of this, and to assure the safety of a colony that could only rest on unremitting labour and mutual assistance, Phillip was forced to bring in severe penalties, as he told his master back home:

> Your Lordship will not be surprized that I have been under the necessity of assembling a Criminal Court. Six men were condemned to death. One, who was the head of the gang, was executed the same day; the others I reprieved. They are to be

exiled from the settlement, and when the season permits, I intend they shall be landed near the South Cape, where, by their forming connexions with the natives, some benefit may accrue to the public.

The behaviour of the convicts was bad, but an even more serious bar to progress was their incompetence and lack of skill. Phillip found that little could be done, against the burden of the land and the weather, with so few craftsmen:

As there are only twelve convicts who are carpenters, as many as could be procured from the ships have been hired to work on the hospital and store-houses. The people were healthy when landed, but the scurvy has for some time appeared amongst them, and now rages in a most extraordinary manner. Only sixteen carpenters could be hired from the ships, and several of the convict carpenters were sick. It was now the middle of February; the rains began to fall very heavy, and pointed out the necessity of hutting the people; convicts were therefore appointed to assist the detachment in this work.

As a consequence, the colony was already falling behind in the road to self-sufficiency and would need, as Phillip pointed out, care, provisions and reinforcements from England for some time to come:

The great labour in clearing the ground will not permit more than eight acres to be sown this year with wheat and barley. At the same time the immense number of ants and field-mice will render our crops very uncertain.

Part of the live stock brought from the Cape, small as it was, has been lost, and our resource in fish is also uncertain. Some days great quantities are caught, but never sufficient to save any part of the provisions; and at times fish are scarce.

Your Lordship will, I presume, see the necessity of a regular supply of provisions for four or five years, and of clothing, shoes and frocks in the greatest proportion. The necessary implements for husbandry and for clearing the ground brought out will with difficulty be made to serve the time that is necessary for sending out a fresh supply.

The labour of the convicts shall be, as is directed, for the public stock, but it is necessary to permit a part of the convicts to work for the officers, who, in our present situation, would otherwise find it impossible to clear a sufficient quantity of ground to raise what is absolutely necessary to support the little stock they have; and I am to request that your Lordship will be pleased to direct me to what extent that indulgence may be granted the officers of the garrison.

The Sirius shall be sent to the northward to barter for stock, and which shall be employed solely for the purpose of increasing the breed of such cattle as she may procure. The Supply is no ways calculated for this service, as in the least sea her decks are full of water.

The very small proportion of females makes the sending out an additional number absolutely necessary, for I am certain your Lordship will think that to send for women from the Islands, in our present situation, would answer no other purpose than that of bringing them to pine away in misery.

In the midst of his woes, the Governor had one piece of good fortune. The native inhabitants – the aborigines – from whom the colony might well have expected resentment and aggression, were in fact little trouble. So long as the natives were treated fairly and decently they responded in kind. Phillip's Instructions had commanded him 'to open an intercourse with the natives, and to conciliate their affections, enjoining all our subjects to live in amity and kindness with them.' But considering the ruffians involved, this injunction was easier said than done. The Governor, however, was determined to lead by example; the evidence of his actions and his writing shows that his interest in and benevolence towards the aborigines came from the heart:

With respect to the natives, it was my determination from my first landing that nothing less than the most absolute necessity should ever make me fire upon them, and tho' persevering in this resolution has at times been rather difficult, I have hitherto been so fortunate that it never has been necessary.

When I first landed in Botany Bay the natives appeared on the beach, and were easily persuaded to receive what was

73

offered them, and, tho' they came armed, very readily returned the confidence I placed in them, by going to them alone and unarmed, most of them laying down their spears when desired; and while the ships remained in Botany Bay no dispute happened between our people and the natives. They were all naked, but seemed fond of ornaments, putting the beads of red baize that were given them around their heads or necks. Their arms and canoes being described in 'Captain Cook's Voyage', I do not trouble your Lordship with any description of them.

When I first went in the boats to Port Jackson the natives appeared armed near the place at which we landed, and were very vociferous, but, like the others, easily persuaded to accept what was offered them, and I persuaded one man, who appeared to be the chief, or master, of the family, to go with me to that part of the beach where the people were boiling their meat. When he came near the marines, who were drawn up near the place, and saw that by proceeding he should be separated from his companions, who remained with several officers at some distance, he stopped, and with great firmness seemed by words and acting to threaten if they offered to take any advantage of his situation. He then went on with me to examine what was boiling in the pot, and exprest his admiration in a manner that made me believe he intended to profit from what he saw, and which I made him understand he might very easily by the help of some oyster-shells. I believe they know no other way of dressing their food but by broiling, and they are seldom seen without a fire, or a piece of wood on fire, which they carry with them from place to place, and in their canoes, so that I apprehend they find some difficulty in procuring fire by any other means with which they are acquainted. The boats, in passing near a point of land in the harbour, were seen by a number of men, and twenty of them waded into the water unarmed, received what was offered to them, and examined the boats with a curiosity that gave me a much higher opinion of them than I had formed from the behaviour of those seen in Captain Cook's voyage, and their confidence and manly behaviour made me give the name of Manly Cove to this place.

The first meetings between two peoples so strange to each other – between the Age of Enlightenment and the Age of

Innocence – were naturally fraught with tension. Captain Hunter of the *Sirius* related an encounter during the first days at Port Jackson:

> The armed men with the boughs posted themselves together just by and every one of the men now took up their spears and kept them poised ready for throwing, standing close to the edge of the beach and rocks. When the boat landed, the Old Man came to the side of her and wanted the things which we had held out to the women, to take to them; which we refused and signified to them that we must give the things to the women ourselves. The Old Man, finding us determined, spoke to the women and one of them came into the water to the side of the boat. We ornamented this naked beauty with strings of beads and buttons round her reck, arms and wrists. She appeared rather frightened, altho' she affected a laugh and seemed pleased with her presents. When she retired several of the other women came to the side of the boat, attended by the Old Man. We ornamented these the same as the first. Some came without fear, others trembling and laughing, hesitating before they would come and some just near enough to reach the things. Two of them could not be persuaded to come within 2 or 3 yards of the boat; to those we threw some things and gave the Old Man some for them. The whole of this time the men, who kept their lances ready, were silent and attentive to what was doing. Two men were placed on a separate rock, we supposed to keep a lookout upon the longboat. After having disposed of our trifling presents, we went off to the long boat. As soon as we put off, the men held their spears carelessly and began shouting, laughing and dancing. We counted 72 besides women and children.

It was an occasion, like so many others, resting on the edge of disaster. One wrong step by either party could have plunged the whole community into an abyss in which lay death, warfare and a perpetual blood-feud. That this was on the whole avoided may be put down, first of all, to the geniality of the aborigines and, secondly, to the good endeavours of the English officers under the example and guidance of the Governor. For, as Captain Hunter admitted:

The Governor's plan with respect to the natives was, if possible, to cultivate an acquaintance with them, without their having an idea of our great superiority over them, that their confidence and friendship might be more firmly fixed.

Of course, given the nature of the colony, it was hardly possible that harmony should reign forever. Many of the convicts were only too well tutored in theft, larceny, cheating and fraud, and the aborigines, so candid and open with the newcomers, suffered many acts of injustice which led to friction and sometimes to bloodshed. David Collins, the Judge-Advocate, reported this friction with judicial impartiality:

It was natural to suppose that the curiosity of these people would be attracted by observing, that, instead of quitting, we were occupied in works that indicated an intention of remaining in their country; but during the first six weeks we received only one visit, two men strolling into the camp one evening, and remaining in it for about half an hour. They appeared to admire whatever they saw, and after receiving each a hatchet (of the use of which the eldest instantly and curiously shewed his knowledge, by turning up his foot, and sharpening a piece of wood on the sole with the hatchet) took their leave, apparently well pleased with their reception. The fishing boats also frequently reported their having been visited by many of these people when hauling the seine; at which labour they often assisted with cheerfulness and in return were generally rewarded with part of the fish taken.

Every precaution was used to guard against a breach of this friendly and desirable intercourse, by strictly prohibiting every person from depriving them of their spears, fizgigs, gum, or other articles, which we soon perceived they were accustomed to leave under the rocks, or loose and scattered about upon the beaches.

We had however great reason to believe that these precautions were at first rendered fruitless by the ill conduct of a boat's crew belonging to one of the transports, who, we were told afterwards, attempted to land in one of the coves at the lower part of the harbour, but were prevented, and driven off with stones by the natives. A party of them, consisting of sixteen or eighteen persons, some time after landed on the island, where the people of the Sirius were preparing a garden, and with much artifice, watching their opportunity, carried off a shovel, a spade, and a pick-axe. On their being fired at and hit on the legs by one of the people with small shot, the pick-axe was dropped, but they carried off the other tools.

To such circumstances as these must be attributed the termination of that good understanding which had hitherto subsisted between us and them, and which Governor Phillip laboured to improve whenever he had an opportunity. But it might have been forseen that this would unavoidably happen: the convicts were everywhere straggling about, collecting animals and gum to sell to the people of the transports, who at the same time were procuring spears, shields, fishing-lines, and other articles from the natives to carry to Europe, the loss of which must have been attended with many inconveniences to the owners, as it was soon evident that they were the only means whereby they obtained or could procure their daily subsistence.

From time to time relations became strained and sour, a state of affairs that several officers regretted but had to admit that the fault lay largely on the side of the settlers. Watkin Tench had this to say:

Our intercourse with them was neither frequent or cordial. They seemed studiously to avoid us, either from fear, jealousy or hatred. When they met with unarmed stragglers, they sometimes killed, and sometimes wounded them. I confess that, in common with many others, I was inclined to attribute this conduct, to a spirit of malignant levity. But a farther acquaintance with them, founded on several instances of their humanity and generosity which shall be noticed in their proper places, has entirely reversed my opinion; and led me to conclude, that the unprovoked outrages committed upon them, by unprincipled individuals among us, caused the evils we had experienced. To prevent them from being plundered of their fishing-tackle and weapons of war, a proclamation was issued, forbidding their sale among us; but it was not attended with the good effect which was hoped for from it.

Governor Phillip was ready for trouble from the aborigines; what he did not expect, and what gave him far more aggravation, was trouble with his own force of marines and particularly with their commander Major Robert Ross, the Lieutenant-Governor of the colony. Ross interpreted his orders from England in the narrowest sense only. He was a garrison officer and his men would undertake nothing but garrison duties. And as the danger to the colony from outside forces was slight indeed, the marines looked forward to an idle time. Ross refused to have anything to do with the internal administration of the settlement. He would not administer justice nor, more seriously, would he police the convicts, though he demanded the use of convict labour for his own food and comfort.

This attitude set Phillip an awkward and potentially dangerous problem. His greatest difficulty in the colony was the supervision of the convicts. Without firm discipline, they were liable to get out of hand, and if the marines would not act as guardians Phillip was forced, through lack of manpower, to use convict-overseers – a system of 'trusties'. The system did not work very well and Ross was the first to complain. He resented the Governor's authority, though it was partly Ross's own indifference that had caused Phillip to concentrate power in his own hands. Ross was petty, obstructive and very touchy about his own dignity. He wrote embittered letters back to England:

Take my word for it, there is not a man in this place but wishes to return home; and indeed they have no less than cause, for I believe there never was a set of people so much upon the parrish as this garrison is, and what little we want, even to a single nail, we must not send to the Commissary for it, but must apply to his excellency; and when we do, he always sayes, 'There is but little come out,' and of course it is but little we get, and what we are obliged to take as a mark of favour.

If you want a true description of this country, it is only to be found amongst many of the private letters sent home; however, I will in confidence venture to assure you that this country will never answer to settle in; for altho' I think corn will grow here, yet I am convinced that if ever it is able to maintain the people here, it cannot be in less time than probably a hundred years hence. I therefore think it will be cheaper to feed the convicts on turtle and venison at the London Tavern, than be at the expense of sending them here.

The Governor answered the charges against him with stiff dignity, but the two men – the two most powerful in the colony – could not be reconciled and the antipathy between them was a running sore throughout the difficult first months of the settlement, leading to inefficiency, grievances and mistrust. More than that, Ross, with his narrow military punctilio, indirectly threatened the success of the whole venture; for if the ill-disciplined convicts were unable to get crops sown and reaped in time the settlement might well go down.

In this unsteady manner the little colony was launched on its way. Having to contend with a lack of forethought and care from ministers in England, dissension among his own officers, and an unruly and incompetent convict populace, Governor Phillip was thrown back on his own good judgement and strong sense of responsibility. On the whole he was optimistic, though those around him became less and less so.

It was the little tragedies, the bruising blows of circumstance, that preoccupied the diarists and letter-writers. To some, these seemed overwhelming. Crimes, licentiousness, floggings, sickness, burials. At the lowest point, sometimes an execution. And to raise the spirits a little, an occasional wedding, an occasional birth. The weather, in the first months, was tricky, high but very variable temperatures with sudden violent storms. The streams around Sydney Cove were drying up. The stock animals were coming to the end of the available pasture. Wild dogs had killed some sheep. There was scurvy and then dysentery in the camp, the latter being treated quite effectively with a local red gum.

March continued unsettled. Exploration was undertaken to the north, around Broken Bay, but this was no improvement on Port Jackson. David Collins reported:

The weather proved very unfavourable to an excursion in a country where the residence for each night was to be provided by the travellers themselves; and some of the party returned with dysenteric complaints. The weather at Port Jackson had been equally adverse to labour, the governor finding at his return upwards of two hundred patients under the surgeon's care, in consequence of the heavy rains that had fallen. A building for the reception of the sick was now absolutely necessary, and one, eighty-four feet by twenty-three, was put in hand, to be divided into a dispensary, (all the hospital-stores being at that time under tents,) a ward for the troops, and another for the convicts. It was to be built of wood, and the roof to be covered in with shingles, made from a species of fir that is found here. The heavy rains also pointed out the necessity of sheltering the detachment, and until barracks could be built, most of them covered their tents with thatch, or erected for themselves temporary clay huts.

Construction of the barracks began despite poor workmanship and rotten timber. The lines of a main street were marked out where hogs got underfoot. The approach of the southern winter gave the building work a note of urgency. As usual, the convicts (Collins noted) were not up to the tasks demanded of them:

Although several thefts were committed by the convicts, yet it was in general remarked, that they conducted themselves with more propriety than could have been expected from people of their description; to prevent, however, if possible, the commission of offences so prejudicial to the welfare of the colony, his excellency signified to the convicts his resolution that the condemnation of any one for robbing the huts or stores should be immediately followed by their execution. Much of their irregularity was perhaps to be ascribed to the intercourse that subsisted, in spite of punishment, between them and the seamen from the ships of war and the transports, who at least one day in the week found means to get on shore with spirits.

Notwithstanding it was the anxious care of every one who could prevent it, that the venereal disease might not be introduced into the settlement, it was not only found to exist amongst the convicts, but the very sufferers themselves were known to conceal their having it. To stop this evil, it was ordered by the governor, that any man or woman having and concealing this disorder should receive corporal punishment, and be put upon a short allowance of provisions for six months.

In May 1788, the foundation stone of the Governor's house was laid and Phillip found it necessary to bring to Lord Sydney's attention the unhelpful conduct of Major Ross. The secretary made a list of the livestock, which included only one stallion and three mares, two bulls and five cows, but there were adequate numbers of sheep, pigs and poultry.

On Wednesday, 4 June, the birthday of King George III was celebrated in some style. There was a naval salute and a parade and a band. The convicts were free for the day and each one was issued a pint of grog. All those under sentence were pardoned in honour of the King. And then there was 'a very good entertainment, considering how far we are from Leaden-hall Market.' Surgeon Worgan gave the details:

> It consisted of Mutton, Pork, Ducks, Fowls, Fish, Kanguroo, Sallads, Pies & Preserved fruits. The Potables consisted of Port, Lisbon, Madeira, Teneriffe & good Old English Porter. These went merrily round in bumpers. The toasts after dinner were The King, Queen & Royal Family, the Prince of Wales, Prince William Henry. After this toast, the Governor in a very facetious & judicious manner, mentioned the necessity there was of having a county in order to circum-scribe the situation of our new settlement. He would there-fore take this opportunity of giving it the name of Cumber-land County, mentioning the limits to be Botany Bay to the Southward, Broken Bay to the Northward, & some high land (which he would call Lansdown & Carmathen Hills) about 40 or 50 miles to the westward. He then gave as a toast – The County and the Cumberland Family.

The occasion had all the trappings of established success but Collins was not deceived. The Judge-Advocate knew there was a canker in the rose, for the shortage of provisions was beginning to be felt among the convicts:

> Exemplary punishments seemed about this period to be growing daily more necessary. Stock was often killed, huts and tents broke open, and provisions constantly stolen about the latter end of the week; for among the convicts there were many who knew not how to husband their provisions through the seven days they were intended to serve them, but

were known to have consumed the whole at the end of the third or fourth day. One of this description made his week's allowance of flour (eight pounds) into eighteen cakes, which he devoured at one meal: he was soon after taken speechless and senseless, and died the following day at the hospital, a loathsome putrid object.

The obvious consequence of this want of œconomy was, that he who had three days to live, and nothing to live on, before the store would be again open to supply his wants, must steal from those who had been more provident. . . . And although the convicts, previous to the birth-day, were assembled, and their duty pointed out to them, as well as the certain consequence of a breach or neglect thereof, both by his excellency the governor and the lieutenant-governor, yet it soon appeared that there were some among them so inured to the habits of vice, and so callous to remonstrance, that they were only restrained until a favourable opportunity presented itself.

In July, the transports were due to set sail from Port Jackson, and in the reports that went with them to the Home Department in England, Governor Phillip took stock of his colony. In the long account of his progress Phillip included many shrewd observations of aboriginal life. He noted that the women frequently cut off two joints of the little finger on the left hand, while the men knocked out the right front tooth in the upper jaw and stuck a bone or a stick through the gristle of the nose:

The men hang in their hair the teeth of dogs and other animals, lobsters' claws, and several small bones which they secure by gum, but I never saw the women do this. Their food is chiefly fish – the shark, I believe, they never eat – the fern root, wild fig, and the kernels of a large fruit, that is not unlike a pine-apple, but which when eaten by the French seamen occasioned violent retchings. Their hooks are made from shells, and their lines and nets, I believe, from the flax plant; but I have some that were made from the fur of some animal, and others that appeared to be made of cotton. The cray-fish and lobsters they catch in small hoop-nets, the making of which shows some art, yet they have no kind of cloathing; at the same time they appear to be sensible of the cold, and to dislike the rain very much, putting on their heads when it rains a piece of bark, under which I have seen them shiver. Their huts are generally surrounded by oyster and mussel shells, and their bodies smell of oil. They cannot be called a very cleanly people, yet I have seen one of them, after having in his hand a piece of pork, hold out his fingers for others to smell to, with strong marks of disgust, and though they seldom refused bread or meat, if offered them, I have never been able to make them eat with us, and when they left us they generally threw away the bread and meat; but fish they always accepted, and would broil and eat it.

As well as these notes on native life, Phillip also sent Lord Sydney a comprehensive analysis of the climate, land and natural resources around Port Jackson and concluded, from what he had seen, that the colony would prosper under proper management:

Of the convicts, thirty-six men and four women died on the passage, twenty men and eight women since landing, eleven men and one woman absconded, four have been executed, and three killed by the natives. The number of convicts now employed in erecting the necessary buildings and cultivating the lands only amounts to three hundred and twenty-six, and the whole number of people victualled amounts to nine hundred and sixty-six – consequently we have only the labour of a part to provide for the whole.

Your lordship will doubtless see the necessity of employing a considerable force in the country, and I presume an addition of five hundred men will be absolutely requisite to enable me to detach three or four companies to the more open country near the head of the harbour.

I could have wished to have given your lordship a more pleasing account of our present situation, and am persuaded I shall have that satisfaction hereafter; nor do I doubt but that this country will prove the most valuable acquisition Great Britain ever made; at the same time no country offers less assistance to the first settlers than this does; nor do I think any country could be more disadvantageously placed with respect to support from the mother country, on which for a few years we must entirely depend.

But success could not be achieved unless the policy makers in London took certain prudent steps. The Governor pressed this point very clearly:

> Farmers and people used to the cultivation of lands, if sent out (and without which agriculture will make but a very slow progress), must be supported by Government for two or three years, and have the labour of a certain number of convicts to assist them for that time, after which they may be able to support themselves, and to take the convicts sent out at the expense which Government is put to for their transportation; but then, I presume, none should be sent whose sentence is for a less term than fourteen years. A yearly fine to be paid for the lands granted, after the fifth year, the fine to be in grain, and in proportion to the crop; and this, I should hope, would be the only tax laid on the crops, giving the Church lands in the room of tythes.
>
> The sending out settlers who will be interested in the labour of the convicts, and in the cultivation of the country, appears to me to be absolutely necessary.
>
> Lands granted to officers or settlers will, I presume, be on condition of a certain proportion of the land so granted being cultivated or cleared within a certain time, and which time and quantity can only be determined by the nature of the ground and situation of the lands. And, in that case, when lands are granted to officers the garrison must be sufficient for the service of the place, and to permit such officers occasionally to be absent at the lands they are to cultivate, and for a certain time. They likewise must be allowed convicts, who must be maintained at the expense of the Crown.

Despite its optimistic tone, the message that Phillip sent to London held encouragement and a warning. Development was possible, but an isolated *convict* settlement, without constant support from England and without a reinforcement of farmers and free settlers, was not likely to succeed. Convicts were by nature poor workers and careless citizens at best:

> Every day proves the necessity of proper persons being sent out to superintend the convicts. If a small number of

carpenters and bricklayers are sent out with proper people, who are capable of superintending the convicts, they will soon be rendered serviceable to the State, and without which they will remain for years a burden to Government.

Thus situated, your Lordship will excuse my observing a second time that a regular supply of provisions from England will be absolutely necessary for four or five years, as the crops for two years to come cannot be depended on for more than what will be necessary for seed, and what the Sirius may procure can only be to breed from.

I should hope that few convicts will be sent out this year or the next, unless they are artificers, and after what I have had the honour of observing to your Lordship I make no doubt that proper people will be sent to superintend them. The ships that bring out convicts should have at least the two years' provisions on board to land with them, for the putting the convicts on board some ships and the provisions that were to support them in others, as was done, I beg leave to observe, much against my intimation, must have been fatal if the ship carrying the provisions had been lost.

If the Governor had to rely on the labour and skill of convicts alone, then all the advantage that was likely to accrue to England in this far-flung part of the world might well be lost.

And if the ministers in London read Phillip's reports with attention they had reason to worry; for below the Governor's official good cheer there was a strain of depression and irritability:

The want of temper & the want of harmony in the detachment would not have been mentioned to your Lordship, but that I thought our situation required that a clear idea was given of it. At the same time, I beg leave to assure your Lordship that with regular supplys of provisions, for which we must depend on the Mother Country for a time, I see no difficultys but what a little time & perseverance will do away. A small number of familys to be sent out would do more in cultivating the land than all the convicts under our present circumstances, for they destroy & rob in spight of every possible precaution, & punishments have no effect. They will be better when they are seperated, but I have only two people in the Colony capable of taking charge of a farm.

The very heavy rains we have had for some days has put a stop to all labour, & the natives find it very difficult to support themselves in this season, as few fish are caught. I hope after the ships have sailed to be able to persuade some of them to live near us and every possible means shall be used to reconcile them to us, & to render their situations more comfortable. At present I think it is inferiour to that of the beasts of the field, yet they seem intelligent & merit a better character than what will be given them by Monsieur La Perouse, from what he said to some of our officers.

Governor Phillip, in fact, was not well. He complained of pains in his side aggravated by a fall in rough country. The desperate daily grind of trying to coerce his band of ruffians into necessary labour was wearing him down. The lack of cooperation from Ross and the marines was an extra burden. Nor was the weather kind:

All public labour was suspended for many days in the beginning of the month of August by heavy rain; and the work of much time was also rendered fruitless by its effects; the brick-kiln fell in more than once, and bricks to a large amount were destroyed; the roads about the settlement were rendered impassable; and some of the huts were so far injured, as to require nearly as much labour to repair them as to build them anew. It was not until the 14th of the month, when the weather cleared up, that the people were again able to work. The public works then in hand were the barracks for the marine detachment; an observatory on the west point of the cove; the houses erecting for the governor and the lieutenant-governor; and the shingling of the hospital.

Thefts among the convicts during the bad weather were frequent and a sheep was stolen from the farm on the east side a few nights prior to the birth-day of his royal highness the Prince of Wales, for celebrating of which it had been for some time kept separate from the others and fattened.

Provisions were growing short. Attempts at agriculture were disappointing and livestock was dwindling. The cows were gone, leaving no milk and no butter. The ration for the men was barely sufficient, consisting chiefly of salt meat, flour, rice

The early settlement at Sydney Cove, from the south. From David Collins, *Account of New South Wales*, 1798

and pease, with a few vegetables from the garden. The women had two-thirds of the men's ration, and the children only a third. Phillip gave up his special privileges and had the same ration as the men. Clothes were falling apart without needles or thread to mend them. There was no leather for shoes. There was not even bedding for the sick children. The search of the horizon became more and more anxious, awaiting supply ships from England. The Governor decided to send the *Sirius* to the Cape of Good Hope for emergency provisions. No tea remained, and only a little bad Portuguese wine from Rio de Janeiro. As the *Golden Grove* and the *Fishburn* prepared to depart, the colony seemed utterly abandoned. A woman convict sent home this dejected account:

I take the first opportunity that has been given us to acquaint you with our disconsolate situation in this solitary waste of the creation. Our passage, you may have heard by the first ships, was tolerably favourable; but the inconveniences since suffered for want of shelter, bedding, &c., are not to be imagined by any stranger. However, we have now two streets, if four rows of the most miserable huts you can possibly conceive of deserve that name. Windows they have none, as from the Governor's house, &c., now nearly finished, no glass could be spared, so that lattices of twigs are made by our people to supply their places. At the extremity of the lines, where since our arrival the dead are buried, there is a place called the church-yard; but we hear, as soon as a sufficient quantity of bricks can be made, a church is to be built, and named St. Philip, after the Governor. Notwithstanding all our presents, the savages still continue to do us all the injury they can, which makes the soldiers' duty very hard, and much dissatisfaction among the officers. I know not how many of our people have been killed. . . . The separation of several of us to an uninhabited island was like a second transportation. In short, every one is so taken up with their own misfortunes that they have no pity to bestow upon others. All our letters are examined by an officer, but a friend takes this for me privately. The ships sail to-morrow.

But Phillip continued to battle against failure and in his official correspondence, without glossing over the difficulties, still held out the strong possibility of success:

The Spirit of the Times and some few unexpected difficultys, which already begin to wear away, have prevented my pub-lick letters being so satisfactory as I could wish them. Various accounts will I dare say be given of this country, but I can assure you, my Lord, that the climate is equal to any I ever was in, and the greatest difficultys are already surmounted, or will be before this letter is received. When we first landed a great and voluntary exertion of everyone was necessary, and I felt the disappointment, but which is now no longer of consequence, then as it prevented so much being done as might, if every one had felt themselves interisted as Settlers. We have about 20 acres of ground in cultivation, and those who have gardens have vegitables in plenty and exceeding good in kind. I have no doubt but that a very few years will make this settlement a very desirable one, and fully to answer the end proposed by Government.

And in a progress report prepared for Lord Sydney towards the end of September, the Governor weighed in the balance the trials and the achievements of the infant colony in the first year of its life:

It was now found that very little of the English wheat had vegetated, and a very considerable quantity of barley and many seeds had rotted in the ground, having been heated in the passage, and some much injured by the weevil. All the barley and wheat, likewise, which had been put on board the *Supply* at the Cape were destroyed by the weevil. The ground was, therefore, necessarily sown a second time with the seed which I had saved for the next year, in case the crops in the ground met with any accident. The wheat sent to Norfolk Island had likewise failed, and there did not remain seed to sow one acre. I could not be certain that the ships which are expected would bring any quantity of grain, or, if put on board them, that they would preserve it good by a proper attention to the stowage, to the want of which I impute our present loss.

The colony not being in a state to support any considerable quantity of live stock, many being under the necessity at present of frequently killing a part of what they have for want of food to support them, I should be obliged to kill what the *Sirius* night procure, and which could not be expected to exceed ten or fourteen days' provision for the settlement; and we now have not more than a year's bread in store, having been obliged to furnish the *Sirius* and the *Supply* with provisions. On these considerations, but more immediately from the fear of not having grain to put into the ground next year, when we shall have a more considerable quantity of ground to sow, I have thought it necessary to order the *Sirius* to go to the Cape of Good Hope in order to procure grain, and at the same time what quantity of flour and provisions she can receive. Captn. Hunter is likewise ordered to purchase what necessarys the surgeon of the hospital demands for six months, no necessarys of any kind, according to his letter, which is inclosed, having been sent out. Fifteen pipes of wine were purchased at Rio de Janeiro, which were all that could be procured; and I presume, as thirty pipes were ordered, the remainder will be sent out by any ship that may stop at Teneriffe. I have only ordered a sufficient quantity of necessarys to be purchased for that time, as a demand has been made in my first letter to your Lordship. The cellar for receiving the spirits will be finished, and the *Fishburn* store-ship cleared and ready to sail by the time the *Golden Grove* returns from Norfolk Island, when both ships shall be immediately ordered to England.

The hutting the detachment has been going on under the direction of the Major-Commandant. The officers have all separate houses, and except one or two are now under cover. The barracks are still in hand.

The detachment is now inclosing ground for their gardens and we have about six acres of wheat, eight of barley, and six acres of other grain, all which, as well as such garden seeds as were not spoiled, promise well, and though the soil is in general a light sandy soil, it is, I believe, as good as what is commonly found near the sea-coast in other parts of the world. The great inconvenience we find is from the rocks and the labour of clearing away the woods which surround us, and which are mostly gum-trees of a very large size, and which are only useful as firewood, though I think that when we can cut them down in the winter and give them time to season they may be made useful in building.

The climate is equal to the finest in Europe, and we very seldom have any fogs. All the plants and fruit-trees brought from the Brazil and the Cape that did not die in the passage thrive exceeding well; and we do not want vegetables, good in their kind, which are natural to the country.

Stone houses that will not be in danger from fire will, if possible, be erected in the course of the summer, as likewise a place of worship; and if ships coming out bring limestone as ballast these very necessary works will go on fast. At present we are obliged to lay the bricks and stones in clay, and of course to make the walls of an extraordinary thickness, and even then they are not to be depended on.

This country is supposed to have mines of iron and tin or silver by those who have been used to work in mines; but I give no encouragement to search after what, if found in our present situation, would be the greatest evil that could befal the settlement.

A couple of decked vessels of 30 or 40 tons burthen, if sent out in frames, and two or three good shipwrights, would be of great service.

In December 1788, David Collins drew up the mortality figures for a year of settlement.

Dead through sickness or injury	56
Killed by natives	4
Executed	5
Gone missing	14

To lose less than a hundred in the first year, under all the stress of occupation and establishment, seemed to confirm, at least tentatively, Governor Phillip's high hopes for the future.

*

But even the Governor's confidence in the future was hedged by doubts and qualifications, and other members of the colony were downright sceptical of its chances. Major Ross, who seemed to oppose Phillip in everything, naturally opposed him also in his vision of what was to come:

Might I presume to intrude an opinion on their Lordships with respect to the utility of a settlement upon this coast, at least upon this part of it. It should be that it never can be made to answer the intended purpose or wish of Government, for the country seems totally destitute of everything that can be an object for a commercial nation, a very fine harbour excepted, and I much fear that the nature of the soil is such as will not be brought to yield more than sufficient sustainance for the needy emigrants whose desperate fortunes may induce them to try the experiment. Here I beg leave to observe to their Lordships that the above is but a private opinion. The Governor's I am unacquainted with, as he has never done me the honor of informing me of his or asking me for mine.

When the chaplain, Richard Johnson, sketched the conditions of the country for a friend in England, though he was a more temperate observer than the gloomy Commandant of Marines, he nevertheless agreed with Ross that New South Wales, in its situation and resources, had no attraction for permanent settlers:

> Port Jackson is without doubt the finest harbour in the known world. It extends from 15 to 20 miles into the country, forming beautiful bays and coves on every side, with deep water everywhere for ships of any burden. Sidney Cove, which is the seat of government, is 5 miles within the entrance of the harbour. The country all round the harbour is similar to that of Botany Bay, only more rocky, some few spots excepted, which may admit of cultivation with a deal of labour. The soil is in general sandy, and no freshwater river or spring has as yet been discovered; still fresh water is found in many places, which is only the overflowing of swamps, consequently cannot be very wholesome. It has on our arrival here, and still does occasion many complaints, such as dysentery and worms. The climate is fine and temperate, and seems to be considerably influenced by the moon, as we have a deal of thunder and lightning at every change of that planet, besides torrents of rain. The lightning has done some damage by killing all the sheep belonging to the Lieutenant-Governor and others. We have had a great deal of rain in the months of June, July, and part of August, which seem to constitute the rainy season here.
>
> The country, as far as we know, produces few quadrupeds. The largest is the kangaroo; they make use of their hind legs only in jumping or escaping from their enemies. The female carries and nurses its young in the pouch under its belly. The opossum is next in size; they are easily tamed, and eat anything. There are flying squirrels – a spotted animal of the cat kind, but larger bodied – extremely destructive to fowls; and three sorts of rats – the kangaroo rat, which partakes of that animal; the flying rat, which by the assistance of its bushy tail flies from tree to tree, which are numerous and very

Kangaroo. From John White, *Journal of a Voyage to New South Wales*, 1790

92

A Kangaroo.

London Published as the Act directs Dec 20 1789 by I Debrett.

troublesome. These are all the quadrupeds we have seen here yet except the native dogs, some of which are large, and seem to be of the fox kind.

The birds are not so numerous as you would expect in a wild country, but very beautiful in general, especially those of the parrot kind. The ostrich is here, and the black swan: one of each has been killed and several seen, besides many other birds, large and small, which I cannot describe. Twelve miles from this settlement I have shot wild ducks, pigeons, and quail.

The country produces five or six kinds of trees, two of which produce the same sort of gum, viz., a red astringent gum well known in England. These gum-trees grow to an amazing size, but are scarce worth cutting down. The only tree fit for building or any other use is the fir-tree, and even that is bad. There are here many shrubs, plants, and flowers totally unknown in Europe, some of which have been used medicinally with success by our surgeon, Mr. Considen, particularly the yellow gum, as a substitute for balsam of tolu.

There is neither ore nor mineral as yet found, except iron, which is very common, and a small portion of copper.

The natives do not appear numerous, but the most wretched of the human race; they are dressed in nature's garb, subsist chiefly on fish and roots we are unacquainted with; they inhabit chiefly the cavities of rocks and trees; their miserable huts, which are few, are constructed of the bark of trees. They do not wish to cultivate our acquaintance or friendship; they are treacherous, for they have murdered several of the convicts and one marine, besides wounding many more; indeed, they attack every person they meet unarmed, and appear civil to all those they meet armed; this is what induces me to call them treacherous. They have spears which they use in fishing and in assailing their enemies, besides stone hatchets and chisels.

The kangaroo is a very timid animal, incredibly strong for its size, and can jump faster than a hare can run; its flesh is not bad eating – something like coarse mutton.

Having given you a sketch of the country, I shall leave you to form your own opinion of it; at the same time I beg to give mine, which is, that it will never answer the intentions of the Government, for two reasons: first, because it is at too great a distance from every trading country; and secondly, it will never make any return to the mother country, nor can it support itself independent of the mother country these twenty years. I could adduce many other reasons beside these.

The common opinion agreed with the Reverend Johnson. The colony was doomed by its distance from the homeland and by lack of opportunities for trade and commerce. New South Wales was, wrote Surgeon White, 'so much out of the world and tract of commerce that it could never answer.' But Governor Phillip, with a wisdom ripened through the experience of his administration, saw that the real problem was not so much remoteness or lack of trade but rather the constitution of the colony itself: a convict dump dependent for survival on convict efforts:

Experience, sir, has taught me how difficult it is to make men industrious who have passed their lives in habits of vice and indolence. In some cases it has been found impossible; neither kindness nor severity have had any effect; and tho' I can say that the convicts in general behave well, there are many who dread punishment less than they fear labour; and those who have not been brought up to hard work, which are by far the greatest part, bear it badly. They shrink from it the moment the eye of the overseer is turned from them.

I wish, sir, to point out the great difference between a settlement formed as this is and one formed by farmers and emigrants who have been used to labour, and who reap the fruits of their own industry. Amongst the latter few are idle or useless, and they feel themselves interested in their different employments. On the contrary, amongst the convicts we have few who are inclined to be industrious, or who feel themselves anyways interested in the advantages which are to accrue from their labours, and we have many who are helpless and a dead-weight on the settlement. Many of those helpless wretches who were sent out in the first ships are dead, and the numbers of those who remained are now considerably increased. I will, sir, insert an extract from the surgeon's report, who I directed to examine these people.

'After a careful examination of the convicts, I find upwards of one hundred who must ever be a burden to the settlement, not being able to do any kind of labour, from old age and chronical diseases of long standing. Amongst the females there is one who has lost the use of her limbs upwards of three years, and amongst the males two are perfect idiots.'

Such are the people sent from the different goals and from the hulks, where it is said the healthy and the artificers are retained. The sending out of the disordered and the helpless clears the gaols, and may ease the parishes from which they are sent; but, sir, it is obvious that this settlement, instead of being a colony which is to support itself, will if the practice is continued, remain for years a burthen to the mother country.

England must decide. Did the mother country want a graveyard for criminals, or did she want to plant a new, viable community in a new land? Captain Watkin Tench, one of the few officials with some sympathy for the settlement and its future, set out the alternatives for England in his straightforward soldierly way:

If only a receptacle for convicts be intended, this place stands unequalled from the situation, extent, and nature of the country. When viewed in a commercial light, I fear its insignificance will appear very striking. . . . After what we have seen, the idea of being soon able to breed cattle sufficient for our consumption, must appear chimerical and absurd. From all which it is evident, that should Great Britain neglect to send out regular supplies, the most fatal consequences will ensue. To men of small property, unambitious of trade, and wishing for retirement, I think the continent of New South Wales not without inducements. One of this description, with letters of recommendation, and a sufficient capital (after having provided for his passage hither) to furnish him with an assortment of tools for clearing land, agricultural and domestic purposes; possessed also of a few household utensils, a cow, a few sheep and breeding sows, would, I am of opinion, with proper protection and encouragement, succeed in obtaining a comfortable livelihood, were he well assured before he quitted his native country, that a provision for him until he might be settled, should be secured; and that a grant of land on his arrival would be allotted him.

To men of desperate fortune and the lowest classes of the people, unless they can procure a passage as indented servants, similar to the custom practised of emigrating to America, this part of the world offers no temptation: for it can hardly be supposed, that Government will be fond of maintaining them here until they can be settled, and without such support they must starve.

CHAPTER FIVE

THE CONVICT COLONY

The good sense of Governor Phillip, the luck of the times and the endurance of the community had carried the infant colony through its critical first year. As 1789 began, and the problems mounted, optimism was in short supply. Now, and for several years to come, the resilience of the colony was to be continually defeated by despondency and want. Rationing became a tedious constant of life and the ghost of famine looked over all shoulders. Everything that was eaten, except for fish and a few vegetables, came from abroad. Captain Watkin Tench watched the stocks diminish:

> When the age of the provisions is recollected its inadequacy will more strikingly appear. The pork and rice were brought with us from England: the pork had been salted between three and four years, and every grain of rice was a moving body from inhabitants lodged within it. We soon left off boiling the pork as it had become so old and dry that it shrank one-half in its dimensions when so treated. Our usual method of cooking it was to cut off the daily morsel and toast it on a fork before the fire, catching the drips which fell on a slice of bread, or in a saucer of rice.

Tench, one of the official class, wrote with a certain wry humour, but the true state of desperation was well beyond humour, as a convict letter of 1790 made clear:

> I seize this opportunity of letting you know, by a vessel that will sail very soon, our wretched situation, which has been occasioned by the miscarriage of our supplies, and that perhaps you have not yet heard of. To give a just description of the hardships that the meanest of us endure, and the

anxieties suffered by the rest, is more that I can pretend to. In all the Crusoe-like adventures I ever read or heard of, I do not recollect anything like it; for though you may be told of the quantity of salt meat that is allowed us, its quality in boiling does not make it above half as much, besides other inconveniences I cannot now mention, and which I think make so many of the children very unhealthy. On the same account, I believe few of the sick would recover if it was not for the kindness of the Rev. Mr. Johnson, whose assistance out of his own stores makes him the physician both of soul and body. All our improvements, except our gardens, have lately been quite at a stand, neither do I think they will go on again till we have more assistance from England. God only knows what our Governor thinks of it, or what word he has sent home; but for my part, from the highest to the lowest, I see nobody that is so contented as they were at first. We fear the troops, and they are not contented with seeing those who live better than themselves, nor with us who live worse; and I think if the savages knew that we were as short of powder as we are of provisions they would soon be more daring than they are. We have heard that some convicts at home, who might have been pardoned for capital crimes, have chosen their former sentence rather than come here; and which, though it was contradicted, we cannot help thinking is true. We cannot tell, if they have heard of our situation, how it could be, unless from the Cape or Norfolk Island, which we hear no more from than from England.

By 1790, Tench also was writing with renewed seriousness, lamenting the isolation and the scarcity in the colony:

Our impatience of news from Europe strongly marked the commencement of the year. We had now been two years in the country, and thirty two months from England, in which long period no supplies, except what had been procured at the Cape of Good Hope by the Sirius, had reached us. From the intelligence of our friends and connections we had been entirely cut off, no communication whatever having passed with our native country since the 13th May, 1787, the day of our departure from Portsmouth. Famine besides was approaching with gigantic strides, and gloom and dejection overspread every countenance. Men abandoned themselves to the most desponding reflections, and adopted the most extravagant conjectures.

The expected supply of provisions not having arrived, makes it necessary to reduce the present ration. And the commissary is directed to issue, from the 1st of April, the undermentioned allowance, to every person in the settlement without distinction.

Four pounds of flour, two pounds and a half of salt pork, and one pound and a half of rice, per week.

The distress of the lower classes for clothes was almost equal to their other wants. The stores had been long exhausted, and winter was at hand. Nothing more ludicrous can be conceived that the expedients of substituting, shifting, and patching, which ingenuity devised, to eke out wretchedness, and preserve the remains of decency. The superior dexterity of the women was particularly conspicuous. Many a guard have I seen mount, in which the number of soldiers without shoes, exceeded that which had yet preserved remnants of leather.

Nor was another part of our domestic economy less whimsical. If a lucky man, who had knocked down a dinner with his gun, or caught a fish by angling from the rocks, invited a neighbour to dine with him, the invitation always ran, 'bring your own bread.' Even at the governor's table, this custom was constantly observed. Every man when he sat down pulled his bread out of his pocket, and laid it by his plate.

The insufficiency of our ration soon diminished our execution of labour. Both soldiers and convicts pleaded such loss of strength, as to find themselves unable to perform their accustomed tasks. The hours of public work were accordingly shortened; or rather, every man was ordered to do as much as his strength would permit; and every other possible indulgence was granted.

In March, the *Sirius* was wrecked while taking convicts and stores to Norfolk Island, the daughter colony 900 miles out in the Pacific. The little *Supply* came back alone with a story, wrote David Collins, 'that was of itself almost sufficient to have deranged the strongest intellect among us.' At last, in June 1790, two-and-a-half years after landing in Botany Bay, the first news and the first relief arrived from England. Tench expressed the general feelings of joy and renewed hope:

June. At length the clouds of misfortune began to separate and on the evening of the 3rd of June, the joyful cry of 'the flag's up', resounded in every direction.

I was sitting in my hut, musing on our fate, when a confused clamour in the street drew my attention. I opened my door, and saw several women with children in their arms running to and fro with distracted looks, congratulating each other, and kissing their infants with the most passionate and extravagant marks of fondness. I needed no more; but instantly started out, and ran to a hill, where, by the assistance of a pocket-glass, my hopes were realised. My next door neighbour, a brother officer, was with me; but we could not speak; we wrung each other by the hand, with eyes and hearts overflowing.

Finding that the governor intended to go immediately in his boat down the harbour, I begged to be of his party.

As we proceeded, the object of our hopes soon appeared:– a large ship, with English colours flying, working in, between the heads which form the entrance of the harbour. The tumultuous state of our minds represented her in danger; and we were in agony. Soon after, the governor, having ascertained what she was, left us, and stept into a fishing boat to return to Sydney. The weather was wet and tempestuous; but the body is delicate only when the soul is at ease. We pushed through wind and rain, the anxiety of our sensations every moment redoubling. At last we read the word *London* on her stern. 'Pull away, my lads! she is from Old England! a few strokes more, and we shall be aboard! hurrah for a belly-full, and news from our friends!' – Such were our exhortations to the boat's crew.

A few minutes completed our wishes, and we found ourselves on board the Lady Juliana transport, with two hundred and twenty-five of our countrywomen, whom crime or misfortune had condemned to exile. We learned that they had been almost eleven months on their passage, having left Plymouth, into which port they had put in July, 1789. We continued to ask a thousand questions on a breath. Stimulated by curiosity, they inquired in turn; but the right of being first answered, we thought, lay on our side. 'Letters! letters!' was the cry. They were produced, and torn open in trembling agitation. News burst upon us like meridian splendor on a blind man. We were overwhelmed with it; public, private, general, and particular. Nor was it until some days had elapsed, that we were able to methodize it, or reduce it into form. We now heard for the first time of our sovereign's illness, and his happy restoration to health. The French revolution of 1789, with all the attendant circumstances of that wonderful and unexpected event, succeeded to amaze us. Now, too, the disaster which had befallen the Guardian, and the liberal and enlarged plan on which she had been stored and fitted out by government for our use, was promulged. It served also, in some measure, to account why we had not sooner heard from England. For had not the Guardian struck on an island of ice, she would probably have reached us three months before, and in this case have prevented the loss of the Sirius, although she had sailed from England three months after the Lady Juliana.

June, 1790. Good fortune continued to befriend us. Before the end of the month, three more transports, having on board two companies of the New South Wales corps, arrived to add to our society. These ships also brought out a large body of convicts.

The relief of the colony could only be temporary, for the very arrival of the ships underlined most strongly the vulnerability of the settlement and its utter dependence on events beyond the shores of New South Wales. Thoughtful men remained gloomy. Given the nature of the colony and the neglect from England, what real hope was there for the future? Surgeon White saw only a bleak present:

Much cannot now be done, limited in food and reduced as people are, who have not had one ounce of fresh animal food since first in the country; a country and place so forbidden and so hateful as only to merit execration and curses; for it has been a source of expence to the mother country, and of evil and misfortune to us, without there ever being the smallest likelihood of its repaying or recompensing either. From what we have already seen, we may conclude that there is not a single article in the whole country that in the nature of things could prove of the smallest use or advantage to the mother country or the commercial world.

In the name of Heaven, what has the Ministry been about? Surely they have quite forgotten or neglected us; otherwise they would have sent to see what had become of us, and to know how we were likely to succeed. However, they must soon know from the heavy bills which will be presented to them, and the misfortunes and losses which have already happened to us, how necessary it becomes to relinquish a scheme that in the nature of things can never answer. It would be wise by the first steps to withdraw the settlement, at least such as are living, or remove them to some other place.

This is so much out of the world and tract of commerce that it could never answer. How a business of this kind (the expence of which must be great) could first be thought of without sending to examine the country, as was Captain Thompson's errand to the coast of Africa, is to every person here a matter of great surprise. Mons. Peyrouse and Clonard, the French circumnavigators, as well as us, have been very much surprised at Mr. Cook's description of Botany Bay. The wood is bad, the soil light, poor, and sandy, nor has it anything to recommend it. Accurate observers have surveyed the country without being able to see anything like the meadow land that Mr. Cook and others mention. The Frenchmen declare the same, and that in the whole course of their voyage they never saw a place half so unpromising for a settlement as this . . . They made an observation with respect to it which, from its singularity, propriety, and force I cannot suppress, that it was only a place fit for angels and eagles to reside in.

Another correspondent told the Home Office in London, in forthright terms, that the colony was doomed and should be abandoned:

The country, my lord, is past all dispute a wretched one – a very wretched – and totally incapable of yielding to Great Britain a return for colonising it. There is no wood fit for naval purposes; no fibrous grass or plant from which cordage can be made; no substance which can aid or improve the labours of the manufacturer; no mineral productions; no esculent vegetable worth the care of collecting and trans- porting to other climes; and lastly, which is of the most serious consideration, no likelihood that the colony will be able to support itself in grain or animal food for many years to come; so that a regular annual expense is entailed on the mother country as long as it shall be kept.

But ministers in England had no thought of abandoning the colony nor were they, despite the volume of complaints from Port Jackson that rang in their ears, displeased with the progress being made. They had priorities other than the ones so urgently put forward by Governor Phillip. London had decided, as Lord Sydney made plain in 1789, 'to send out all the convicts sentenced for transportation . . . in order that his Majesty's gaols in this kingdom may be at once quite cleared.' And when, in the House of Commons in 1791, William Pitt reviewed the penal policy in New South Wales, he had reason to feel that the government was well satisfied:

If Botany-Bay was not capable of receiving them, he would freely acknowledge, that ministers were highly reprehensible for sending out so many as were now on the point of going there; but government had no reason to suppose it to be the case. In point of expense, no cheaper mode of disposing of the convicts, he was satisfied, could be found. The chief expense of the establishment of the colony was already passed and paid. Why, then, were they, unless strong reasons indeed operated to enforce the measure, to begin *de novo*, and make a new colony? And where it could be made to more advantage he really was a stranger. That it was a necessary and essential point of police to send some of the most incorrigible criminals out of the kingdom, no man could entertain a doubt, since it must be universally admitted, that it was the worst policy of a state to keep offenders of that description at home to corrupt others, and contaminate the less guilty, by communicating their own dangerous depravity.

Nor would Pitt allow the accusation that English neglect left convicts in want: 'In respect to Botany Bay, as transportation appeared to him to be a very fit punishment for incorrigible offenders, he saw no reason to hold out a prospect of luxury to exiles; nor did he wish that the effect of their conviction should be so described.' No, the government objective of clearing the gaols at minimum expense was being achieved and convicts would continue to flow to the penal colony as quickly as ships could be found for them. In the face of the cry from the colony that supplies were inadequate and the colonists unfit for the task, the ministers allowed a little grudging help in men and materials. But really, they chided the starving settlement, internal development and self-sufficiency must be the aim. If the colonists – convicts and officials alike – wanted a better world, they must make it themselves.

With the destiny of New South Wales thus firmly placed in his hands, Governor Phillip, who was not a man to shirk responsibility, set about his task. He faced two urgent yet related problems – firstly, to increase food production so as to lessen dependence on English supplies, and secondly, to induce discipline and self-respect in a mob of feckless, half-starved convicts so that agriculture, and indeed any sort of development, could proceed. Long-term he had to try to determine the future form and scope of the whole colony, to work out a balance between penal punishment and the settlement of a new land. Arthur Phillip governed the colony for a little less than five years, but the remedies and plans that he attempted, for better or worse but always with the best intentions, determined the course of history in New South Wales for many years after his departure.

The need for agriculture was urgent. The population grew fast – in 1791 alone, eleven convict transports arrived, bringing useless mouths to be fed from official stores. And as Watkin Tench wisely remarked, 'It can hardly be supposed, that Government will be fond of maintaining them here until they can be settled, and without such support they must starve.'

Despite the praise heaped upon the country by Captain Cook, the first colonists discovered a hard land. Some thirty years after the first landing, the enterprising settler who wrote much sound observation and a little fiction under the name of Alexander Harris pictured an untamed and rugged landscape visited by extremes of weather:

The spot where we had pitched our tent was a small grassy forest on the hill side; and everywhere around it, down below in the endless ravines, and up above towards the insurmountable heights of the range, was thick tangled brush growing amidst lofty trees, so thick set that beneath them was perpetual shadow, or rather something more gloomy still. The ground was covered with decaying leaves and old water-logged windfall trees, so rotten that the foot could break its way deep into the substance of that gnarled wood which at one time would have stopped a cannon-ball. Wherever you went, creeks of crystal ice-like water, plunging down the mountain side, each in its stony bed, kept up a murmur day and night; never changing save when increased by rains into the roar of a torrent. This mountain, or, more properly, heap of mountains, ran down, where we were at work, nearly into the sea, and for many miles every way the character of the vegetation was as I have described. Here and there certainly a little patch of grassy forest would assert a place for itself on the shoulder of a hill, and partly down the side; but generally the entire surface of this mountain, for many miles up and down the coast every way, was clothed with this thick brush; beside which so irregular and broken and confused was the surface of the range itself that even the best bushmen felt timid of committing themselves to it. Thus, in one of these little grassy forests in the midst of the bush, on the shoulder of an easy ridge about two miles back from the sea, and so far up that we could see the sea like a broadish sheet of water below us, was pitched our little hut. It was no more than a few sheets of the bark that we had stripped off our black butts, leaned together, top to top, tent like, with one end stopped by another sheet, and the fire a few feet in front on the ground at the other. Here we had been, say ten days, when it began to rain; and, as is the case generally at this season of the year in Australia, when it sets in for a week's rain, it rained with a will. I began to be initiated into the disasters of a bush life. The rain came through the roof of the hut as if we had been making arrangements in its favour; and no sooner had we stopped it there than, coming down the hill, it began to run through the bottom of the hut like a mill-stream; and as we had, in our confidence of fine weather, laid our beds on the ground, they got thoroughly soaked.

For twenty-five years the unpenetrated barrier of the Blue Mountains hemmed in the settlement. Botany Bay was soon abandoned. Port Jackson, though possessing a magnificent harbour, was considered by Phillip to lie in 'a poor, sandy heath, full of swamps'. Cultivation was first attempted at Farm Cove, below the site of Sydney, but failed comprehensively. Greater success leading to the first proper agricultural development was achieved some miles above Sydney, at Rose Hill, at the place that later became the town of Parramatta. From there, the axe and the plough made slow progress up the river valleys, along the banks of the Parramatta, the Hawkesbury, the Nepean and Cook's River.

When one looks today at this prosperous and orderly countryside, it is hard to imagine the early challenge that the land held. Even at Rose Hill, where the Governor established his house and gardens began to take form under his servant, Henry Dodd, the wilderness snapped at the heels. To step from the path was to court danger, and a remarkable number of early colonists were lost almost within reach of the settlement. David Collins recorded a typical case at Rose Hill, in May 1789:

From that settlement, early in the month, two soldiers of the detachment doing duty there were reported to be missing; and, though parties had been sent out daily in different directions to seek for them, yet all was unavailing. It was supposed that they must have lost their way in some of the thick and almost impenetrable brushes which were in the vicinity of Rose Hill, and had there perished miserably. They had gone in search of the sweet tea plant already mentioned; and perhaps when they resigned themselves to the fate which they did not see how to avoid, oppressed with hunger, and unable to wander any farther, they may have been but a short distance from the relief they must so earnestly have defired. A dog that was known to have left the settlement with them reached Rose Hill, almost famished, nine days after they had left it. The extreme danger attendant on a man's going beyond the bounds of his own knowledge in the forests of an unsettled country could no where be more demonstrable than in this. To the westward was an immense open track before him, in which, if unbefriended by either sun or moon, he might wander until life were at an end. Most of the arms which extended into the country from Port Jackson and the harbour on each side of Port Jackson, were of great length, and to round them without a certain and daily supply of provisions was impossible.

But at Rose Hill, in particular, after much effort the wilderness began to give way to productive land. In November 1790, Tench noted some of the steps taken in that struggle for food:

Cultivation, on a public scale, has for some time past been given up here, (Sydney) the crop of last year being so miserable, as to deter from farther experiment; in consequence of which, the government-farm is abandoned, and the people who were fixed on it, have been removed. Necessary public buildings advance fast; an excellent storehouse, of large dimensions, built of bricks, and covered with tiles, is just completed; and another planned, which will shortly be begun. Other buildings, among which I heard the governor mention an hospital, and permanent barracks for the troops, may also be expected to arise soon. Works of this nature are more expeditiously performed than heretofore, owing, I apprehend, to the superintendants lately arrived, who are placed over the convicts, and compel them to labour. The first difficulties of a new country being subdued, may also contribute to this comparative facility.

Vegetables are scarce, although the summer is so far advanced, owing to want of rain. I do not think that all the showers of the last four months put together, would make 24 hours rain. Our farms, what with this, and a poor soil, are in wretched condition. My winter crop of potatoes, which I planted in days of despair, (March and April last) turned out very badly, when I dug them about two months back. Wheat returned so poorly last harvest, that very little, besides Indian corn, has been sown this year. The governor's wound is quite healed, and he feels no inconveniency whatever from it. With the natives we are hand and glove. They throng the camp every day, and sometimes by their clamour and importunity for bread and meat (of which they now all eat greedily) are become very troublesome. God knows, we have little enough for ourselves! Full allowance (if eight pounds of flour, and either seven pounds of beef, or four pounds of pork, served

The Governor's House at Rose Hill. From David Collins, *Account of New South Wales*, 1798

alternatively, per week, without either pease, oatmeal, spirits, butter, or cheese, can be called so) is yet kept up; but if the Dutch snow does not arrive soon it must be shortened, as the casks in the storehouse, I observed yesterday, are woefully decreased.

The convicts continue to behave pretty well; three only have been hanged since the arrival of the last fleet, in the latter end of June, all of whom were new comers. The number of convicts here diminishes every day; our principal efforts being wisely made at Rose Hill, where the land is unquestionably better than about this place. Except building, sawing, and brick-making, nothing of consequence is now carried on here. The account which I received a few days ago from the brick-makers of their labours, was as follows: Wheeler (one of the master brick-makers) with two tile stools, and one brick stool, was tasked to make and burn ready for use 30000 tiles and bricks per month; he had 21 hands to assist him, who performed every thing; cut wood, dug clay, &c. This continued (during the days of distress excepted, when they did what they could) until June last. From June, with one brick and two tile stools he has been tasked to make 40000 bricks and tiles monthly, (as many of each sort as may be) having 22 men and two boys to assist him, on the same terms of procuring materials as before. They fetch the clay of which tiles are made, two hundred yards; that for bricks is close at hand. – He says that the bricks are such as would be called in England, moderately good; and he judges they would have fetched about 24s. per thousand, at Kingston-upon-Thames, (where he resided) in the year 1784: their greatest fault is being too brittle. The tiles he thinks not so good as those made about London: the stuff has a rotten quality, and besides wants the advantage of being ground, in lieu of which they tread it.

November 16th. Got to Rose Hill in the evening: Next morning walked round the whole of the cleared and cultivated land, with the Rev. Mr. Johnson, who is the best farmer in the country. Edward Dod, one of the governor's household, who conducts every thing here in the agricultural line, accompanied us part of the way, and afforded all the information he could. He estimates the quantity of cleared and cultivated land at 200 acres. Of these 55 are in wheat, barley, and a little oats, 30 in maize, and the remainder is either just cleared of wood, or is occupied by buildings, gardens, &c. Four inclosures of 20 acres each, are planned for the reception of cattle, which may arrive in the colony, and two of these are already fenced in. In the centre of them is to be erected a house, for a person who will be fixed upon to take care of the cattle. All these inclosures are supplied with water.

Two months later Tench was able to record a minor triumph:

No circumstance, however apparently trivial, which can tend to throw light on a new country, either in respect of its present situation, or its future promise, should pass unregarded. – On the 24th of January, two bunches of grapes were cut in the governor's garden, from cuttings of vines, brought three years before from the Cape of Good Hope. The bunches were handsome; the fruit of a moderate size, but well filled out; and the flavour high and delicious.

This production took place on government land, worked by convicts. But Phillip, anxious for the future, had always resolved not to rely on convict labour alone. His Instructions permitted him to make grants of land, either to free settlers, or to soldiers and officials, or to convicts who had served their sentence and even to those who merited reward for good conduct. In 1789 he made grants to twenty-seven emancipated convicts. This was a crucial experiment to prove whether ex-convicts could make good farmers and good citizens. And in the case of James Ruse, at least, the Governor was vindicated, for here was a type of successful settler such as the colony needed. Captain Tench visited him at Rose Hill towards the end of 1790 and learnt his history:

I next visited a humble adventurer, who is trying his fortune here. James Ruse, convict, was cast for seven years at Bodmin assizes, in August 1782; he lay five years in prison and on board the Dunkirk hulk at Plymouth, and then was sent to this country. When his term of punishment expired, in August 1789, he claimed his freedom, and was permitted by the governor, on promising to settle in the country, to take in December following, an uncleaned piece of ground, with an assurance that if he would cultivate it, it should not be taken from him. Some assistance was given him, to fell the timber, and he accordingly began. His present account to me was as follows. 'I was bred a husbandman, near Launcester in Cornwall. I cleared my land as well as I could, with the help afforded me. The exact limit of what ground I am to have, I do not yet know; but a certain direction has been pointed out to me, in which I may proceed as fast as I can cultivate. I have now an acre and a half in bearded wheat, half an acre in maize, and a small kitchen garden. On my wheat land I sowed three bushels of seed, the produce of this country, broad cast. I expect to reap about 12 or 13 bushels. I know nothing of the cultivation of maize, and cannot therefore guess so well at what I am likely to gather. I sowed part of my wheat in May, and part in June. That sown in May has thriven best. My maize I planted in the latter end of August, and the beginning of September. My land I prepared thus: having burnt the fallen timber off the ground, I dug in the ashes, and then hoed it up, never doing more than eight, or perhaps nine, rods in a day, by which means, it was not like the government-farm, just scratched over, but properly done; then I clodmoulded it, and dug in the grass and weeds: this I think almost equal to ploughing. I then let it lie as long as I could, exposed to air and sun; and just before I sowed my seed, turned it all up afresh. When I shall have reaped my crop, I purpose to hoe it again, and harrow it fine, and then sow it with turnip-seed, which will mellow and prepare it for next year. My straw, I mean to bury in pits, and throw in with it every thing which I think will rot and turn to manure. I have no person to help me, at present, but my wife, whom I married in this country: she is industrious. The governor, for some time, gave me the help of a convict man, but he is taken away. Both my wife and myself receive our provisions regularly at the store, like all other people. My opinion of the soil of my farm, is, that it is middling, neither good or bad. I will be bound to make it do with the aid of manure, but without cattle it will fail. The greatest check upon me is, the dishonesty of the convicts, who, in spite of all my vigilance, rob me almost every night.'

There were few ex-convicts like James Ruse and, with a growing colony, it was still a long and hard road to self-sufficiency. But by the time Governor Phillip left the colony, in December 1792, he was able to report modest progress, a base to build on year by year:

Of the present state of this settlement, I have the satisfaction of assuring you that the soil and its produce more than answer the expectations which I have formerly given. Our last year's crop of maize, notwithstanding the long drought, was 4,844½ bushels, of which 2,649½ bushels have been issued as bread for the colony, 695 bushels were reserved for seed and other purposes, and not less than 1,500 bushels were stolen from the grounds, notwithstanding every possible precaution was taken to prevent it. From the time the corn began to ripen to the time it was housed, the convicts were pressed by hunger, and great quantities were stolen and concealed in the woods; several convicts died from feeding on it in its crude state, when carrying the grain to the public granary. But in speaking of these people, it is but just to observe that I can recollect very few crimes during the last three years but what have been committed to procure the necessaries of life.

One thousand acres of ground are in cultivation on the public account, of which 800 are in maize, the rest in wheat and barley, at Parramatta and a new settlement formed about three miles to the westward of Parramatta, and to which I have given the name of Toon-gab-be, a name by which the natives distinguish the spot. The soil is good, and in the neighbourhood of this place there are several thousand acres of exceeding good ground. The quantity of ground in cultivation by the settlers is 416 acres, and they have 97 acres more ground cleared of timber. By the land in cultivation some judgment may be formed as to the corn, which may next year be carried into the store towards the support of the colony. And I flatter myself that the time now approaches in which this country will be able to supply its inhabitants with grain; but no dependence must be placed on a crop while it is in the ground, consequently regular supplies of flour, &c., from Europe will be necessary until there is sufficient quantity in store to serve the colony for one year at least. The grub, as in all new grounds, is very destructive. The crop may fail from a dry season, or be lost from fire or other accidents, and to which it may naturally be supposed the crops in this country are more exposed than in Europe.

This was a message of some hope. But if he had let matters rest there Phillip, an honest man, would not have been true to his responsibility. So the final words that the Governor addressed to London were not words of optimism but of warning – if England deserted the settlement, it would fail:

My letters by the Supply, Gorgon, and Pitt will have shewn that I look to England for the necessary supplies, of which we still stand in great need, and which I doubt not are now on their passage; but the great length of time in which this colony has remained in its present state takes away hope from many, and the consequences must be obvious. It has, sir, been my fate to point out wants from year to year; it has been a duty the severest I have ever experienced. Did those wants only respect myself or a few individuals I should be silent; but here are numbers who bear them badly; nor has the colony suffered more from wanting what we have not received than from the supplies we have received not arriving in time.

For nothing – neither effort nor development nor progress – could be relied on in a convict colony. Everything that had been done had only been achieved under the pain and groans of the whip. Even agriculture, which was urgently needed for the benefit of the half-starved prisoners themselves, could only be practised under conditions of forced labour. Most convicts regarded all work as an extra dimension added to their punishment and had to be driven to it, often by brutal overseers taken from their own ranks. George Thompson, who arrived in the colony in 1792, described the sorry lot of the convicts on the Toongabbie government farm:

> They are allowed no breakfast hour, because they seldom have anything to eat. Their labour is felling trees, digging up the stumps, rooting up the shrubs and grass, turning up the ground with spades or hoes, and carrying the timber to convenient places. From the heat of the sun, the short allowance of provisions and the ill-treatment they receive from a set of merciless wretches (most of their own description) who are the superintendents, their lives are truly miserable.
>
> At night they are placed in a hut, fourteen, sixteen or eighteen together (with a woman, whose duty it is to keep it clean, and to provide victuals for the men when at work), without the comfort of either beds or blankets, unless they take them from the ship they came out in, or are rich enough to purchase them when they come on shore. They have neither bowl, plate, spoon nor knife, but what they can make of the green wood of the country, only one small iron pot being allowed to dress their poor allowance of meat, rice, etc.; in short, all the necessary conveniences of life they are strangers to, and suffer everything they could dread in their sentence of transportation. Some time ago it was not

uncommon for seven or eight to die in one day, and very often while at work, they being kept in the field till the last moment, and frequently while being carried to the hospital. Many a one has died standing at the door of the storehouse, while waiting for his allowance of provisions, merely for want of sustenance and necessary food.

After Phillip's departure, when the rule of the military introduced an even lower standard of humanity into the government of the colony, more frequent and cruel punishment became the rule, as a subsequent victim of the Toongabbie system made clear:

We were yoked to draw timber in a gang. We held a stake between us six feet long and six men abreast, and dragged with our hands. Only occasionally were we given scraps of food. 800 convicts died in six months. We cleared the scrub and timber. Each man was expected to clear an acre of ground a week, but the ground was as hard as iron, the timber tough, and the few tools we had were useless. We were dreadfully weak for want of food.

I have seen 70 men flogged in a day. 25 lashes each was the usual flogging, but I saw Maurice Fitzgerald, an Irish political prisoner, receive 300 lashes. The unfortunate man had his arms extended round a tree, his wrists tied tightly with cords, and his breast pressed close to the tree so that flinching was out of the question. It was impossible for him to stir. He was flogged by two men – a left-hand man and a right-handed one, so that every one of the 300 blows were given the maximum force. Blood spouted from Fitzgerald's shoulders, and I turned my head away from the sickening sight. Though he was cut to the bone, Fitzgerald never even whimpered.

It had long been accepted, even by humane men like Governor Phillip and Captain Tench, that the natural depravity of the convicts required exceptional measures. As early as September 1789 Tench had written:

But all our attention was not directed to explore inlets, and toil for discovery. Our internal tranquillity was still more important. To repress the inroads of depredation; and to secure to honest industry the reward of its labour, had become matter of the most serious consideration; hardly a night passing without the commission of robbery. Many expedients were devised; and the governor at length determined to select from the convicts, a certain number of persons, who were meant to be of the fairest character, for the purpose of being formed into a nightly-watch, for the preservation of public and private property, under the following regulations, which, as the first system of police in a colony, so peculiarly constituted as ours, may perhaps prove not uninteresting.

And the Judge-Advocate, David Collins, pointed out the peculiar difficulties of disciplining and policing such a lawless colony:

But orders, in general, were observed to have very little effect, and to be attended to only while the impression made by hearing them published remained upon the mind; for the convicts had not been accustomed to live in situations where their conduct was to be regulated by written orders. There was here no other mode of communicating to them such directions as it was found necessary to issue for their observance; and it was very common to have them plead in excuse for a breach of any regulation of the settlement, that they had never before heard of it; nor had they any idea of the permanency of an order, many of them seeming to think it issued merely for the purpose of the moment.

It was much to be regretted, that there existed a necessity for placing a confidence in these people, as in too many instances the trust was found to be abused: but unfortunately, to fill many of those offices to which free people alone should have been appointed in this colony, there were none but convicts.

This early problem of order had been compounded by the attitude of Major Ross of the Marines, who refused to have anything to do with the convicts, forcing Phillip to adopt the system of 'trusties' under whom discipline was often capricious, arbitrary and brutal. Even when, after 1789, the colony received its own military regiment, the New South Wales Corps, the severity and lack of due process of the already established discipline appealed to military notions of justice. The brutality inherent in Phillip's system was allowed a freer rein under the military, affecting the judgements of convict overseers and official magistrates alike. At the turn of the century, Joseph Holt observed the whipping of the convicted Irish rebel Maurice Fitzgerald. He wrote that 'Fifteen yards from the sufferer's blood, skin and flesh blew in my face as the executioners shook it from their cats – the day being windy. After feeling the convict's pulse during the punishment, Dr Mason's only remark was: "Go on, this man will tire you both before he fails".'

Through repetition of scenes like this flogging became a cancer that ran a long course through the future of Australia. It was part of a way of life, an ordinary adjunct of a convict colony. When Alexander Harris arrived as a fresh young settler in the early part of the nineteenth century, he was soon introduced to the Australian realities by a cynical old hand:

'You may wonder, my lad,' he said, 'at what you read about the treatment of prisoners: most people do when they first come. But you'll see things yet up the country that these Sydney doings are only child's play by the side of.'

'You don't mean to say,' I replied, 'that I shall meet with anything worse than this case I have just read? Here is an offence called by three different names; three several charges are made upon it; three several trials, three several sentences, and three several punishments following! A man gets drunk, has his clothes stolen, and is afraid to go home to his master: he is tried first for drunkenness, a second time for making away with his clothing, and a third time for absconding. His sentence is in sum total one hundred lashes, which with the cat-o'-nine-tails is really nine hundred lashes.'

'Why, I have known the same act to be called by *five* different names, and *five* sentences passed upon the prisoner for it. It was in the case of a government servant belonging to a magistrate near me. The man, as in the case you read, had got a drop of liquor from a travelling dealer; his master's son, a very pert young fellow, began to curse at and threaten him; the man retorted; a constable was sent for, whom he knocked down and escaped from. He then ran off into the bush,

taking with him, as he passed his own hut, about three parts
of a cake he had by him ready baked. The young fellow
prosecuted him for drunkenness, insolence, theft (the piece
of bread, for rations are considered the master's till used),
and bushranging; and then the magistrate made the constable swear the assault against him. He got twenty-five lashes
for drunkenness, twenty-five for insolence, fifty for bushranging, six months to an iron-gang for stealing the cake, and
three months for assaulting a peace-officer in the execution
of his duty. The flogging he got before going to the iron-
gang frightened him; and on receiving sentence for some
trivial offence at the iron-gang, he escaped before the punishment was inflicted, took the bush, joined a gang of
bushrangers who had arms, committed several robberies with
them, was taken with arms in his hands, and hanged. The
man was a quiet, hardworking, honest fellow; but he could
not stand flogging, and he was fond of liquor. The crime he
was sent here for he committed when drunk, and it was
perhaps the only one he had to answer for. That man was
murdered! And so hundreds upon hundreds have been, and
are being, every year in this cursed country.'

Young Harris was shocked. But his experienced guide cheer-
fully informed him that such punishments were quite normal,
just a little quirk of local life:

'But the fact is, flogging in this country is such a common
thing that nobody thinks anything of it. I have seen young
children practising on a tree, as children in England play at
horses. I have now got a man under me who received 2600
lashes with the cat in about five years, and his worst crime was
insolence to his overseer. The fact is, the man is a red-hot
Tipperary man; and when his blood gets up, you could not
make him hold his tongue if you were to threaten to hang
him. Since I have had him he has never had a lash, just
because I take no notice of what he says. The consequence is,
there is nothing in the world that man would not do for me
if he could. Some years ago, a little way up the country, a
man actually died under the cat; of course it was all quietly
hushed up.'
'But do you really think such things can be true?'

'Ah! you must not judge of this country by England. What I tell you now, I tell you on the authority of my own eyes. I was sent for to Bathurst Court-house to identify a man supposed to have taken the bush from the farm I have charge of. I had to go past the triangles, where they had been flogging incessantly for hours. I saw a man walk across the yard with the blood that had run from his lacerated flesh squashing out of his shoes at every step he took. A dog was licking the blood off the triangles, and the ants were carrying away great pieces of human flesh that the lash had scattered about the ground. The scourger's foot had worn a deep hole in the ground by the violence with which he whirled himself round on it to strike the quivering and wealed back, out of which stuck the sinews, white, ragged, and swollen. The infliction was a hundred lashes, at about half-minute time, so as to extend the punishment through nearly an hour. The day was hot enough to overcome a man merely standing that length of time in the sun; and this was going on in the full blaze of it. However, they had a pair of scourgers, who gave one another spell and spell about; and they were bespattered with blood like a couple of butchers. I tell you this on the authority of my own eyes. It brought my heart into my mouth.'

'Well, I can only say that, for disgusting brutality, it exceeds anything I ever yet heard of as practised under the sanction of British law.'

'It is nevertheless true; and many much worse things than any I have yet enumerated are true. . . . I know of several poor creatures who have been entirely crippled for life by these merciless floggings; and, which is worst of all, oftentimes for offences which no considerate and right-thinking person would dream of considering heinous and unpardonable. I will give one instance more of the summary jurisdiction of magistrates. The commandant at ——, a police station near my hut, was walking out one summer-evening about twelve months ago with his lady; he was in plain clothes, all but his military foraging cap, an article of dress that many private gentlemen wear. Two men accosted him, and asked the way to a farm in the vicinity, to whose owner they had been assigned. Considering they did not address him quite respectfully enough, he gave them some sharp language, which they returned: hereupon, but still without telling them that he was a magistrate, he laid hands on one of them, who immediately tripped him up. On this his lady began to shout out most lustily, which brought the soldiers of the party under his command out of their hut close by. The men were presently seized and confined. The next day the worshipful peace-breaker deposed against them himself, before himself, pronounced them guilty himself, and sentenced them himself to twelve months at an iron-gang.'

After some years in New South Wales, Harris was able to form his own opinion on the custom of flogging, which he saw as a consequence of a corrupted penal system, a custom that still thrived because it suited the established order of society:

There was thus afforded me an opportunity of becoming acquainted, by personal observation and inquiry, with the real character of our British penal institutions in New South Wales. There was one man being flogged for theft, whose crime it was acknowledged was the consequence of the hunger of a three days' fast. His miserable pittance had been stolen, and, after enduring his hunger as long as he could, he had swum the river in the night, and broken into an adjacent settler's granary. Another poor wretch had a sentence of twenty-five lashes for laziness in not doing his task. The fact was, it would not have been laziness in the same man, in the condition he was in, to have lain abed for a month. Besides these, a number of men received twenty-five lashes each, on the charge of disobedience of orders. That disobedience was, that, their rations not having come by the proper time, they had refused to go to work till they got them, under the very natural impression that they could not be compelled to work when they were not fed. It would be in vain to try to depict the looks of mingled astonishment, indignation, and dogged sullenness that they exchanged as they came out of the Court-house door after hearing their sentence, and as they filed off into the prison-yard to be tied up to receive it. The constable who went in last left the gate partly open. I heard the flogger say, 'Well, who's the first?' After an instant or two I heard the answer; it seemed to be the voice of a Scotch lad: 'Here, I'm the first, you ——; but —— my eyes if I don't have satisfaction one way or another, if I get hanged for it.'

I heard, awhile after, the dull, heavy fall of the cat on the flesh, and the constable's count – ONE, TWO, THREE, FOUR, &c., mingling with the flogger's *hiss* each time, as he sent the blows home, dallying between each to spin out the punishment to the utmost. But there was no cry, no groan, no prayer for mercy. It was not long I listened. My heart began to beat chokingly, and I got away from the legalised abomination as fast as I could. I often heard people in Sydney afterwards expressing their astonishment and horror when some of these iron-gang overseers were killed by the men; but from this time I never found any difficulty in comprehending the how and why.

All this was the sad legacy of Governor Phillip's well-intentioned efforts to get a struggling colony out of the waters of chaos onto safe land.

Agriculture and discipline were problems that permitted immediate solutions, for good or bad. But always, at every step, the early governors came face to face with the unsolved puzzle: how was this colony, a place designated for the reception and punishment of convicts, to survive and develop? The Home Office in England cared little for events in New South Wales; its only concern was to clear the gaols and limit expense. But all the early governors, thrust into this uncomfortable berth 12,000 miles from home, echoed to some degree the judgement of Captain Watkin Tench. 'Punishment,' he wrote, 'when not directed to promote reformation is arbitrary and unauthorized.' A growing colony needed a sounder foundation than this on which to base its life. If the colony was to prosper, it needed to grow in the direction of freedom.

But how was this to be done? The earliest Instructions permitted land grants for settlement and Phillip's policy had been to seek free settlers from wherever he could find them: from immigration, from among emancipated convicts, officials of the colony, and all ranks of the military. Not all were as industrious as James Ruse, but slowly they came forward. In December 1791, Tench recorded that three corporals, one drummer and fifty-nine privates from the departing marine battalion accepted land grants, to settle at Norfolk Island and Rose Hill.

And the terms granted to encourage settlers were attractive:

BEYOND THE BLACK STUMP

free land, free of all charges for ten years, two convict servants
supported at official expense for a period that varied according
to the rank of the settler, and a further chance to use convicts as
assigned labourers provided the settler undertook to feed and
clothe these workers. The assignment system pleased ministers
in England partly because it gave a boost to agriculture, and
was thus a help towards self-sufficiency, but more particularly
because it removed from the government the necessity to
provide for a large number of convicts. The settlers liked the
system because it gave them cheap, almost free, labour which
they could use as they wished subject only to a very lax,
negligent supervision.

A system connived at so willingly by both government and
privileged landowners was ripe for abuse. The history of
convict assignment in Australia was another long lurid story,
tenaciously maintained, and distasteful to relate. Alexander
Harris soon saw how the system worked. 'The Australian
settler,' he wrote, 'undertakes, as a matter of course, to supply
his labourers with rations; but he never thinks there is the
slightest obligation on himself to make that supply a constant
one.' Wandering through the bush, Harris noted several
examples of assigned convicts at work:

These men I discovered were all convicts, lent by the government to the settler on whose land they were at work. There
was no restraint on their personal liberty beyond that of fear
of consequences if they left the farm or neglected the work;
their huts were at the edge of the piece of tobacco ground,
and were merely a few upright sheets of bark with interstices
of many inches and only part of a roof – in short many a
countryman in England provides his pig a snugger shelter. In
fine weather this would matter but little, but in wet it must
have been the source of much discomfort. They received no
wages, but were provided with a scanty suit of slop clothing at
certain seasons specified by law; and also every Saturday
afternoon with as much coarse beef and flour as would just
keep them till the same period of the succeeding week.
Occasionally their master opened his heart so far as to give
them a little tobacco, tea, and sugar beyond the allowance
ordered by law. Altogether their cost might be about half that
of free labourers: whilst between fear of being flogged and

hope of getting a little indulgence in the matter of ration, their labour was nearly or quite equal – so that the master's clear gain was just the wages a free servant would have been paid over and above his ration at the same kind of work.

Only too often the assignment system, for the convict, was nothing less than a tyranny. Harris recorded an instance of this kind:

Besides the two shepherds there was at this station of Mr. ——'s also a hut-keeper or watchman. To him it belonged to watch the sheep by night and the hut by day. He was a prisoner, and if he had either suffered the hut to be robbed by day or the sheep to be attacked by the native dogs at night, he would have been flogged. I say he *would have been*, because his predecessor, a prisoner also, *had been*. Perhaps it is a peculiarity of the office to enable a man to do without sleep, – perhaps there is something in being a convict that deprives him of the right to any, as it does of many other rights; perhaps there is some grand reformatory experiment carrying on of which this is a particular, and of which we are not permitted to know anything publicly. This fellow (for really I have not the impression on my mind of his being a man) had been flogged over and over and over again; and, I verily believe, for nothing else than that naturally he was remarkably stupid and gruff. He was in short just a type of a class of individuals you may meet with in New South Wales at every step; men perfectly crushed by being flogged month after month and year after year for a natural stupidity and abruptness which continually betrays them into blunders, and then by the manner they reply to reproof making them seem insolent and their blunders wilful. At the same time let me be well understood – no person of any discrimination, or whose penetration of character passes beneath the surface, would fall into such a misconception; yet, superintended as they generally are by overseers who have crept up from their own ranks by cunning and sycophancy, and because they would do any dirty work rather than submit to bodily toil, it is only just such a result as might be looked for. The effect of this monstrous and irrational treatment of this convict had been that an almost maniac spitefulness at times took possession of him; and I assure the reader (morally frightful as it may seem) that this very kind of feeling, induced and fostered by the atrocious severities to which they have been and to a still serious extent *are* subjected, may be constantly detected among the lower order of the labourers, but especially among the pastoral class. This poor fellow had been fifteen years in bondage, and I suppose had never passed a year of that time without (let me be permitted to use a phrase not thought by any means too expressive to be regularly used at the tables of gentlemen in the colony) – without his master 'making him a present of a red shirt' (a scarified back).

Nor was there any room in this system for complaint. The assigned convict was on parole, working his way towards his 'ticket of leave' – his emancipation. If he displeased his master, one word to the local magistrate (who was also a landowner) sent him back into irons or onto the government road-gang. Assigned convicts were, as Earl Grey declared in the 1830s, 'in fact slaves'.

Among those who benefited most from the early days of the assignment system were the officers of the military. In the first years of the colony it seemed to be the lot of the military to play the role of villain. Major Ross of the Marines had troubled the plans of Governor Phillip. The New South Wales Corps, the colony's own regiment that took over in 1791, gave later governors no easier ride. The Corps was a collection of misfits rejected by other English regiments and the officers were sharp dealers with a keen desire to grow rich. In the long-term, the best way to achieve this was through the free land grants, which the officers grabbed with both hands and, with the help of assigned convict labour, consolidated into large estates on the best land within reach of Sydney.

But the rewards from landholding only accumulated slowly. The officers also looked for some other capitalist enterprise where their power and position in the colony would give them an advantage. In 1792, they secretly clubbed together £2,000 to charter the *Britannia*, sending her on a round trip to the Cape of Good Hope and raising a very handsome profit.

At this moment, fortune played into the officers' hands. Governor Phillip retired from the colony at the end of 1792 while his successor, Captain John Hunter, was away. The governorship devolved on the highest ranking military officer, who was Major Francis Grose of the New South Wales Corps. In the three years of military rule, Grose made sure that the financial and political interests of the officers had priority within the colony. His rule established the military as the power-brokers and the trading monopolists of the colony, a fraught inheritance that worried later governors for seventeen years, until Governor Macquarie arrived with his own regiment and broke the power of the Corps.

The system was simple, as the wife of Captain John Macarthur demurely explained in 1795 to a friend in England:

> The officers in the colony, with a few others possessed of money or credit in England, unite together and purchase the cargoes of such vessels as repair to this country from various quarters. Two or more are chosen from the number to bargain for the cargo offered for sale, which is then divided amongst them, in proportion to the amount of their subscriptions. This arrangement prevents monopoly, and the impositions that would be otherwise practiced by masters of ships. These details which may seem prolix are necessary to show you the mode in which we are in our infant condition compelled to proceed.

But what this ingenuous lady failed to explain was that the monopoly of the carriers (the ship masters) had been superceded by the monopoly of the importers (the military); and that the activity these officers encouraged and speculated in most was trade in alcohol.

'Rum' – as spirits of any kind were called – was the dangerous life-blood of the new colony. The attraction of drink to the convict population was obvious; for a little while, stupified by bad liquor, the convicts could forget their misery and exile. In his last days Governor Phillip had permitted some sale of alcohol. David Collins noted:

> At Sydney and at Parramatta shops were opened for the sale of the articles of private trade brought out in the Royal Admiral. A licence was given for the sale of porter; but, under the cover of this, spirits found their way among the people, and much intoxication was the consequence. Several

of the settlers, breaking out from the restraint to which they had been subject, conducted themselves with the greatest impropriety, beating their wives, destroying their stock, trampling on and injuring their crops in the ground, and destroying each other's property.

Within two years, Collins was lamenting a destructive rage for strong drink gripping the whole colony:

The passion for liquor was so predominant among the people, that it operated like a mania, there being nothing which they would not risk to obtain it: and while spirits were to be had, those who did any extra labour refused to be paid in money, or any other article than spirits, which were now, from their scarcity, sold at six shillings per bottle. Webb, the settler near Parramatta, having procured a small still from England, found it more advantageous to draw an ardent diabolical spirit from his wheat, than to send it to the store and receive ten shillings per bushel from the commissary. From one bushel of wheat he obtained nearly five quarts of spirit, which he sold or paid in exchange for labour at five and six shillings per quart.

This was the craving that the military monopolists set out to exploit. Indeed, so universal and popular was alcohol that it soon, in a colony without any settled coinage, assumed the place of money. When the Reverend Richard Johnson erected the first church in Sydney, a little thatched wattle building put up, at his own expense, in Rushcutter Bay for £67.12s.11½d., he partly paid for it in half-gallons of spirits. So successful were the military rum traders in impressing on the colony the stamp of their business that ever after Sydney, to the delight of some travellers and to the despair of the moralists, seemed the mecca of alcoholics. The whole town was rife with the dens of 'the sly grog-sellers'. Here was a typical one – the *Sheer Hulk* – encountered by Alexander Harris on his rambles about Sydney:

It was kept at this time by a man of the name of D——, a convict free by servitude (so convicts are designated whose term of sentence has expired), as a lodging-house for sailors.

He had a partner in the speculation who still further cloaked the character of the house by putting up a barber's pole at the door. There is no doubt nevertheless that such a nest would have been rooted out long before but for the handsome 'sweeteners' (bribes) which old D——'s profits enabled him to give the constables. At this time almost every constable in Sydney and indeed in the colony had been a prisoner of the crown; I believe there were two or three old soldiers in the force, but their principles were not a whit superior, so far as I heard and observed, to those of the convict class. These sly grog shops sold rum only, or rather grog; though, adulterated as it was, it hardly deserved even that name.

These places were a reproach to order and good government, but the early governors, derided at every turn by the entrenched power of the military, were unable to curb the use of alcohol. Nor were these governors any more successful in curbing the officers themselves. As Philip King, the third Governor, complained during his long battle with Captain Macarthur:

His employment during the eleven years he has been here has been that of making a large fortune, helping his brother officers to make small ones (mostly at the publick expence), and sewing discord and strife. Experience has convinced every man in this colony that there are no resources which art, cunning, impudence, and a pair of baselisk eyes can afford that he does not put in practice to obtain any point he undertakes.

The influence of the military was not broken until 1809, when Governor Lachlan Macquarie arrived with his own regiment, the 73rd Highlanders, to displace the New South Wales Corps. But by then drink had an unshakable hold on the community. It had become a colonial tradition, just another part of the convict inheritance.

*

Was New South Wales a penal outpost, a convict dump, or was it a colonial venture to people a new land? The puzzle remained. It was, for very many years, a country in the grip of a

127

mild schizophrenia. The early history of piecemeal, improvised development had irretrievably intermixed the world of the bound and the world of the free. The convict needed the free settler for his support, the settler needed the prisoner for his success. Beasts of a very different kind, they were yoked together and they dragged behind them the new civilization of Australia. But it was a civilization that remained shot through with the rivalries and suspicions of the two classes.

The convict, quite naturally, envied the settler his freedom and took every chance to remind the free man of his privilege. Harris, at a dangerous meeting with bushrangers, soon discovered the latent divisions within Australian society:

> 'My mate,' said Dick, 'is hardly a month in the country.'
> 'Oh! we know that; he's one of the free objects – bad luck to 'em! what business have they here in the prisoners' country? But after all, it's prisoners that's worse to one another than these emigrants are to them.'
> 'To be sure,' said another; 'there's bad and good of all sorts, mate. I never think a bit worse of a man for being of one country than for being of another; there's bad and good of all sorts as there is of all religions. If you act as a man, lad (addressing me), you will be respected by every man that knows himself, let you be free or bond.'

Another time, it was an occasion for some of that rough banter so common among working men:

> My share was to answer all the questions (rather all that were answerable) which any and all thought proper to put to me on the subject of affairs in England; and to pocket with the best grace I could (for most of these men had been convicts) the jokes they not very sparingly, but I must say with very good humour, cut on me for having come to the colony 'to make a fortune', or for being 'a free object' (subject), or for having 'lagged myself for fear the king should do it for me'. All these little matters notwithstanding, the evening passed away very pleasantly; if there were many things in these men which I could not approve, there was much more that I could not but admire. There was a sort of manly independence of disposition, which secured truthfulness and sincerity at least among themselves.

And the suspicion worked in reverse also. Free immigrants were likely to arrive with a prejudice against criminals. Moreover, the convict, through the assigned servant system, competed more and more with the free worker in the labour market, as Harris also found to his cost:

Travelling on I found very few free labourers in this district; almost all the work seemed done by the settlers, their sons, and their convict servants. Of course there were a few free men, but the proportion was much less than in the non-agricultural parts. As I have not yet mentioned it, it may be as well to notice here a peculiar characteristic of the free labouring population of Australia: it is in a state of constant migration. The man who has a contract job or is a hired servant here this year, probably spends the next at the other end of the colony. It is less so about the Hawkesbury than elsewhere, occasioned, I have always had a strong surmise, by so many of the little settlers having daughters. Some stalwart young Briton transported at fifteen weathers his seven years, and at two and twenty gets his certificate of freedom and goes off to seek his fortune. The Hawkesbury arrests his weary footsteps; some crabbed old emancipist offers him a job, which, too new in liberty to be fastidious, he takes; there is but one hut, and man and master eat together; a few days domesticates the stranger; and every night when the 'laughing jackass', the settler's clock, a common bush bird, calls him home from the field, the pleasant piano-voice of Nance or Nelly sends him unresisting to the river for a bucket of water or to the bush for a log; till joke gets transformed into serious earnest, and the wandering servant owns the heiress of the soil.

It even happened that certain convicts, because of their position, were able to exercise a control, and sometimes a tyranny, over free men:

The farm-constables I have promised to describe are prisoners of the crown actually serving their sentence, who have been authorised to act ostensibly for the purposes of convict restraint on the farm. But no one ever questions (so that I suppose it cannot be questioned) their right to arrest under the Bushranging Act; and now that the settlers have commenced building private lock-ups on their own farms this really becomes a very serious matter. I could point out plenty of estates which are always short of free labour for no other reason than that free men travelling for work are afraid to go to them, on account of the intolerable conduct of their farm-constable; indeed this is one of the reasons why some of the settlers who have been examined before public committees have been able to give such very explicit evidence of their own want of labourers. Free men do not like being continually called upon by prisoner constables to 'show their freedom'; and emigrants very often have nothing to show, while at the same time their bare word will not go for a straw; and thus, after going a couple of hundred miles up the country for work, they may be marched back in handcuffs, and eventually turned adrift in Sydney with not a penny in their pockets. At the same time, if it has all been regularly done under 'The Bushranging Act', there is no redress.

But this situation, where the convict had the last laugh, was the exception. In relation to the free settlers, the convicts' lot, as the candid Harris admitted, was in general nothing to laugh about. And that was not all. The pernicious attitude which the landowning settlers had developed towards their assigned convicts, who were treated as contemptuous chattels, had crept over into the landlords' dealings with the free workers and poisoned the relations of the labour market:

The fact is, the upper classes of New South Wales settlers have so long been used to deal with the poor wretched convicts, and to tell them they have no rights, and to taunt and mock them if they talk about seeking redress for any ill treatment, that the habit and the feeling at the bottom of it have become rooted in their very nature; and they would wish to treat free people in the same way. 'Is not the free labourer here for our convenience – as a substitute for convicts who can no longer be found in sufficient numbers to supply us? What more profit is one to us that the other? Why should we treat one better than the other?' Such is positively the feeling. And peculiarly suited as these colonies are for the settlement of the surplus labouring population of the British Islands, this feeling has become an effectual bar to both the

welfare of the class that might be benefited and the advance-
ment of the colony. For this same feeling extends itself to
the land question, and has poisoned all the information and
the counsel which the higher settlers and the council of the
colony and the governors have given to the British government at home. Thousands of pounds are now spent in
drinking, &c., in New South Wales, by the labouring class,
which, if small portions of land were to be had, they would
lay out in its purchase. But such a practice the upper class of
settlers universally regard as detrimental to their interests,
and therefore an infringement of their rights; as if no man
had a right to land but themselves.

It was a strange life. The circumstances of their loneliness in
a far country and the history of its curious development made
for the inhabitants a hard, manly, competitive, angry existence.
It was a land in which women were needed to soften masculine
rigour; but it was a land in which women, for many years, had
little place beyond that of bedfellows.

As in most pioneering colonies, there was always a serious
imbalance between the sexes. Throughout the history of transportation, far fewer women than men were sent to New South
Wales, nor was it a place to attract unattached women as free
settlers. Women, to put it bluntly, were a commodity in short
supply, prized most of all for sexual gratification. They were
snapped up by lonely men. The process began at once, on the
convict transports, as John Nicol, sailing in 1790 on the *Lady
Juliana*, admitted:

> Once we put to sea every man on board took a wife from
> among the convicts, they nothing loath. I must confess that I
> was as bad on this point as the others. The girl with whom
> I lived was Sarah Whitelam, a native of Lincoln, a girl of
> modest and reserved turn, as kind and true a creature as ever
> lived. I courted her for a week and upward and would have
> married her on the spot if there had been a clergyman on board.
> I fixed my fancy upon her from the moment I knocked the
> rivets out of her irons.

The Reverend John West went so far as to call the transports
'floating brothels' and added sadly: 'These practices were first

tolerated, and after justified as politic.' The practice of selecting women for concubinage became an official perk. Governor King calmly acknowledged his illegitimate child, from the days of his lonely administration on Norfolk Island. In 1812, a House of Commons select committee, examining the practice of the early years, described its full enormity in prim parliamentary language:

> In the distribution of female convicts great abuses have formerly prevailed; they were indiscriminately given to such of the inhabitants as demanded them, and were in general received rather as prostitutes than as servants; and so far from being induced to reform themselves, the disgraceful manner in which they were disposed of, operated as an encouragement to general depravity of manners. Upon the arrival of Governor Bligh, two-thirds of the children annually born within the Colony were illegitimate. Marriages have latterly become more frequent, consequently prostitution is stated to have been less prevalent; and Governor Macquarie is directing his endeavours under order from the Government here, 'to keep the female convicts separate till they can properly be distributed among the inhabitants, in such a manner as they may best derive the advantages of industry and good character.' . . . Let it be remembered too, how much misery and vice are likely to prevail in a society in which the women bear no proportion to the men; in the Colony at present, the number of men compared to that of women is as 2 to 1; to this, in great measure, the prevalence of prostitution is reasonably to be attributed; but increase that proportion, and the temptation to abandoned vices will also be increased, and the hopes of establishing feelings of decency and morality amongst the lower classes will be still farther removed.

The problems, as this account made clear, could not be solved easily. No one had considered what role women were expected to play in the new society. And female convicts, most of them tough specimens, were, as successive governors found to their cost, a turbulent, obstructive, disorderly presence in a society designed for men. Too many were like the riotous, spirited, foul-mouthed Nancy Ferrel on the *Lady Juliana* whom the captain at first straight-jacketed by means of an empty flour barrel but was later forced 'to tie her up like a man and give her twelve with the cat-o'-nine tails'.

In the face of their official helplessness, the rulers of the colony – all men – could find no better solution for these displaced women convicts than to put them to hard labour in the factory built for them at Parramatta. Their miserable life there was related by Commissioner Bigge:

On their arrival there, they are allowed to remain in a wooden building that is near the factory; and if they have succeeded in bringing their bedding from the ships, they are permitted to deposit it there, or in the room in which the female prisoners are confined for punishment. The first of these apartments is in the upper floor of a house that was built for the reception of pregnant females. It contains another apartment, on the ground floor, that is occupied by the men employed in the factory. It is not surrounded by any wall or paling; and the upper room or garret has only one window, and an easy communication with the room below. No accommodation is afforded for cooking provisions in this building; nor does there exist either inducement to the female convicts to remain in it, or the means of preventing their escape. The greater portion, therefore, betake themselves to the lodgings in the town of Paramatta, where they cohabit with the male convicts in the employ of government, or with any persons who will receive them. Their employment in the factory consists of picking, spinning and carding wool. They are tasked to perform a certain quantity in the day, and when their task is finished, which is generally at one o'clock, they are allowed to return to their lodgings. Their weekly ration consists of four pounds ten ounces of flour, and the same quantity of meat, or two pounds of pork; and the same ration is issued to the females who are confined for punishment. The children who accompany their mothers to Paramatta are maintained by government, and receive one half of the ration last described. As there is a general objection amongst the settlers, to receive into their families female convicts who are accompanied by children, it is their lot to remain longer in Paramatta, and at the factory, than others. The factory itself consists of one long room that is immediately above the gaol, having two windows in front that look into the gaol yard, one in the end of the building, and two windows looking into a yard that is immediately behind. The dimensions of the room are 60 feet by 20; and at one end are store-rooms, where the wool, yarn and cloth are kept. There is one fire-place, at which all the provisions are cooked. The women have no other beds than those they can make from the wool in its dirty state; and they sleep upon it at night, and in the midst of their spinning wheels and work. No attempt has been made to preserve cleanliness in this room, as the boards had shrunk so much, that when they were washed, the water fell through them into the prison rooms below. The walls of the room and the roof bore equal marks of neglect; and the drains in the yard were in the highest degree offensive.

The only punishment that it inflicted was that of moral and physical degradation, beyond the low state of existence from which many of them had previously been taken; and reducing those who had been in better situations, nearly to the same level. The women who had become most profligate and hardened by habit, were associated in their daily tasks with those who had very lately arrived, to whom the customs and practices of the colony were yet unknown, and who might have escaped the consequences of such pernicious lessons, if a little care and a small portion of expense had been spared in providing them with a separate apartment during the hours of labour.

But this tidy practice did nothing to stop the sexual market and the men, instead of waiting for the transports, trooped to the factory:

If a master has a convict that he is anxious to keep, and whom he believes to be well behaved, it is considered a great indulgence if he gives him permission to get a wife from the factory; but the master must enter into an agreement with the Government to feed and support the woman and, in fact, the offspring, to prevent its being a burden on the Government. This being done, the man goes, and he gets an order to the matron of the factory, and, of course, this is for a wife. The women are turned out, and they all stand up as you would place so many soldiers, or so many cattle, in fact, at a fair.

It is requisite for me to state that the same sort of ceremony, and the same mode, occurs with a free-man; for there are free-men that go to the factory to select a wife. . . . I have known of convicts going, and having the pick of one or two hundred without finding one to please them; the lowest fellows you can fancy have said, it wouldn't do; they could not get one to suit. But if he finds one to please him, they get married.

Neither forced labour nor involuntary marriage constituted a proper social policy for female convicts. So long as the penal system lasted in Australia, the fate of women convicts was on the whole a sad one, thrown into a sexual lottery and exploited for what little comfort they could lend to a man's world. Even as late as 1850, the Reverend Fry saw them degraded in the penal settlements of Van Diemen's Land (later Tasmania):

The treatment of the women has long been deemed by the colonists a violation of reason and justice, in direct opposition to the interests of the community. The depôt into which they are received, when discharged from their services, is a scene of feasting, complete idleness and vicious indulgence. The women are occasionally let into the town, and have free communication with their associates. When they bring forth illegitimate children they are received into a nursery, where they live on the same abundant fare, and with nothing to do but nurse their infants; as soon as the children are of proper age, they are sent to the Orphan School which should be called the school for illegitimate children of the convicts, and the mothers are dismissed to repeat the same expensive course of conduct.

To gain a measure of social justice, women in Australia had to wait for the decline of the penal system and the fuller burgeoning of a free society.

If this closed male society, dominated by the necessity of punishment but struggling to expand and free itself through immigrant land settlement, was hard on women, it was not likely to be any easier with the native inhabitants. Governor

Phillip had first instituted an enlightened policy towards the aborigines and for a while, despite scuffles and a little bloodshed, things went well enough. But inevitably the intrusion of the strangers caused increased friction. Phillip then had the curious notion of capturing some natives and forcing on them the supposed benefits of civilization so that they would become missionaries to their own people. Men were duly captured and two of them, Bennelong and Yemmerawanine, even accompanied Phillip back to England, from where Bennelong returned to the colony, a strange, affected mannikin who belonged to neither world. His influence with his own people was negligible, and he is remembered chiefly because his name was given to Bennelong Point, on which the Sydney Opera House now stands.

Captain Watkin Tench was an interested observer of the early native policy. If civilization was supposed to be persuasive in itself, Tench, at least, could see no evidence of it:

> One of the principal effects which we had supposed the seizure and captivity of Arabanoo would produce, seemed yet at as great a distance as ever; the natives neither manifested signs of increased hostility on his account, or attempted to ask any explanation of our conduct through the medium of their countrymen who was in our possession, and who they knew was treated with no farther harshness than in being detained among us. Their forbearance of open and determined attack upon us can be accounted for only by recollecting their knowledge of our numbers, and their dread of our fire-arms.

Nor, when some convicts were flogged for mistreating the aborigines, was the captured Arabanoo gratified by this display of civilized justice. 'Arabanoo was present at the infliction of the punishment,' wrote Tench, 'and was made to comprehend the cause and necessity of it; but he displayed on the occasion symptoms of disgust and terror only.'

Almost the first gift of the Europeans to the natives of New South Wales, as Tench noted in April 1789, was smallpox:

> An extraordinary calamity was now observed among the natives. Repeated accounts brought by our boats of finding

Aboriginal funeral practice – burning the corpse. From David Collins, *Account of New South Wales*, 1798

bodies of the Indians in all the coves and inlets of the harbour, caused the gentlemen of our hospital to procure some of them for the purposes of examination and anatomy. On inspection, it appeared that all the parties had died a natural death: pustules, similar to those occasioned by the small pox, were thickly spread on the bodies; but how a disease, to which our former observations had led us to suppose them strangers, could at once have introduced itself, and have spread so widely, seemed inexplicable. Whatever might be the cause, the existence of the malady could no longer be doubted. Intelligence was brought that an Indian family lay sick in a neighbouring cove: the governor, attended by Arabanoo, and a surgeon, went in a boat immediately to the spot. Here they found an old man stretched before a few lighted sticks, and a boy of nine or ten years old pouring water on his head, from a shell which he held in his hand: near them lay a female child dead, and a little farther off, its unfortunate mother: the body of the woman shewed that famine, superadded to disease, had occasioned her death: eruptions covered the poor boy from head to foot; and the old man was so reduced, that he was with difficulty got into the boat.

This exchange between white and black, so cruelly destructive to the natives, was sadly symbolic. For despite some determined, good-hearted efforts from both sides, there was no meeting point. And this was not because the natives lacked intelligence or humanity. The astute Tench had a chance to study the captured aborigines:

But Baneelon, though haughty, knew how to temporize. He quickly threw off all reserve; and pretended, nay, at particular moments, perhaps felt satisfaction in his new state. Unlike poor Arabanoo, he became at once fond our our viands, and would drink the strongest liquors, nor simply without reluctance, but with eager marks of delight and enjoyment. He was the only native we ever knew who immediately shewed a fondness for spirits: Colbee would not at first touch them. Nor was the effect of wine or brandy upon him more perceptible than an equal quantity would have produced upon one of us, although fermented liquor was new to him.

His powers of mind were certainly far above mediocrity. He acquired knowledge, both of our manners and language, faster than his predecessor had done. He willingly communicated information; sang, danced, and capered: told us all the customs of his country, and all the details of his family economy. Love and war seemed his favourite pursuits; in both of which he had suffered severely. His head was disfigured by several scars; a spear had passed through his arm, and another through his leg; half of one of his thumbs was carried away; and the mark of a wound appeared on the back of his hand. The cause and attendant circumstances of all these disasters, except one, he related to us. 'But the wound on the back of your hand, Baneelon! how did you get that?' He laughed, and owned that it was received in carrying off a lady of another tribe by force. 'I was dragging her away:

she cried aloud, and stuck her teeth in me.' – 'And what did you do then?' 'I knocked her down, and beat her till she was insensible, and covered with blood. – Then' ——

Whenever he recounted his battles, 'poized his lance, and shewed how fields were won,' the most violent exclamations of rage and vengeance against his competitors in arms, those of the tribe called Cam-ee-ra-gal in particular, would burst from him. And he never failed at such times to solicit the governor to accompany him, with a body of soldiers, in order that he might exterminate this hated name.

Tench was, on the whole, favourably impressed:

It is, I think, fair to conclude, that these people are not of a sanguinary and implacable temper. Quick indeed of resentment, but not unforgiving of injury. There was not one of them that did not testify strong abhorrence of the punishment, and equal sympathy with the sufferer. The women were particularly affected; Daringa shed tears; and Barangaroo, kindling into anger, snatched a stick, and menaced the executioner. The conduct of these women, on this occasion, was exactly descriptive of their characters. The former was ever meek and feminine; the latter, fierce and unsubmissive.

And his final judgement contained a firm, warm appreciation of native character and ability.

But if from general view we descend to particular inspection, and examine individually the persons who compose this community, they will certainly rise in estimation. In the narrative part of this work, I have endeavoured rather to detail information, than to deduce conclusions; leaving to the reader the exercise of his own judgment. The behaviour of Arabanoo, of Baneelon, of Colbee, and many others, is copiously described; and assuredly he who shall make just allowance for uninstructed nature, will hardly accuse any of those persons of stupidity, or deficiency of apprehension.

To offer my own opinion on the subject, I do not hesitate to declare, that the natives of New South Wales possess a considerable portion of that acumen, or sharpness of intellect, which bespeaks genius. All savages hate toil, and place happiness in inaction: and neither the arts of civilized life can be practised, or the advantages of it felt, without application and labour. Hence they resist knowledge, and the adoption of manners and customs, differing from their own. The progress of reason is not only slow, but mechanical. – The tranquil indifference, and uninquiring eye, with which they surveyed our works of art, have often, in my hearing, been stigmatized as proofs of stupidity, and want of reflection. But surely we should discriminate between ignorance and defect of understanding. The truth was, they often neither comprehended the design, nor conceived the utility of such works: but on subjects in any degree familiarized to their ideas, they generally testified not only acuteness of discernment, but a large portion of good sense. I have always thought that the distinctions they shewed in their estimate of us, on first entering into our society, strongly displayed the latter quality: – when they were led into our respective houses, at once to be astonished and awed by our superiority, their attention was directly turned to objects with which they were acquainted. They passed without rapture or emotion, our numerous artifices and contrivances: but when they saw a collection of weapons of war, or of the skins of animals and birds, they never failed to exclaim, and to confer with each other on the subject. The master of that house became the object of their regard as they concluded he must be either a renowned warrior, or an expert hunter. Our surgeons grew into their esteem from a like cause. In a very early state of intercourse, several natives were present at the amputation of a leg: when they first penetrated the intention of the operator, they were confounded; not believing it possible that such an operation could be performed without loss of life; and they called aloud to him to desist: but when they saw the torrent of blood stopped, the vessels taken up, and the stump dressed, their horror and alarm yielded to astonishment and admiration, which they expressed by the loudest tokens. – If these instances bespeak not nature and good sense, I have yet to learn the meaning of the terms.

By 1796, Judge-Advocate Collins was convinced that relations between natives and colonists were now running smoothly:

After many untoward occurrences and a considerable lapse of time, that friendly intercourse with the natives which had been so earnestly desired was at length established; and having never been materially interrupted, these remote islanders have been shown living in considerable numbers among us without fear or restraint; acquiring our language; readily falling in with our manners and customs; enjoying the comforts of our clothing, and relishing the variety of our food. We saw them die in our houses, and the places of the deceased instantly filled by others, who observed nothing in the fate of their predecessors to deter them from living with us, and placing that entire confidence in us which it was our interest and our pleasure to cultivate.

But he was too sanguine. The spread and development of white settlements (which was very rapid), the rude incursion of strangers into untamed native country, put too much pressure on the small aboriginal population with its stable but fragile stone age economy. Though there were still fights and misunderstandings, the aborigines seemed to withdraw from the white world. It was as if they had, by secret agreement, rejected the bargain that civilization proposed. The colonists were too much for them; they were overwhelmed.

The native inhabitants processed, slowly and almost without struggle, down the road to defeat and Alexander Harris, writing of the first quarter of the nineteenth century, gives us many glimpses of the stages of that road:

Before we started this morning some of the blacks that I saw encamped a few evenings ago at the foot of the mountains came up to the station. They seemed spiritless and fast verging to the usual fate of the tribes – extinction. The stock-keeper told us that when he first came here to live, and there were as yet no white men about within miles, they were so savage that on the occasion of one of the tribe being killed in an affray, they kept his body unburied for months, till they could take revenge for his death.

And even more to the point:

Even the deep water-holes on the runs already taken up were very much reduced. The blacks say, 'Plenty water before white man come, plenty pish (fish), plenty kangaroo, plenty 'possum, plenty everything: now all gone. Poor fellow now, black fellow! By and bye that got nothing at all to patter. Then *that* tumble down' (then *he* will die).

Yet Harris felt drawn towards these people, and like Tench, could not help but notice their finer qualities. He had every reason for respect and affection – gratitude, too, because they saved his life:

Far in the night as I rose out of one of these creeks on to the hip of a scrubby hill, there gleamed out bright before me, not half a quarter of a mile off, the fires of a blacks' camp; and the dogs at the same instant, attracted by the cracking of the bush, sprang forward yelping by scores. I knew there were none but quiet tribes here, and, filled with new strength, was in a few minutes more among them, as heartily pleased as ever I had been at any thing in my whole life. They gave me plenty of baked fish and cabbage-tree, and a 'bangola' of 'sugar-bag' (water sweetened with native honey), for which I rewarded them with nearly the remainder of my tobacco – about half a pound. There were about a hundred of them; several of them I knew well from their coming to my hut some years before, when in the Long-Brush, behind Kiama. They put me in one of their best gunyahs (a sort of hut of bark, shaped much like those of the English gypsies), and gave me two very large opossum cloaks for the night, with many an exclamation of '*Poor fellow you, binghi* (brother): *most dead you, I believe: what for you stupid like that? what for you not fetch 'em gun and shoot 'em parrot, and patter* (eat)? *bail boos got it chop* (the bush has got no shops).' For an hour the camp was all astir with the white fellow's adventure; the young men shouted and laughed, triumphing in their superior faculties; the old men talked gravely and shook their heads; and the gins, true to their sex, passed to and fro among themselves, from fire to fire, their exclamations of pity with each new bit of information about my mishap, as one or other of the black fellows, by some fresh question, extracted it from me. Human nature is the same from the throne to the gunyah.

And they were able to do this, as Harris acknowledged, only because their traditional lives had endowed them with powers that were beyond the white man:

Aboriginal tribal group – night scene near Sydney. From David Collins, *Account of New South Wales*, 1798

In the morning, though dreadfully tired, stiff, and weak, I set off under the guidance of two of the old men for the rendezvous. I easily made them understand where I wanted to go. You can scarcely name any particular tree in the bush but the blacks know it. This hut they recognised immediately I described it; and I found that my opinion of its original use was perfectly correct. They told even the stockman's name who used to 'sit down' (live) there. He had been dead some time, or they probably would not have done so. Instead of going all round by the road, the blacks took me a short cut; and on my arrival I had the gratification of finding R—— was behind his time, and not yet there. As I made full sure it would not be much longer before he made his appearance, we knocked up a fire in the hut, and I passed the remainder of the time in explaining to my guides that I wished them not to say anything to other white men of my being here. This they promised, and they are a people with whom a promise made under such circumstances is very rarely, if ever, broken. In my many years' dealings with them I never knew an instance.

A remarkable people! And why, Harris indignantly wanted to know, should we expect them to take on the attributes of a cruel, destructive and avaricious civilization?

On the contrary, all the thanks we get from the black native for attempting to introduce our religion into his tribes is the laugh of derision, or the silence of a yet deeper scorn. 'You!' he says, 'you who tie one another up, and flog one another within an inch of life, for some little hasty word; you who begrudge one another enough to eat; you who deprive me of my hunting grounds, only to increase possessions for mere possessions' sake; you, a people divided into two classes, the one hateful and the other contemptible, the tyrant and the slave; you who keep, and clothe, and train men to human slaughter as a trade – you teach me to be better! Me who walk the forest free, who appropriate no more than I need, who never fight but as a deeply injured man, who would not lay your bloody lash upon my dog, much less my brother; who "in wrath remember mercy", and give even the public culprit, against whom I am to direct my spear at the command of the tribe, his shield to defend himself with; – YOU convert ME! preposterous!' Oh! that mankind would but have common sense.

*

At the heart of the new country stood the convict. The colony existed, in theory, for the punishment, correction and perhaps reformation of prisoners. And though many vigorous shoots were being thrown out in the direction of freedom, all ventures started out from that forlorn figure, the prisoner on the government chain-gang:

The convicts in the service of Government, are divided into gangs, – every gang has an overseer, and every two or three gangs a superintendent; these are frequently chosen from amongst those convicts who best conduct themselves. They work from six in the morning till three in the afternoon, and the remainder of the day is allowed to them, to be spent either in amusement or profitable labour for themselves. They are clothed, fed, and for the most part lodged by the Government; and though in the early periods of the Colony, inconvenience and distress may have arisen from the irregularity of supply from this Country, latterly the food and clothing have been good, and, generally speaking, in sufficient abundance. Should the convicts misconduct themselves at their work, the superintendents have no power of inflicting punishment, but are for that purpose obliged to take them before a magistrate; the sitting magistrate of the week at Sydney, may order a punishment of 25 lashes; a regular Bench, which consists, at least, of three, may order as many as 300; and in distant parts of the colony, a single magistrate has the same power with the Bench at Sydney; but a heavy punishment is not executed without the previous approbation of the Governor. Another mode of correction, and that which Your Committee would recommend to be preferred, in as many cases as possible, is to sentence the culprit to work for a certain number of days in the gaol gang; he is here obliged to labour at some public work in irons, from six in the morning to six at night, and no hours are allowed to him for profit or amusement.

But even when the convict's central position was acknowledged, it still remained a problem to know what to do with him. More and more, the convicts came to be regarded merely as slave labour, a cheap resource to be used for public works, chiefly land clearance and road-making. A House of Commons select committee investigating in the 1830s described their life:

The convicts under the immediate charge of the Government in the Australian Colonies, may be divided into those who are retained in the service of the Government merely because they are required as labourers, those who are returned by their masters as unfit for service, those who having suffered for some offence committed in the colony, are retained for a certain period of probation in the employment of the

Government, and those who, for crimes committed in the colonies, are worked on the roads generally in irons, or are sent to the penal settlements.

To commence with a description of the first class of convicts, those who are retained in the service of the Government, not as an additional punishment. On the arrival of a convict vessel in the penal colonies of Australia, an application is made to the assignment commissioner from the proper authorities for the number of the convicts who are required for the service of the Government. These convicts are selected without reference to their past conduct, except that prisoners who are described to be of very depraved character are not usually assigned to settlers, and remain under the charge of the Government; in some few cases directions to this effect are sent out from England. In Van Diemen's Land all mechanics are retained in the service of the Government, and placed either in the engineer department or in the loan-gang; a few convicts likewise are selected out of every ship for the police. In the year 1835, out of 14,903 convicts in Van Diemen's Land there were in the road department, 1,687; engineer ditto, 516; miscellaneous, including marine survey, &c., 716; constables and field-police, 338; total, 3,257. There are no returns of a similar description with regard to New South Wales. It appears, however, that the number of convicts retained (not as punishment) on the public works in the latter colony, has of late years considerably decreased; and most of those works are now performed by contract.

Convicts in the employment of Government are generally worse off than those assigned as servants; they are employed chiefly on the public works of the colony; some of them are, however, in situations of comparative ease, such as clerks, messengers, constables in the police and so forth, in which services it is a necessary evil to employ convicts. That it must be an enormous evil to employ convicts, or persons that have been convicts, in the police, especially in such communities as New South Wales and Van Diemen's Land, seems to Your Committee to be a self-evident proposition. Many of the convicts so employed appear to have been of the worst possible character; willing to take bribes; conniving at the offences of the convict population; when employed as scourgers, defeating the sentence of the law; sometimes bringing false accusations against innocent persons, other times screening the guilty from justice; committing outrages on female prisoners committed to their charge; and, in short, frequently defeating all the efforts of the Government to prevent crime. In the present state of Van Diemen's Land, Sir George Arthur thought it impossible to obtain a police of free emigrants: some three or four years ago he said that he took into the police a number of Chelsea pensioners and of free emigrants, but they proved worse than the convicts.

Large parties of convicts, called road parties, are employed in making roads in New South Wales and Van Diemen's Land; these parties consist mostly of convicts, who have been returned to Government by their masters as being unfit for service, and of convicts who, having been convicted of some offence in the colony, have been sent, on the expiration of their sentence, to work for a certain period on the roads before they were re-assigned. Composed entirely of criminals, some of them of the very worst character (all of them ultimately degraded and demoralised by associating together), these parties were dispersed over a wide extent of country, under a most incomplete and inefficient system of superintendence, with overseers most of whom had been convicts, and in many cases with convicts for the deputy overseers, to whose sole charge the road-parties were sometimes left for many days. Prisoners in the road-parties were sometimes in league with the convict servants of the neighbouring settlers, upon whose property they committed every description of depradation, the fruits of which were consumed in intoxication and other debauchery. The conditions of convicts in the road-parties on the whole appears to be a more disagreeable one that that of assigned servants; the former are subject to a greater degree of restraint than assigned convicts. The nature of the work of convicts in road-parties, particularly that of breaking stones under a hot sun, was irksome, though the quantity of work which they performed was very slight. . . . Many persons connected with that colony consider that, in its present state, the road-parties are a necessary evil because, in their opinion, it would be impossible to obtain a sufficient supply of free labour to repair the roads, and free labourers would consider themselves degraded by an occupation, that had been a punishment for convicts. Moreover, free labourers would not submit to the same degree of superintendence and discipline as convicts; and it is said they would probably, therefore, commit outrages as great, if not greater, than those committed by convicts. General Bourke likewise observed, 'that great as the complaints are which are made by a certain portion of the colonists on account of the crimes committed by the road-parties, still greater is the demand for good roads; and if those parties were broken up, they would probably be regretted in the colony.'

Here was a tacit recognition that the convict system in New South Wales had broken down by about 1840. The convict was little more than a nuisance and an embarrassment to a society that had grown beyond him. Only in certain restricted areas, in Van Diemen's Land and Norfolk Island, were the original penal aims still followed:

In Van Diemen's Land the employment of convicts out of chains on the roads has not occasioned evils to the same extent as in New South Wales. This result is partly to be attributed to the better system of management which is in force in that colony, and partly to the nature of the general system of government which has been pursued in Van Diemen's Land, which, aided by the limited extent of the island, renders it easier for the Government to enforce its regulations, to preserve discipline, and to prevent escape from the road-parties, than in the other penal colony. For New South Wales is not only a penal, but a large and flourishing free colony. Though the free inhabitants are subjected, on account of dwelling there, to greater restraints than if they were residing in the mother country, and are obliged to submit to laws 'which, (according to Sir R. Bourke) nothing but the peculiar case of the colony could render tolerable to Englishmen,' yet they claim, and on the whole, enjoy most of the privileges of free men in this country. Van Diemen's Land, on the contrary, was looked upon by Sir George Arthur as intended to be a vast goal or penitentiary.

New South Wales was evolving a life of its own, rugged, vulgar, vital, with many elements drawn from the convict past, but beginning to be recognizably Australian. It was a life that was often the despair of the governors. Governor King, when he began his rule in 1800, was not impressed by his citizens:

> Vice, dissipation, and a strange relaxation seems to pervade every class and order of people. One shipload of spirits is not more than half sold. Cellars, from the *better sort of people* in the colony to the blackest character among the convicts, are full of that fiery poison. The children are abandoned to misery, prostitution, and every vice of their parents, and, in short, nothing less than a total change in the system of administration must take place immediately I am left to myself. But it must be done by degrees. I shall have to begin everything anew.

And when Governor Bligh, the disciplinarian of the mutiny on the *Bounty*, followed King in 1806, he found the task must begin yet again:

> In the customs and manners of the people here a great deal is to be corrected. The Settlers in general, and particularly those from Prisoners, are not honest, have no prudence and little industry, besides being burthened with debts; great chicanery is used in all their dealings, and much litigation. All this will require a vast deal of attention on my part to remove, to which end the rising generation shall be watched over and educated, while the pernicious customs of the place shall be checked by every means in my power.

These men, inundated by the worries of government, were much too pessimistic. Taking the short view, they could not see that there was a ferment at work that carried society irresistibly onward. What was lacking in morals and good order was compensated for by energy, spirit and hard work. Even the convict type was not without its virtues:

> He was a sturdy, gray-headed, old man from the north of Ireland; a convict, but still a Presbyterian; combining a singular sternness with an unconquerable cheerfulness; a man who did a great deal of work, more by long hours than by speed, who never seem tired, and never was an instant

behind time at his meals; he had been an overseer, but lost the office because he would not have men flogged, and had invariably for many years past drank all his earnings every fifteen or eighteen months: then on coming out of his spree, and finding himself penniless, and suffering from the blue devils almost to madness, he would resolve again, and again lay by his hoard to be in like manner subjected to the periodical fit of dissipation. Although I was now only second in command and one does not very easily fall into the whims and put up with the blunders of an inferior workman, I must say I liked the old man very much. There was a natural conscientiousness about him which commanded my confidence.

And the familiar watchwords in the colony, as Harris found, were early rising and long hours:

I was awakened by our host coming in from his work to breakfast. It was about eight o'clock, and his brother, who had also been up some time, had lit the fire, boiled a piece of salted beef, baked a cake on the hot hearth, and made the tea. This sort of readiness and activity is a remarkable feature in the character of the working population of the Australian colonies.

Driven by such energy, the world was briskly on the move. Only thirty-four months after the first landing, Captain Tench was enthusiastically casting his eye over Rose Hill, the future town of Parramatta:

The main street of the new town is already begun. It is to be a mile long, and of such breadth as will make Pall-Mall and Portland-Place 'hide their diminished heads.' It contains at present 32 houses completed, of 24 feet by 12 each, on a ground floor only, built of wattles plaistered with clay, and thatched. Each house is divided into two rooms, in one of which is a fire place and a brick chimney. These houses are designed for men only; and ten is the number of inhabitants allotted to each; but some of them now contain 12 or 14, for

Design for a church at Parramatta. From David Collins, *Account of New South Wales*, 1798

PLAN & ELEVATION of a CHURCH.

Built at Paramatta New South Wales during the Government of John Hunter Esq.r 1800.

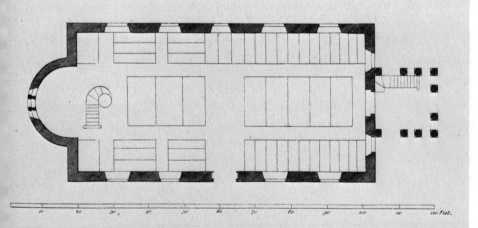

want of better accommodation. More are building; in a cross street stand nine houses for unmarried women: and exclusive of all these are several small huts where convict families of good character are allowed to reside. Of public buildings, besides the old wooden barrack and store, there is a house of lath and plaister, 44 feet long by 16 wide, for the governor, on a ground floor only, with excellent out-houses and appurtenances attached to it. A new brick store-house, covered with tiles, 100 feet long by 24 wide, is nearly completed, and a house for the store-keeper. The first stone of a barrack, 100 feet long by 24 wide, to which are intended to be added wings for the officers, was laid to-day. The situation of the barrack is judicious, being close to the store-house, and within a hundred and fifty yards of the wharf, where all boats from Sydney unload. To what I have already enumerated, must be added an excellent barn, a granary, an inclosed yard to rear stock in, a commodious blacksmith's shop, and a most wretched hospital, totally destitute of every conveniency. Luckily for the gentleman who superintends this hospital, and still more luckily for those who are doomed in case of sickness to enter it, the air of Rose Hill has hitherto been generally healthy. A tendency to produce slight inflammatory disorders, from the rapid changes of the temperature of the air, is most to be dreaded.

The hours of labour for the convicts are the same here as at Sydney. On Saturdays after ten o'clock in the morning they are allowed to work in their own gardens: these gardens are at present, from the long drought, and other causes, in a most deplorable state: potatoes, I think, thrive better than any other vegetable in them. For the public conveniency a baker is established here in a good bakehouse, who exchanges with every person bread for flour, on stipulated terms; but no compulsion exists for any one to take his bread; it is left entirely to every body's own option to consume his flour as he pleases. Divine service is performed here, morning and afternoon, one Sunday in every month, when all the convicts are obliged to attend church, under penalty of having a part of their allowance of provisions stopped, which is done by the chaplain, who is a justice of the peace.

Buildings were one thing, but the life of the spirit was not totally forgotten either. Already, in June 1789, the first Australian theatrical performance had taken place. Farquhar's comedy *The Recruiting Officer* providing, as Tench said, relief in the midst of some miserable days:

> The exhilarating effect of a splendid theatre is well known: and I am not ashamed to confess, that the proper distribution of three or four yards of stained paper, and a dozen farthing candles stuck around the mud walls of a convict hut, failed not to diffuse general complacency on the countenances of sixty persons, of various descriptions, who were assembled to applaud the representation. Some of the actors acquitted themselves with great spirit, and received the praises of the audience: a prologue and an epilogue, written by one of the performers, were also spoken on the occasion; which, although not worth inserting here, contained some tolerable allusions to the situation of the parties, and the novelty of a stage-representation in New South Wales.

Quick though progress was, aspirations ran ahead even faster. In December 1791, Watkin Tench was contemplating for Parramatta a future of European resplendence:

> In a colony which contains only a few hundred hovels, built of twigs and mud, we feel consequential enough already to talk of a treasury, an admiralty, a public library, and many other similar edifices, which are to form part of a magnificent square. The great road from near the landing place to the governor's house is finished, and a very noble one it is, being of great breadth, and a mile long, in a strait line: in many places it is carried over gullies of considerable depth, which have been filled up with trunks of trees, covered with earth. All the sawyers, carpenters, and blacksmiths will soon be concentred under the direction of a very adequate person of the governor's household.

This was a little too much expectation. The reality did not quite match that vision. George Cayley, a plant collector for Sir Joseph Banks, first saw the colony in about 1800:

> The best public building in the colony is a new church at Parramatta which is not yet finished. Another is also begun in

Sydney, at which place there is a good jail, which is but lately finished. There are three windmills at Sydney, two of them built by Government. People are better clothed now than when I first came here. After making a list of what one wants, one must apply to the Governor, who looks over the list. If it meets with his approval he signs it. Then one must go to the Commissary for him to sign it. After that one goes to the stores and perhaps may wait a long time before one gets served. The goods are not exposed for sale but left in a large storehouse with a sentinel placed at the foot of a step-ladder, where the people sometimes form a waiting crowd, as only one person is permitted to go up at once.

There are a few schools, but badly managed. At Sydney there is an orphan school; none but girls are admitted, yet children with parents are admitted too.

Nor was agriculture, from which so much was expected, quite as thriving as had been hoped. Cayley, a botanist himself, was not impressed.

The method of farming is conducted upon a bad principle, and carried on in a slovenly manner. Nothing more is done than break up the ground with a hoe and throw in the wheat, which again is chopped over with a hoe. I have never seen any people weed their wheat, though it is generally overrun with weeds.

Gardening is in an infant state. It is not uncommon for the colonists to be without vegetables for some months of the year. Potatoes were very bad and stinking on my first coming here, but have improved of late. Watermelons are much thought of . . . Houses are nothing more than simple wretched huts, especially the farmers'. The walls are wattled and plastered with clay, the roof thatched, the floor nothing more than the bare ground. They generally consist of two rooms, and the furniture coincides with them.

The general mode of living is very mean and wretched. I have known worn-out bullocks killed and issued. Had this meat been exposed for sale in an English market it would have been publicly burnt, but here it was considered prime meat. Though the colony is yet but in infancy, there are a deal of lawsuits and people arrested for debt. A settler, if though he is poor, yet he is out of debt, may consider himself a happy man.

It took another twenty years or so for cultivation in New South Wales to produce the excellent results that Alexander Harris noticed:

My way to the farm of the first settler I had been advised to go to, a miller, lay along the lowlands ascending the river. On making my way down into this tract I found all sorts of vegetables and fruit trees flourishing; at least all the settlers troubled themselves to plant. There were excellent figs, gooseberries, currants, lemons, oranges, melons, peaches as large as a good sized breakfast cup and of the most exquisite flavour; potatoes, pumpkins as big as a large bucket, cabbages, radishes, onions, beans, pease; in short everything of the kind profusely produced and of the most superior quality. In one place I saw a whole cart-load of the most delicious peaches going along the road; and on asking the driver where he was taking them to market, he told me they were for the pigs, and that all the season through they gathered a similar load every other day from under the trees in the orchard for the same purpose. In another place I found a large tract planted with what at first glance seemed to be a species of cabbage; but on inquiring of some men who were working among the plants hilling them up, I found it to be tobacco. They said there would be about twelve hundredweight to the acre, and that, if well cured, it would be worth 150*l.* per acre; and that really well cured Australian tobacco would sell about that part as well as American; but few people could succeed, from want of a knowledge of the true process, in effecting a good cure of their leaf.

And Harris, though he found parts of Sydney squalid enough, saw other evidence of large-hearted man-made grandeur, the 'government roads' in particular:

Surveyors lay down the best course for the line, and gangs then occupy it, felling in one unbroken line a space of bush of many fathoms wide, and burning off the timber as they go. Finally, where the ground needs it, it is levelled; and where bridges are wanted they are made. The effect of these vast avenues, particularly before the grass is worn away, and all but the mere opening remains in its primitive and natural state, is singularly fine and striking; perhaps the term sublime would not be too strong to apply to the effect. In some places you may see miles along these magnificent openings; the timber on each side is sometimes of gigantic growth; tall regal-looking gums; black, gnarled, grim iron-barks, or stringy-barks swathed in their soot-mantles from the bush-fires: there, if the air be clear, and you catch sight of some other traveller a mile away, the sense of his *conspicuous little-ness* is irresistible; and this the next act of reflection can scarcely fail to transfer to yourself.

In twenty-five years remarkable things had been achieved. To view the urban vitality of Sydney and the tranquil spread of Parramatta, to see the communities at Windsor, Richmond and Kiama, the rich settlements along the Parramatta River and in the valleys of the Nepean and the Hawkesbury, to wander among the cattle stations and the first of the sheep ranges, all this was to see just how far the world had come from those miserable days so graphically described, in 1845, by an old man whose memory stretched back to the time of Governor Phillip:

I arrived in the colony fifty-six years since; it was Governor Phillip's time, and I was fourteen years old; there were only eight houses in the colony then. I know that myself and eighteen others laid in a hollow tree for seventeen weeks, and cooked out of a kettle with a wooden bottom: we used to stick it in a hole in the ground, and make a fire around it. I was seven years in bondage, and then started working for a living wherever I could get it.

There was plenty of hardship then: I have often taken grass, pounded it, and made soup from a native dog. I would eat anything then. For seventeen weeks I had only five ounces of flour a day. We never got a full ration except when the ship was in harbour. The motto was 'Kill them, or work them, their provision will be in store.' Many a time have I been yoked like a bullock with twenty or thirty others to drag along timber. About eight hundred died in six months at a place called Toogabbie, or Constitution-hill.

I knew a man so weak, he was thrown into the grave, when he said, 'Don't cover me up; I'm not dead; for God's sake don't cover me up!' The overseer answered, 'Damn your eyes, you'll die to-night, and we shall have the trouble to come back again!' The man recovered; his name is James Glasshouse, and he is now alive at Richmond.

They used to have a large hole for the dead; once a day men were sent down to collect the corpses of prisoners, and throw them in without any ceremony or service. The native dogs used to come down at night and fight and howl in packs, gnawing the poor dead bodies.

Any man would have committed murder for a month's provisions: I would have committed three murders for a week's provisions! I was chained seven weeks on my back for being out getting greens, wild herbs. The Rev. Marsden used to come it tightly to force some confession. Men were obliged to tell lies to prevent their bowels from being cut out by the lash. The laws were bad then. If an officer wanted a man's wife, he would send the husband to Norfolk Island.

Old Jones killed three men in a fortnight at the saw by overwork. We used to be taken in large parties to raise a tree; when the body of the tree was raised, Old Jones would call some men away – then more; the men were bent double – they could not bear it – they fell – the tree on one or two, killed on the spot. 'Take him away; put him in the ground!' There was no more about it.

After seven years I got my liberty, and then started working about for a living where I could get it.

But in the midst of development, the ghost of tyranny still remained. The convict system still existed – modified, ineffi- cient, negligently applied – but still casting dark shadows, corrupting colonial society. What else could one expect, cried Alexander Harris, 'under this system of white slavery?'

The master's interest is to get as much as possible for as little as possible. Thus when the thing to be done is a fixed amount, not liable to increase or decrease, as shepherding or hut-keeping, the master naturally says, 'Well, the very lowest amount of strength a man can walk about with will suffice for this work: consequently if I only give this man a diet that keeps him alive, I get all I want.' This leads to bitter, ineradicable animosity in the men, which year by year gets deeper and stronger; until at last the magistrate, himself a settler too, and equally a party in the iniquitous system, is appealed to by the master. Of course he orders the man a flogging, and I am sorry to say generally with much such nonchalance as the housewife sends for a pound of candles. Then come bushranging – robbery – murder – and capture and execution.

'The free settlers,' Harris added, 'governed their men with capriciousness and by terror.' A society that lent itself so willingly to bondage would never be able to grasp the full flower of free development. Too many whose lives were painful and unfulfilled, themselves objects of exile and contempt, welcomed at last the final exile in the Sand-Hills of Sydney:

Every body in New South Wales knows the import of the phrase *the Sand-Hills*. It is one of the still trophy yards of death – one of the stillest – one of the saddest. Here in a cloudy winter day, a chiller and more waillike breeze goes stealing along each little knoll that breasts up along the barren hollow; and here too in the summer's prime the sand, gathering the solar heat, glows upward again into the descending beams, intensifying them till it is faintness and blindness and something near suffocation to stand still anywhere within the dread precinct. If the world were searched from end to end, nowhere could you find such another volume of unutterable woe as is bound up in this little spot. In yonder corner lie the Jews, in this the Protestants; here the Presbyterian, there the Catholic: but *all* wanderers far from home and kin. Take any group of those masses and analyze it. What elements! – Misfortunes wonderful – incredible delusions – pure suffering – and direst criminality.

CHAPTER SIX

FROM GAOL INTO FREEDOM

When Governor Lachlan Macquarie landed in New South Wales, on the last day of 1809, he found the colony, as usual, in a deplorable state:

> I found the colony barely emerging from infantile imbecility, and suffering from various privations and disabilities; the country impenetrable beyond forty miles from Sydney; agriculture in a yet languishing state; commerce in its early dawn; revenue unknown; threatened with famine; distracted by faction; the public buildings in a state of dilapidation and mouldering on decay; the few roads and bridges formerly constructed rendered almost impassable; no public credit nor private confidence; the morals of the great mass of the population in the lowest state of debasement, and religious worship almost wholly neglected.

But the time was ripe for change, and Macquarie, an honest, persevering, rather humourless Scot, was the man to set things in motion. The 'Rum Rebellion' of the officers of the New South Wales Corps had fizzled out. The populace, tired of military authority that greedily lined its own pocket, was ready for properly constituted civilian rule and welcomed Macquarie with a display of enthusiasm by the light of blazing tar-barrels. With his own regiment about him, and the old military withdrawn, the new Governor had a freer hand than any of his predecessors.

His first task was to introduce a little sobriety and order into a place characterized by the Reverend Samuel Marsden as one given over to 'riot, dissipation and depravity'. 'Drunkenness, murder and robbery,' the chaplain went on, 'had become common crimes.' But the more important task was to give direction to the growing colony, and here Macquarie was determined to follow the policy that Governor Phillip had been edging towards from the very beginning, to swing the new land away from the cruelty and restricted life of a penal settlement and throw it open to the fresh, boisterous winds of free colonization.

The policy Macquarie began, and the one his successors followed, sometimes doubtfully and sometimes with the rush of true faith, had two aims: to emancipate as many convicts as possible, thereby turning government drones into working citizens, and to encourage by all means the immigration of free settlers.

The first aim was controversial and clashed with the established privileges and perks of the colonial officials. Macquarie persevered:

> I was very much surprised and concerned, on my arrival here, at the extraordinary and illiberal Policy I found had been adopted by the Persons who had preceded me in office respecting those Men who had been originally sent out to this country as Convicts but who, by long Habits of Industry and total Reformation of Manners, had not only become respectable, but by many degrees the most useful members of the community. These persons have never been countenanced or received into Society. I have, nevertheless, taken upon myself to adopt a new Line of Conduct, conceiving that Emancipation, when united with Rectitude and long-tried good Conduct, should lead a man back to that Rank of Society which he had forfeited, and do away, in so far as the Case will admit, All Retrospect of former bad conduct. This appears to me to be the greatest Inducement that can be held out towards the Reformation of the Manners of the Inhabitants and I think it is consistent with the gracious and humane intentions of His Majesty and his Ministers in favour of this Class of People.

And eventually the policy succeeded, proving once again (though governments in all ages are reluctant to learn the lesson) that the reformation and encouragement of prisoners pay better dividends for society than repression and revenge.

The second aim, to increase immigration, was more easily accepted, but over the years it proved troublesome to regulate and became, in time, a matter for regret.

The colony wanted free people. But what kind of people? Official instinct at first preferred development by a landowning capitalist middle class. Free labourers, it was thought, were not needed. Their place was already occupied by convicts working as assigned servants. The ship's surgeon, Peter Cunningham, who was something of a propagandist for the colony, expressed it like this:

> I would counsel no man encumbered with a family, however, to risk emigration to New South Wales with a capital of *less* that 1200*l.*, and even then he should proceed cautiously and economically. If Australia is better suited to the agricultural *capitalist* than America, the latter is probably more advantageous to the agricultural *labourer*. In Australia, farm labour is performed almost entirely by convicts, whose only remuneration consists of food and clothing; to which arrangement they are compelled to submit; and as their numbers are generally abundant, farm labour is kept low. . . . I question much, however, whether many *English* labourers live better than our convict servant here, whose weekly ration consists of a sufficiency of flour to make four quartern loaves at least; of seven pounds of beef; two ounces of tea, one pound of sugar, and two ounces of tobacco, with the occasional substitution of two or three quarts of milk daily for the tea and sugar allowance. Numbers of the English working poor would doubtless be happy to bargain for such a diet; and thus their situation might in these points be bettered, by their being placed upon an equality with *convicts!* (Mechanics, nevertheless, of all descriptions, earn here liberal pay.) The wages of labour therefore being so low, and the price of farm produce comparatively so high, it must be apparent to all how profitably capital may be invested here.

As long as the colony remained locked into its little world by the barrier of the Blue Mountains, and the assignment system worked with reasonable efficiency, there was perhaps adequate labour. But in 1812 the barrier was pierced and the colony began to expand fast by means and into places that the government would rather not contemplate. Soon there was a need for all sorts of workers and the settlers themselves were clamouring for labour. The government slowly responded. Assisted passages for immigrants were introduced, bounties were given as encouragement, land policies were tinkered with to allow easier access and freer competition.

All this caused trouble with one or other settled interest. Only on the question of women was there agreement – there were not enough of them:

NOTICE
TO
YOUNG WOMEN

Desirous of bettering their condition by an
Emigration to New South Wales.

In New South Wales and Van Diemen's Land there are very few women compared with the whole number of people, so that it is impossible to get women enough as Female Servants or for other Female Employments. The consequence is, that desirable situations, with good wages, are easily obtained by Females in those Countries; but the passage is so long that few can pay the expense of it without help. There is now, however, the following favourable opportunity of going to New South Wales.

The Committee has been formed in London for the purpose of facilitating Emigration, which intends to send out a Ship in the course of the Spring, expressly for the conveyance of Female Emigrants, under an experienced and respectable Man and his Wife who have been engaged as Superintendents. The parties who go in that Vessel must be *Unmarried Women or Widows*; must be *between the ages of 18 and 30*; and must be of *good health and character*. They must also be *able to pay* £6 towards the expense of their Passage. The remainder of the expense will be paid by the Society. Every arrangement will be made for the comfort of the Emigrants during the voyage; and Medical Assistance provided: they will also be taken care of on their first landing in the Colonies; and they will find there, ready for them, a list of the different situations to be obtained, and of the wages offered, so that they may at once see the different opportunities of placing themselves. The women sent out in this manner will not be bound to any person whatsoever, but will be, to all intents and purposes, Free Women.

But all other immigrants, especially labourers with little capital, appeared as a threat to one or other section of colonial society. Perhaps the new arrivals would not serve their purpose. Breathing the heady air of New South Wales, they might even have the gall to enter the marketplace in competition against their masters:

My own man who had served me for eight years in England, and had often sworn that he would go the wide world over with me, seeing that I was the best of masters, never reached my new abode. He had saved about £150 in my service; and I had advised him to take the money out of a London Savings' Bank, under an idea that he might obtain ten per cent for it at Sydney. He followed my advice. About a month after our arrival I missed him one morning. Before night I received a letter, by which he informed me that he had taken a grant of land near Hunter's River, and that he 'hoped we parted friends'. He is now one of the most consequential persons in the Colony, has grown enormously fat, feeds upon greasy dainties, drinks oceans of bottled porter and port wine, damns the Governor, and swears by all his gods, Jupiter, Jingo, and Old Harry, that this Colony must soon be independent.

Or worse, the newcomers might even be part of a Whig plot to debauch the colony, as the *Sydney Morning Herald* contended in 1840, drawing the attention of the public to 'the scandalous abuses of the Government system of importing immigrants':

These statements are quite sufficient to draw the attention of the public to the scandalous abuses of the Government system of importing immigrants. It has been converted into a contemptible tool for Whig faction purposes, and Popish ascendancy. The interests of the colony are thrown overboard to promote the Irish poor laws. The sale of Land funds are handed over to agents, who sweep the gaols and parishes of the cumberers of the property of popish landlords. The unhappy emigrants are shipped off, to make way for pardoned cut throats released from prison, by the popularity hunting Lord Lieutenant. Will the Government permit this system, so ably exposed by Mr. Pinnock, to exist for one day, will no sense of oppression awaken the torpid energies of the buyers of land and hirers of servants? The nefarious system is open to the glare of the sun. If the monster is not crushed let the sufferers take the consequences, in the embarrassing poor-law begging system it produces, and in the pondrous taxes to be levied for poor-houses, hospitals, gaols, and police, to supress such scenes, as have never been witnessed in this land, comparatively happy with all its disadvantages of convict servants and irresponsible Councils. . . . The system is 'too bad'. It merits the severest censure.

In the matter of immigration, it was almost impossible to balance the colony's needs against its fears. But as the Speaker of the Legislative Council wrote in 1846, 'the fact is, we *must* have labour in some shape or other – free labour if we can get it – if not, this prison labour, and failing either, coolie labour.'

Over the years the immigrants came, sometimes in a head-long rush which reaction and prejudice then reduced to a steady trickle. In the quarter century after 1820 nearly 225,000 came from Great Britain, and a lesser but uncertain number from other countries.

Among those who arrived in the early 1820s was the young hopeful who wrote under the name Alexander Harris. Harris was not one of the respectable capitalists recommended by Surgeon Cunningham, with £1,200 in his pocket and a family to help him. He was a carpenter, just out of his apprenticeship, with about £80 to his name, emigrating to New South Wales with 'the hope of bettering my condition'. He was a typical artisan immigrant, a member of a free class that became the backbone of the new land.

Landing with their expectation and anxiety, the newcomers already detected a breezy urgency in the colonial air:

On getting sight of Sydney you see a waterside town scattered wide over upland and lowland, and if it be a breezy day the merry rattling pace of its manifold windmills, here and there perched on the high points, is no unpleasing sight. It gives, even from the distance, a presage of the stirring, down-right earnest life (be it for good or evil) that so strongly characterizes the race that lives, and breathes, and strives around: a race with whom it is one of the worst reproaches to be *a crawler*.

The town that lay before them was both familiar and strange, with all the turmoil and press of a European city giving way to a relaxed, semi-rural sprawl. Cunningham, writing also of the 1820s, gave this lively portrait:

You land at the government wharf on the right where carts and porters are generally on the lookout for jobs; and on passing about fifty yards along the avenue, you enter George Street, which stretches on both hands, and up which towards the left you now turn, to reach the heart of the town. Near the harbour, where ground is very valuable, the houses are usually contiguous, like those of the towns in England; but, generally speaking, the better sort of houses in Sydney are built in the detached cottage style, – of white freestone, or of brick plastered and whitewashed, one or two stories high, with verandas in front, and enclosed by a neat wooden paling, lined occasionally with trim-pruned geranium hedges; they have besides a commodious garden attached, commonly decked out with flowers, and teeming with culinary delicacies. Into the enclosure immediately around the house, the dogs are usually turned at night, to ward off rogues, – and uncompromising, vigilant watchmen they certainly are, paying little of that respect to genteel exterior which their better-bred brethren in England are so apt to demonstrate. The streets are wide, and neither paved nor lighted at present; but the general dryness of our climate and durable composition of our streets render paving unnecessary; while an elegant set of lamps is now actually in progress, to be placed diagonally at fifty yards distance; and by reason of the whiteness of our houses and clearness of our sky, an illumination will thus be effected equalling some of the best-lighted London streets. Although all you see are English faces, and you hear no other language but English spoken, yet you soon become aware you are in a country very different from England, by the number of parrots and other birds of strange note and plumage which you observe hanging at so many doors, and cagefuls of which you will soon see exposed for sale as you proceed. The government gangs of convicts, also, marching backwards and forwards from their work in single military file, and the solitary ones straggling here and there, with their white woollen Paramatta frocks and trowsers, or grey and yellow jackets with duck overalls, (the different styles of dress denoting the oldness or newness of their arrival,) all daubed over with broad arrows, P. B's, C. B's, and various numerals in black, white, and red; with perhaps the jail-gang straddling sulkily by in their jingling leg-chains, – tell a tale too plain to be misunderstood. At the corners of streets, and before many of the doors, fruit-stalls are to be seen, teeming, in their proper seasons, with oranges, lemons, limes, figs, grapes, peaches, nectarines, apricots, plums, apples, pears, &c., at very moderate prices.

Sydney, from the scattered state of its buildings, necessarily occupies a great extent of ground, stretching from Dawes Point, in the line of George Street, a mile and a half in *length*; and, from the top of the ridge on the left, across that on the right, (quite to Darling Harbour beyond,) about one-fifth of that distance in *breadth*. . . . The streets are commonly named after the various governors, secretaries, and other public officers, who have borne sway among us; thus we have Phillip, Hunter, King, Bligh, Macquarie, Brisbane, O'Connel, Erskine, Campbell, and Goulburn streets; the last of which is gravely pointed out by the Sydney wags as remarkable for no burglary ever having been committed in it; but the mystery is soon unravelled on finding that it does not contain a single house, – being, like many similar instances in America and this colony too, merely a street in *anticipation*.

Obviously, this was not quite London or Manchester, Edinburgh or Dublin. Convicts or parrots were as likely to appear in Sydney streets as horses and drays. But the new settler, unless he were a town tradesman or a shopkeeper, soon put Sydney behind him. Land was his aim, and enthusiasts like Surgeon Cunningham directed him towards the pioneer country:

The inhabited parts of the colony cultivated by free people may be divided into four. *First*, the old settled division, comprehending the county of Cumberland (in which Sydney lies), and the county of Camden, southerly, between Cumberland and Argyle. *Secondly*, the counties of Argyle and Westmoreland, and the unnamed country beyond, to the left, or *southward* of Sydney. *Thirdly*, the counties of Northumberland and Durham to the right or *northward* of Sydney, situated upon Hunter's River: and, *Fourthly*, the counties of Roxburgh and Londonderry, beyond the Blue mountains, interiorly, or *westward* of Sydney, known best by the name of Bathurst. The three first divisions all lie between the barrier range of mountains, stretching parallel to the coast forty miles interiorly, and the sea, consequently all their waters run into the sea *easterly*; while the *fourth* division (Bathurst) lying *beyond* this barrier range, consequently *its* waters run *westerly*, and terminate in the immense interior swamps, the outlet whereof is yet a mystery. Carriage roads lead from Sydney to them all, excepting the *third* division spoken of (upon Hunter's River to the *northward*), to which there is yet but a cattle track.

He was looking for the potential rich pastures, the productive land such as that which Harris noticed around Illawarra:

The Five Islands (by the aborigines much more euphoniously called Illa Warra) is a tract of New South Wales, a short distance south of Sydney, on the sea-coast, and so called from five small islands which lie a short distance off, immediately abreast of it. It may be described loosely as a plot of the richest soil, bounded on one side by the sea, and on the other by enormous masses of mountain, confusedly heaped together. These are covered either with dense dark forests, or low bushy scrub, knee high or higher, with flats of swampy table-land, and gloomy ravines, into whose depths the eye cannot reach. The soil is excellent. I have heard some of the settlers say, that they could dig down 40 feet through the soil of their farms on this sea-side tract without finding a stone as large as a pea. Little crystal brooks of the coldest and purest water, making their way out of the mountain reservoirs above, traverse the ground at all seasons of the year, in their passage to the sea. It was therefore one of the most amiable features of the policy of the best Governor this colony ever had, to give out in this district farms to a number of little settlers; for a poor man's use of land is of course first agricultural, and a fertile soil must be an immense advantage.

But in the lottery of the wilderness not everyone found his ideal haven. Early settlers, in particular, had a hard time of it. The Quaker preacher, James Backhouse, had an account of the first atrocious conditions in Van Diemen's Land:

I had some conversation with a person who was brought to the Colony in 1804, at the time that Lieut. Governor Collins first formed a settlement in V. D. Land. At that period she was but a child; and on landing was lodged with some others under a blanket supported by sticks, near the place where the Commissariat-office now stands in Hobart Town, which at that time was covered with wood. After spending a night there, they were removed to the spot where the village of New Town now stands, and lodged in a hollow tree. Here they were first visited by the Aborigines, with whom the children were often left, and who treated them kindly. Provisions becoming scarce, the people often cooked maritime plants collected on the sea shore, which bear to this day, the name of Botany Bay Greens. Sometimes they collected for food the crap or refuse of the blubber of whales, out of which the oil had been taken by whaling vessels, and which was washed up on the shores. At length the pressure of hunger was so great, as to oblige the Governor to give leave to some of the convicts, to go into the country and shift for themselves. Many of these committed outrages upon the natives, whose animosity toward the white people thus became excited at an early period, notwithstanding many years elapsed before they were in open hostility.

By the 1820s, however, a large and varied body of experience had been brought together to guide the canny new settler:

In searching for a suitable grant, it is a great point to fix upon a place where the land *round* it is all so indifferent that no new settler is likely to place himself near you, for a considerable period at least, enabling you thus to have a free run for your stock for miles without being encroached on; it being a good maxim to consider *near* neighbours as *bad* neighbours, in first settling. A horse, with canvas bags for changes of clothes, &c. slung over behind the saddle, with a blanket under to wrap yourself up in at night, and a light cord round the horse's neck to tether him by, furnish your personal equipment while upon this quest; and if pushing into a country at a distance from settlers, a pack-horse with provisions ought to accompany you. A steady white man who is a good bush-ranger, and a black native, complete your train. The note of the bellbird, tinkling like a dull sheep-bell, announces in our drouthy wilds the welcome presence of water (a very useful thing to know); and toward this sound you may confidently proceed.

The settlers are generally hospitably disposed, and in these jaunts you are always welcome to such fare and such accommodation as they have it in their power to give. A tinder-box, or powder-flask, conjures up a fire when you *bivouac* in the forest; while a few slips of bark, peeled from a tree, shelter you from the cold and wet; – and with a good fire at your feet, and a tin of hot tea before retiring to rest, you may sleep comfortably enough. Your muskets will furnish you with birds of various kinds; – and with a brace of good grayhounds you will never lack kangaroos and emus; so that your *bush*-fare is a true sportsman's feast. You meet with some adventures probably both to astonish and alarm you, but these mostly end in your amusement. . . .

The rankness of the grassy sward is the best criterion to go by in making choice of land; but as the grass is in some instances devoured by the caterpillars, you must be cautious how you decide on its being actually bad. The growth of the apple-tree is another favourable sign; while the conveniences of fencing timber and an abundance of water will decide you in other respects. – Much good land is to be culled yet in the Argyle, Bathurst, and Hunter's River districts, by careful examination; and as your views will naturally be directed rather toward the maintenance of stock than raising cultivatable commodities, you must secure, if possible, a good grazing *back-run* behind your location.

You must pay no attention to what the settlers may tell you regarding the land about their farms; as, it being the interest of every settler to keep others at a distance, the land within twenty miles is sure to be *bad* in his description. When in fact you hear a settler abusing a tract of land as *very bad*, you may generally suspect it to be *very good*.

Armed with admonition and advice, with stout boots and a plentiful supply of courage, the new settler set out for the bush:

At nearly twelve o'clock at night we reached our journey's end. . . . My companion's well-known voice soon aroused the sleeper, who came to the door in his shirt: in his shirt lit the fire; in his shirt got us supper; in his shirt joined us in a feed and a smoke; and in his shirt made our bed, and tumbled into it with us.

The hut itself, which was merely a few sheets of bark stripped from trees, and each varying from the size of a common door to that of a double that width by the same length, was but a single area of about 9 feet one way by 6 the other: the roof too was of bark, and of the usual shape. One of the 6-feet ends was a chimney, throughout its whole width, in which the fire was made by logs of any length and thickness available: on the earthen hearth, at the other 6-feet end, was a sort of berth, also of bark, like the bunks on board ship, fixed at about 3 feet from the ground; whilst at the 9-feet side next the road was the door, which likewise was of bark; and at the opposite parallel side was a little table, and that too was of bark, to wit, a sheet about 3 feet one way by 2 the other, nailed on to four little posts driven into the ground, and having of course its inner or smooth side upwards. The architect of the building had used all his materials whilst they were green, so that in seasoning they had twisted into all manner of forms except planes: and as is usually the case the worst example came from the most responsible quarter; the table was the crookedest thing in the whole hut, not excepting the dog's hind leg.

After a good supper of hot fried beefsteaks, damper bread and tea, which our host, who was a free-hearted, hardworking bushman, gave with many a 'Come, eat, lad, don't be afraid; there is plenty more where this came from,' &c., &c., &c. according to the custom of the colony and especially of his class, we betook ourselves to a smoke of good old Brazil, over the latter part of our quart pots of tea; and then at nearly two o'clock my companion reminded his brother that it was 'time to pig down'. Accordingly our entertainer clearing the floor by making us stand in the chimney, putting the blocks under the table, and giving his dog a kick, which I thought the thing least to his credit that I had seen him do, began to 'make the dab'. This was accomplished by stretching his own bed, which was only adapted for a single person, lengthwise across the hut, at about 6 or 7 feet from the fireplace; then laying down across the hut in the same manner between the bed and the fireplace all the old clothes he could muster of his own; and finally over these he spread about half a dozen good sized dried sheepskins with the wool on. These, with a blanket spread over the whole, really made a very tolerable bed. Certainly towards morning I began to feel a good deal as if I were lying with my body in a field and my legs in the ditch beside.

Certainly, the settler had embarked upon a stern life, full of danger, but it was not without rough, decent fellowship carried out, at least for the first years, amid spectacular discomfort:

A few more steps and turning the corner of this building we stood at the door of the settler's hut, where we were to stop for the night. It was one of those huts which must be ranked among the remarkable objects of Australian life. Situated on some main track and alone in the midst of the wilderness, one of these little 'cribs' necessarily becomes the nightly rendezvous of numbers of travellers. If the traveller have no food with him, a share of what there is is always freely offered him. ... The same hospitality is maintained in accommodations for rest. Those who have a blanket with them contribute it to the general stock; those who have none have equal share with those who have. These customs lead very naturally to a great degree of frankness and cordiality among the persons, most of whom are thus meeting for the first time, and the evenings consequently are for the most part spent in cheerful conversation and merriment.

Meantime such in this respect were our night's quarters. The hut was well built of slabs split out of fine straight-grained timber, with hardly a splinter upon them; and consisted of several compartments, all on the ground floor. The only windows were square holes in the sides of the hut, and a good log fire was blazing in the chimney. On stools, and benches, and blocks about the hut sat a host of wayfarers like ourselves; and several lay at their ease in corners on their saddlecloths or blankets, whilst saddles and packs of luggage were heaped up on all sides. Supper was over, and the short pipes were fuming away in all directions. Our hosts were two Irishmen, brothers, who had got a little bit of good land cleared here in the wilderness, and refused nobody a feed and shelter for the night. They soon put down a couple of quart pots of water before the blazing fire, made us some tea, and set before us the usual fare, a piece of fine corned beef, and a wheaten cake baked on the hearth.

The settler's first home was often rudimentary, but it had the virtues of being easy to make and cheap. And Backhouse, writing in 1832, suggested that thrift and ambition could still make a success of such a poverty-stricken little estate:

171

When a place is first occupied by a settler, a hut of the simplest kind is formed, often like a mere roof resting on the ground; and when other needful things have been effected, one of upright logs is built, and covered with shingles. This is usually divided into two rooms; one of which is fitted up with broad rough shelves, for sleeping berths; and the other, which has a square recess for a fireplace, built of stones, at the outer end, and continued into a rude chimney a little higher than the roof, is used for a cooking and sitting room. The crevices between the logs either remain open, or are filled with wool or some other material. A square opening, closing with a shutter, admits light into each room, and short logs of wood or rude benches, serve for seats. Many families that have been brought up in England in respectable circumstances, live for several years in a hut of this description, until they can find time and means to build themselves a better habitation; and a hut of this kind is generally to be seen contiguous to a better house, and is occupied by the male servants, who are mostly prisoners.

Perhaps a chief reason why some persons make a better livelihood here than in England, is, because they submit to live at a much smaller expense. The original settlers having had free grants of land, subject only to a quit-rent, had also no rent to pay; but no free grants of land are now made. The lowest sum for which land is sold by the Government is £5 per acre. Although convict servants are sentenced to work without wages, they cost a settler in one way or another, from £20 to £25 a year, including maintenance, clothing, &c.

No success, however, was likely to come without constant hard labour:

We were up by day-break, worked for about two hours, and then had our breakfast, which was of damper, salt pork fried, and good tea, – for tea and sugar are used among bush-men very prodigally. My mate and myself often used a pound of tea and six pounds of sugar between us in a week. The same is the case with tobacco. I mostly used close on half a pound weekly, till I found its undermining effect on my constitution, and began to try to leave it off. After breakfast we pelted away again till twelve o'clock, and then had dinner, which was damper, pork, and tea again, and laid down till the heat of the day was over, which was about three o'clock where we were: we then worked for another hour, had a lunch of damper, and tea, and pork, and knocked along till night. After 8 P.M. we had our supper, pork, tea, and damper, and soon after 9 were under the blankets.

That was Harris in his first job, building a house for an established settler. Next, he worked as a sawyer in the cedar forest:

We used to get up in the winter and have our breakfast before going to work, on account of the day being so short in the cedar-brush. But when we did begin to work it was pretty solid eye-balling. A cedar-sawyer's cuts are very deep, and a deep cut makes the saw move stiff. Again the lifts in a cedar-brush are very heavy. I have often worked for half a day together with a lever that I could barely lift into its place. Besides this, the only intermission through the day is one hour at noon for dinner, and perhaps twenty minutes towards the latter part of the afternoon, fifteen of which the topman employs in brightening up his saw, and the pitman in boiling a couple of pots of tea, and throwing the dust out of his pit; the other five are occupied in a very active lunch. Both men, if they are smokers, just light their short pipes and turn to with them in their mouths. If any man can without exaggeration at night say he is a tired as a dog after a hard day's run, it is the cedar-sawyer. A striking peculiarity of the class is their colour, or rather deficiency of all colour. A few months' residence and hard work in the brush leaves most men as pallid as corpses. Probably this is chiefly the effect of shade, but promoted further by excessive perspiration; for it is not necessarily attended by any sensation of illness.

It is during the three or four evening hours that elapse after his work that the sawyer enjoys himself. The success of the day, the prospect of a good cutting or an advantageously shaped log on the morrow, the pleasant perfume of the pipe, the cheering pot of tea again and again repeated, with each new yarn, or joke, or laugh, the busy and pompous excursions and barkings of the dog, the pattering shower, the clouds of fireflies that dance along in their countless angular courses where the cold stream tumbles among great stones in the bed of the creek – such are the objects which occupy his senses and his thoughts.

It was a hard living, but Harris found he was not alone. The bush was full of his own kind, workers striving grimly for their place in the sun:

> The whole bush in this part of the country was then thronged, as indeed it was also almost all round Sydney, with men who get their living by various kinds of bush work. . . . Each of these pairs of bushmen (for owing to the nature of the work it is best to work in pairs) knocks up a little temporary hut on setting in to work; shifting only as the job is finished or as it becomes necessary to move on for fresh timber. But sawyers who have their logs drawn by timber-carriages to their pits often remain a long time at the same hut. Indeed in many places you come across 'camps', as they are termed, of sawyers: these are where some large timber-dealer holds his head station; and comprise the huts and pits of three, five, six, or more pairs of sawyers. Some of these men have wives, some have not. It is generally considered that 'a woman keeps a hut more comfortable'. But really a sawyer's life is one of such incessant labour out of doors that the difference to him must lie chiefly in the carrying of the idea in his mind that his hut is so provided. He is so little in the hut except at meals that the actual difference of comforts can be but small. My own sense was never so much that of absence of comforts and conveniences when living where there was no individual of the female sex, as that I was living an unnatural and incomplete life – that work which robbed me of female society was work which defeated its own end – that the positive loss was far beyond the gain. Still while I could not help myself I was fain to put up with it like the rest.

Very often, hard work was not enough. Fate seemed to be stacked against the new immigrant: older settlers were suspicious; emancipated convicts and 'ticket-of-leave' men feared his competition; bushrangers and disaffected aborigines ambushed him; drought and flood threatened; up-country traders swindled him. And if all this were not enough, there was still, for the poor immigrant, the oppression of the magistrate to overcome:

> About three miles beyond Windsor, towards Sydney, we came up to a group of constables, all armed and gathered round a young man, who evidently by his English dress had

not been long in the colony. This of course they could see as well as I could, and as there was not the slightest indication in any other point of his being a bushranger, there was in fairness and common sense no ground for supposing him anything else than a free emigrant. They however insisted that, as he had 'no protection', they would take him into custody to be sent to Hyde Park Barracks, Sydney, the head convict office, 'for identification'. It was in vain that he remonstrated: their resolution remained unshaken. . . . They marched the poor fellow to Paramatta gaol that night. . . . He had come out to the colony to an old friend of his family, who had emigrated some years before to hold a respectable public situation, but on arrival found him to be dead. After trying to get employment till everything was gone but the clothing he stood in, he had wandered on up the road toward the interior, more from the impulse of hope than of any precise expectation; and had had his journey cut short in the way described. I felt curious to know how the magistrates would deal with the case, for to me it seemed a most flagrant outrage, whilst the constables maintained it was quite legal, and in the common course of things. I had heard of such things before, but did not quite credit them. I also felt interested in the poor fellow, for I recollected how my own heart had often sunk on my first arrival, when I tried day after day to get a job without succeeding. The magistrate, Captain Rossi, long the chief superintendent of the Sydney police, sent him first to the prisoners' barracks, where the documents descriptive of all individuals transported are kept, but he was returned from thence as unknown. . . . Could not Captain Rossi give him 'a pass' to protect him, as he now knew him to be free? Captain Rossi said, No, that was beyond his province: he would recommend the young man to apply to the colonial secretary. The poor fellow was about to reply, when a couple of constables had him turned round, marched off, and set at liberty at the court-house door, before one could count half-a-dozen.

In the face of all these difficulties, Alexander Harris thought it useful to set out some practical rules for new settlers which, if not guaranteeing success, at least made it more likely:

1. I know of nothing in which the axiom of 'More haste worse speed' is so true as in the approach of a new settler to

his undertaking. My advice to him would be on no account to neglect, in the first place, a tour of inspection. He should put his knapsack on his back and penetrate to the farthest limit of colonization. He should travel as unpretendingly as possible; up the country every hut door is open to the traveller. . . . By thus stopping a good deal at the labouring men's huts he will hear the prices of labour, of stock, of land, and of goods, from individuals not interested in deceiving him: whereas I am afraid, if he trust for his information on those points to landowners, he will often be misled. . . . The conversation that passes in the labouring men's huts, when the pipes are lit, after tea in the evening, is certainly both the most varied and the soundest as to facts. They have no pecuniary interest in the matters they talk about, but each relating his observation and experience in different parts of the colony, incites others to do the same.

2. The next general principle I would lay down is this:- To make his undertaking, whenever it does commence, as much as possible *a series of experiments*, rather than *one experiment*. Let him go on by degrees, feeling his way. The banks will give him very high interest for his ready money – at least double what he would get in England; and up-country living really costs next to nothing. After he is well settled in a hut on his land, his personal charges for food can hardly be above 15*l.* or 18*l.*, per year; and, having no rent to pay, clothing need be his only other fixed expense; and on that again a bushman seldom spends more than 10*l.* a year.

3. Another advantage the new settler should by no means set light by, his credit. For there is really not any such difference between the prices he must give in ready cash and those he may give on credit when purchasing his stock as to warrant the nervousness which some persons feel about taking credit. In fact, there is a perfectly definite feeling in the minds of large stockholders, that they would not think of turning away a good bill for 500*l.* at twelve months for a flock of sheep or herd of cattle, though for the same flock or herd they would 'rather of the two' have the 500*l.* in cash. But when the new settler, by merely pressing the point firmly, can turn the 40*l.* interest of the sum into his own concern, he would be very ill fitted for business if he neglected to do so. Such a man had better not begin business in New South Wales.

4. On settling, and always afterwards, till your circumstances and arrangements have become such as to place you beyond all danger, look after every thing yourself; join in all the farm operations yourself; it both ensures their being well done, and makes you so acquainted with them that you can instruct others.

5. If your concerns are extensive enough to permit your having an overseer, take care to have a good one; if not, get a better sort of working hand, and give him 5*l*. or 10*l*. a year higher wages. An adviser of some sort you must have, or you will fall into mistakes, often of a very expensive and pernicious character: and to have an ignorant, weak-minded man in such a capacity is worse than to have none; for your own mistakes alone will be preferable to your own and his together.

6. Treat your hands rather better than worse than your neighbours. The damage to a settler's concerns that arises from the neglect of his people (the intentional, revengeful neglect) is beyond all estimate.

So much for matters of general conduct. To them may be added these directions upon the more immediate business of settling a farm:–

1. Order of operations:–

Immediately you reach your land, traverse it and select the site for your homestead; and let that be a spot a little elevated.

Set your spare hands or any blacks there may be about to strip you forty or fifty sheets of bark. Of these have two tent huts made; the one for yourself and servant, the other for the men. One or at the utmost two days should suffice to construct two good snug weather-tight tent huts.

Next get up a moderate sized stockyard, say five rods by six. Let it be very strong: and let it contain milking bales. . . . Another convenience it must contain is what is called 'the gallows' for hauling up a beast that has been slaughtered, to take the hide off. After the stockyard, you should get a small paddock of ten acres fenced in, and while the fencing is going on other hands should be employed in clearing the timber. Plough it as speedily as possible; let it lie for a couple of months, if time permits, and then cross plough it and put in seven or eight acres of wheat, one of maize for your horse, and another of potatoes and garden seeds.

Next have a couple of yards of good 6 feet paling erected for your sheep (if you have sheep); and if you begin with more than two flocks, have ready also, before purchasing them, a lot of hurdles. . . . Sheep ought never to be brought to a station till there is a secure defence for them from the native dogs. In the same manner if you buy horned cattle, have your stockyard first ready; and yard them every night till they get thoroughly reconciled to the run, sending out with them all day a couple of men.

Having got thus far you may leave your splitters to put you up a better, permanent, roofed hut while you go away to make your purchases of live stock. This hut should be strong; as you will have to appropriate one room of it to the purpose of a store.

With these accommodations you may consider yourself snug – without them your business will be one round of mishap, vexation, and loss.

The Blacks should be kindly treated, as they are of great service in stripping bark, showing new runs, tracking lost bullocks and sheep, &c. &c.; moreover kind treatment will be found the great secret of restraining their tendency to furtive and vindictive depredations. At the same time, with kindness must be mingled a manifestation of the most perfect fearlessness, but it should not be mere parade and bravado. They are very quick at detecting the true feeling that dictates an action. Arms should always be ready, and securely kept, and they should know it too.

I subjoin finally a list of the articles with which it will be advisable to load the dray on proceeding to take possession of a new farm:–

1 ton flour.
Enough meat for the journey: on arrival beasts for slaughter can be purchased of neighbours.
4 or 5 cwt. salt.
1 cwt. soap (or ½ cwt.).
2 chests tea (1 chest).
7 or 8 cwt. sugar (4 cwt.)
3 cwt. tobacco (1 cwt.).
2 frying-pans.
1 doz. tin quart pots.
1 doz. tin pint pots.

Several iron pots.
1 doz. pocket knives.
1 doz. tin plates.
½ doz. tin dishes.
1 doz. blankets.
Bed-ticking.
3 or 4 doz. check shirts.
2 or 3 doz. woollen ditto.
2 or 3 doz. pair of boots.
Jackets, of sorts.
Trousers, of sorts.
Needles, thread, pipes.
3 cross-cut saws: a 6-ft., a 6½, a 7-ft.
1 pit saw, fine space, 7-ft. plate.
Tiller and box for ditto.
Cross-cut and pit saw files.
½ doz. best falling axes.
2 lopping axes.
2 mortising axes.
1 broad axe.
1 heavy adze.
1 light ditto.
Chest of carpenter's tools.
Grindstone and frame.
½ doz. padlocks, hasps, and staples.
Several bags of nails of sizes (100 lbs., of sorts).
Fire-arms, powder and ball.
4 or 5 buckets.
30 or 40 fathoms of good ½in. rope.
A small churn.
½ doz. spades.
½ doz. heavy breaking-up hoes.
A small but very strong plough and tackle (may be left till second load).
½ doz. reaping hooks (ditto).
1 doz. sheep-shears (ditto).
Wool-bagging, and packing needles and twine (ditto).
A good tarpaulin.
Paper, pens, ink, &c.

This was a formidable list. But the new settler should not be intimidated. Success *was* possible; it had been achieved by thousands of ordinary people, unsung in the official records but not without their own small measure of heroism. Here was one whom James Backhouse met in Van Diemen's Land:

> George Dixon emigrated to this colony eleven years ago, he was trained to agricultural pursuits, and has brought a portion of his location of land into cultivation, both in the growth of wheat and other grain; he has also formed a good garden, which is well stocked with fruit trees and has a Hawthorn hedge. The common fences of the country are formed of logs, branches, or posts and rails. His house is built of split wattles, plastered and whitewashed, the roof projecting in front and resting on wooden pillars so as to form a verandah, a common style of building in this country. The house consists of two front rooms with boarded floors, and two behind, – a kitchen and store room, – floored with stone. His land consists of basaltic hills with grassy forest, and he has about a mile of frontage on the Clyde, which at this season of the year is little more than a chain of pools – called here lagoons – of various length and depth, and about 30 ft. in width. In winter this becomes a considerable river. Some parts of its banks are open, others bushy, and some rocky. In one place a rock like a steeple stands between a cliff and the margin of the river.

And here, in note form, were accounts from settlers given to a Committee on Immigration in 1845:

> Came to this country in 1839; on landing, my money and property were worth about £30; was engaged two days after my arrival, at 24s. per week, afterwards 30s. – out of this I got my own food; when I had been three months in service, was engaged as overseer; commenced for myself with the sum of £40, on a clearing lease of ten acres, rent £10 a year; this land I have since purchased for £70; have about half the sum paid; I have 3 horses, 2 carts, and a dray, 10 goats, a number of poultry, and have a tolerable house of my own; I employ two labourers, giving them board and lodgings, and 8s. a week; if I had the capital I could employ more with profit to myself; my young children I send to school, and pay 6d. per week each.

Arrived in 1841; had no money on landing; was engaged as farm servant nine days after my arrival, at the following wages; £20 a year, and a weekly ration of 12 lbs. flour, 10 lbs. meat, 2 lbs. sugar, ¼ lb. tea. I have now eight head of cattle, and am worth in cash £30; the highest wages I ever received before I emigrated to this Colony was £3 10s. a year; I am well known to ——, and to ——; I subscribe to a school, and the Colonial Observer; since in this Colony, I was out of employment about three months, but I must say it was nearly my own fault. I refused, as Mrs. Chisholm knows, £15 a year, and rations; I am now receiving 20s. a week, and board myself; have a nice house, free of rent.

Two years later, Allan Cunningham, the pioneering explorer and rich squatter, summed up the usual case:

I know among my own Servants, those I took out with me, and those that have been taken out by my Friends, there are a large Number now possessed of Property of various Kinds; and I believe that amongst steady and intelligent Men, to set up for themselves after from Five to Eight Years of Labour is the Rule, and to fail in doing so is the Exception.

And another landholder, as usual, found this very success a cause for complaint. 'One slight evil of our present state,' he wrote, 'is that the labourers too rapidly get out of the labour market. The present rate of wages enables the labourers too soon, for a sufficient return to the capitalist, to get out of the ranks of labour.'

*

Australian colonial society was deeply divided from the beginning. The first division, naturally, was between the convicted and the free. After only a few years, a second division developed within the free population, between those convicts who had been emancipated and a section of the older settlers known as the 'exclusionists'. The exclusionists were the officials, the military men, the clergymen, the magistrates of the first settlements, all those free men who had taken advantage of land-grants to build up holdings and establish power in the new land. Emancipists and exclusionists learnt to dislike each other cordially, and Surgeon Cunningham left a sharp little portrait of their enduring struggle:

The grand division, however, of the free classes here, without reference to colonial technicalities, is into that of *emigrants*, who have come out free from England, and *emancipists*, who have arrived here as convicts, and have either been pardoned or completed their term of servitude. It is between portions of these two classes, that there has been so much bickering. One subdivision of the emigrant class alluded to, is termed the *exclusionist* party, from their strict exclusion of the emancipists from their society; while again, a subdivision of emancipists is denominated the *confusionist* party, from their endeavouring to embroil society, as *the others* say. As in all small communities, private feuds, backbiting, and scandal, are commonly to be found in our circles, or rather *have been*, for improvement in this respect seems to be gaining ground. Those thoroughly initiated into the prevailing habits learn, however, to *hear* without *believing* these things, and to repeat them merely for talking's sake, so that the repetitions may go on *ad infinitum* with scarce an atom of credit being attached thereto, even by the retailers.

The first convict had been emancipated by Governor Phillip within two years of the founding of the colony, and from then on the emancipists rose rapidly. Judge Roger Therry, who in thirty years of professional life in New South Wales had dealings with emancipists on both sides of the bench, testified to their importance. By 1829 they formed a section of the community that was 'the wealthiest in the land'. Among them were 'the principal merchants of the city, and the chief contractors with Government.' And there were many others, wrote Judge Therry, 'inferior in wealth to the former, but in general conduct equal and perhaps superior to it.' He instanced the transported members of the gang that tried to kill British ministers in the Cato Street Conspiracy of 1820:

Grievous as was their crime, the three Cato-street conspirators I met with became reformed and useful men in New South Wales. Strange still survives: he was for many years chief constable of the Bathurst district, and was then the terror of bushrangers. His career in the colony showed that the sparing of his life was a humane and well-bestowed act of clemency by the Crown. He was rewarded by the Colonial

Government for having captured several of those daring disturbers of the peace, often after a severe personal conflict with them. The reckless disregard of danger, that in a bad cause made him an apt instrument for the deed that doomed him to transportation, when engaged in a good and righteous one made him an invaluable constable. Strange obtained a ticket of leave soon after his arrival from Sir T. Brisbane, for capturing in a single-handed struggle Robert Story, the notorious bushranger of his time, and many other marauders of less note. If it were known that 'the Cato-street chief' (the name by which as chief constable he was known) was in search of the plunderers who then prowled along the roads, they fled from the district, and his name was quite 'a tower of strength' to the peaceable portion of the community. At the present time, he is the head of a patriarchal home on the banks of the Fish River at Bathurst, surrounded by children and grandchildren, all industrious persons, in the enjoyment of a comfortable competence. Wilson was also for some time an active and brave constable under Strange. On obtaining the indulgence of a ticket of leave he married, and became the fashionable tailor of the district. The signboard over his shop contained a correct description in announcing him 'Wilson, tailor, from London.' Of course the name of Cato-street, the last place of his abode, was suppressed.

Not all emancipists made good. Therry had many examples of colourful and desperate rogues, including the case of a certain Knatchbull, an ex-naval commander and a member of a 'most respectable family':

Knatchbull had been originally transported for picking a pocket in Vauxhall Gardens, but at the time he had exhausted the generosity and kindness of his friends by his profligate course of life. In the Colony his career was one of low vice and habitual crime. The first time I saw him was in the dock in the Supreme Court in Sydney, when he was convicted of forgery and sentenced to be transported to Norfolk Island. On his way to this penal settlement, a conspiracy (of which Knatchbull was the leader) was formed by the convicts to capture the vessel, not with the wicked daring of pirates, but with the low cunning of the basest of criminals. The design was to poison the captain and crew with arsenic, *four pounds* of which were concealed in a pillow-case and stealthily put on board. This was to have been thrown secretly into the cook's galley. It was pre-arranged that, with the exception of the conspirators, the rest of the crew and passengers should be compelled to walk the plank, and that the vessel should then be steered for an American port. The scheme was detected and defeated. Afterwards Knatchbull came back to Sydney, got a ticket-of-leave (which after the commission of such crimes ought not to have been given to him), and obtained the command from a Sydney merchant of a small coasting-vessel of about a hundred tons, on board of which the captain, mate, and sailors, many of them ex-convicts, messed and lived together on terms of equality. What a falling-off, indeed, for a man who had once trod the deck as captain of a British man-of-war! His guilt in the case of murder for which he was subsequently executed was established on the clearest evidence – in fact, he might be said to have been caught *in flagrante delicto*.

But the emancipists were, on the whole, useful and energetic members of colonial society who made up in zeal and ambition for the errors of their convict days. They won applause from Surgeon Cunningham, who also thought it necessary to throw in a little moral instruction for those who might have forgotten the nature of a penal colony:

Our emancipist body, in honest truth, forms the most useful and enterprising portion of our community; – all the distilleries, nearly all the breweries, and the greater portion of the mills and various manufactories, being owned by them; while they have never, so far as I can learn, disgraced themselves by engaging in any of the smuggling transactions, whereby many of those who came out under the proud title of *free men* have tarnished their reputation. Several of our most respectable merchants have told me that in the numerous matters of business wherein they have been concerned with the emancipists, their conduct has always proved *most honourable*, though some here will endeavour to detract from this praise, by saying that their *principles* have suffered no change, the *terror of the law* and *self-interest* alone keeping them honest. This I hold to be an illiberal and unworthy suspicion: – and if otherwise, what retains nineteen-twentieths of mankind in the paths of honesty but these two identical things?

184

Emancipists usually became traders, shopkeepers, contractors, or dealers in anything that was bought and sold; or they
joined the professional classes, even becoming lawyers. But the
exclusionists were the grandees, the landholders, the farmers,
the ranchers, the country gentlemen:

> A little above Emu Plains, the Hawkesbury (or Warragamba,
> as it is here called) emerges from among the mountains,
> sweeping past the rich and picturesque estate of Sir John
> Jamison. His veranda'd cottage and farm-buildings occupy a
> spot near to the bank of the river; but an elegant freestone
> mansion has lately been erected by him on a commanding
> site, which overlooks the rich vale spreading wider and wider
> down the opening vista before you, – the river winding at a
> sluggish pace through this scene of exuberant fertility, and
> the abrupt woody range of the Blue mountains towering
> behind until it steals slowly from your view. A clear cool
> spring of water is seen welling in the immediate vicinity of the
> house, a much-prized article here; – while the land around is
> cleared to the extent of at least one thousand acres, and
> produces most abundantly all the varied productions of our
> clime. Sir John is president of the Agricultural Society,
> and his house the frequent resort of pleasure-parties from
> Sydney.

Or again:

> A road passes to Argyle also, but it is nine miles farther than
> that across the Razor-back. You see Mr. D'Arrieta's, as you
> ride along, on your left, (about five miles off) – a happy,
> good-humoured, hospitable Spanish gentleman, who settled
> some six years back in this colony: but take care how you
> approach his mansion! – for, being of a military turn, he has,
> by way of protection from burglars and bush-rangers, drawn
> a regular chain of videttes around it, in the shape of fierce
> growling devils of dogs, pegged down to the ground at such
> exact mathematical distances, that two can just meet to lick
> each other's faces, and pinch a mouthful out of any intruder's
> hip; and as they are no great respecters of persons, you had
> better 'sound your horn' as you approach, to draw out some
> of the inmates to a reconnoitre and parley, before venturing

in, – unless you are heedless about having your coat-tails pulled off. Mr. D'Arrieta's grant consists of two thousand acres, all fine fertile land, stretching along the river, the banks whereof are here so deep and precipitous, that there is only one solitary spot upon his grounds where cattle can approach to drink. Dr. Douglas's farm, of eight hundred acres, lies immediately adjoining, a large portion of it being cleared and under cultivation. The farms of Major Antill, Messrs. Crawford, Harper, Cowper, and various other gentlemen, lie beyond – all possessing the requisite conveniences, and considerable portions of cleared ground, with flocks or herds pasturing upon the remainder.

These were not the men to get on with such folk as the rich emancipist Solomon Wiseman, a cheerful materialist who 'discarded every other consideration', and who (according to Judge Therry) 'in literary attainments of any kind was sadly deficient, and took unmerciful liberties with the English language'.

The exclusionists considered themselves a privileged caste and wished to keep it that way. They felt they had a right to succeed and consequently many of them, though favoured by free land-grants, managed to fail. Failure seemed, in particular, to afflict military men whose training and idea of their station in life did nothing, as Alexander Harris noted, to help them tame the wilds of New South Wales:

On a splendid blood-horse sat —— ——, late of the —— regiment of foot; he was the new settler. Originally of large fortune, he had spent above thirty years in the army, during which period most of his property had melted from his grasp, through a mere thoughtless indifference to everything except amusement. Having married at an advanced period of life a lady of habits if possible even more thriftless than his own, he had come to the resolution, a few months before the time of which I write, to sell his commission, and with his remaining funds to become a settler. We understood that he had a little family rising around him; and it must no doubt have been very painful to a man of his benevolent temperament to see them growing up with prospects so much narrower than his own education had taught him to look upon as desirable.

Mr. —— was a perfectly well-bred man, in short a gentleman in every sense of the word, in manners, feelings, and
opinions; but he was entirely lacking in independence of
character. Whatever you proposed to him he did directly. . . .
If a brother settler advised him to do this thing or that thing
in the morning, he did it; and if a government man advised
him in the afternoon to undo it, he undid it.

With his dray there was a party of no less than eleven men,
and all those who were doing anything at all were giving
orders; the rest had lit their pipes at the black gin's fire that
was smouldering a few yards away from our hut-door, or
were dispersed into one or other of our men's huts. . . . The
men asked, or rather demanded, whatever their prodigality
suggested; and whatever they asked the overseer gave. If one
of them fixed a covetous eye upon a black fellow's opossum-
skin cloak, he gave his whole week's tea, sugar, and tobacco
for it; and if that were not enough to secure his wish, then the
week's beef and flour were added. 'What odds? there was
plenty more where than came from'; and 'Our cove never
allowances his men, lad!' When bed-time came it appeared
that our new neighbour had neither bed nor blanket. A first-
rate palliasse had been supplied to the dray for him by his
agent who made up his order for stores in Sydney, and with it
blankets befitting; but on the road they had camped one
night at a water-hole in a flat, where there was a sly grog-
seller squatted. Here some of the knowing ones of the party
agreed to 'kick the governor' for 'his footing up the country'.
Of course 'the governor' acceded; and while he was in the hut
paying for 'a gallon of rum among all hands', his bed and
blankets vanished. . . . The rest of the journey Mr. —— had
to content himself with a dirty bed and blanket which one of
the party gave up to him.

The example that officers, and indeed most exclusionists,
had before them was John Macarthur, the best known soldier-
settler of the early colony and the founder of the wool trade on
which the prosperity of Australia came to rest.

Macarthur, a captain in the New South Wales Corps, arrived
in 1790 bringing with him his wife Elizabeth, the first free,
educated lady in the colony. Within three years he had his first
land-grant (from his commanding officer Francis Grose) and

from that point never looked back. In 1794 he wrote to his brother:

> As to myself, I have a farm containing nearly 250 acres, of which upwards of 100 are under cultivation, and the greater part of the remainder is cleared of the timber which grows upon it. Of this year's produce I have sold £400 worth, and I have now remaining in my Granaries upwards of 1,800 bushels of corn. I have at this moment 20 acres of fine wheat growing, and 80 acres prepared for Indian corn and potatoes, with which it will be planted in less than a month.
>
> My stock consists of a horse, 2 mares, 2 cows, 130 goats, upwards of 100 hogs. Poultry of all kinds I have in the greatest abundance. I have received no stock from Government, but one cow, the rest I have either purchased or bred. With the assistance of one man and half a dozen greyhounds, which I keep, my table is constantly supplied with wild ducks or kangaroos. Averaging one week with another these dogs to not kill less than 300 lb. weight. In the centre of my farm I have built a most excellent brick house, 68 feet in front and 18 feet in breadth. It has no upper story, but consists of four rooms on the ground floor, a large hall, closets, cellar, etc.; adjoining is a kitchen, with servants' apartments, and other necessary offices. The house is surrounded by a vineyard and garden of about 3 acres, the former full of vines and fruit trees, and the latter abounding with most excellent vegetables.
>
> This farm being near the Barracks, I can without difficulty attend to the duties of my profession.

John Macarthur had discovered (as his wife naively reported) that 'this country possesses numerous advantages to persons holding appointments under Government.' He consequently set out to exploit these advantages very assiduously. He was a leading rum monopolist and one of the mainstays of the military 'Rum Rebellion'. His business operations undermined all the early governors. He prospered so well that Governor King wrote bitterly: 'Captain Macarthur was £500 in debt when he left England but by 1801 he was said to have a fortune of £20,000.'

In 1810, Macarthur was banished from the colony for eight years for his part in the Rum Rebellion. But his wife, wealth and property remained in New South Wales and Macarthur used the time to promote his main interest. For by now he had firmly established the New South Wales wool trade, which was on its way to becoming the colony's most important business. This was how it happened:

In the year 1794, I purchased from an officer Sixty Bengal Ewes and Lambs, which had been imported from Calcutta and very soon after I procured from the Captain of a Transport from Ireland, two Irish Ewes and a young Ram. The Indian Sheep produced coarse hair and the wool of the Irish Sheep was then valued at no more than 9d. per lb. By crossing the two Breeds I had the satisfaction to see the lambs of the Indian Ewes bear a mingled fleece of hair and wool – this circumstance originated the idea of producing fine wool in New South Wales. In the year 1796 (I believe) the two sloops of war on this station were sent to the Cape of Good Hope, and as their Commanders were friends of mine, I requested them to enquire if there were any wool-bearing sheep at the Cape. At the period of their arrival at the Settlement there was a flock of Merino Sheep for sale, from which about twenty were purchased. Of these I was favoured with Four Ewes and Two Rams, the remainder were distributed amongst different individuals who did not take the necessary precautions to preserve the breed pure and they soon disappeared – Mine were carefully guarded against an impure mixture, and increased in number and improved in the quality of their wool. In a year or two after I had an opportunity of augmenting my flock by the purchase from Colonel Foveaux of 1200 Sheep of the common Cape Breed. In 1801 I took to England specimens of the pure Merino Wool, and of the best of the crossbred, and having submitted them to the inspection of a Committee of Manufacturers, they reported the Merino Wool was equal to any Spanish wool and the Crossbred of considerable value. Thus encouraged I purchased Nine Rams and a Ewe from the Royal Flock at Kew, and returned to this country determined to devote my attention to the improvement of the Wool of my flocks.

After eight years in exile, when Macarthur returned to his home and land in Camden, he was no longer the greedy, obstructive nuisance of former times, but the founder of Australian prosperity and the greatest of the exclusionists. And here, in the late 1820s, Peter Cunningham pictured the great man in all his glory, not only a sheep-rancher, but also a notable horse and cattle breeder, a wine-grower and a master of foxhounds:

The road towards Argyle runs straight forward from this, over the Razor-back hill; but by turning to the left about four miles, you come to Camden, the great agricultural and sheep farm of Mr. John Macarthur, to whom New South Wales owes so much, as the patriotic introducer of the fine-woolled sheep-husbandry, from which in fact this colony has derived nearly all the celebrity it now enjoys. . . . The cottage and out buildings occupy a rising hill about half a mile from the river; a small stream, with ponds at intervals along its bed, stealing quietly through the narrow hollow you have to cross in reaching the house. Mr. Macarthur's property in this county in grants and purchases exceeds thirty thousand acres, all lying contiguous, and consisting chiefly of undulating, thinly-wooded hills covered with a sward of fine dry native pasture, with alluvial plains towards the margin of the river of the most fertile description, producing wheat equalling in quality and quantity the best in England, and maize of the most luxuriant growth. About four hundred acres adjoining the river were originally clear of timber, and being intersected with ponds, having no ready outlet for the discharge of their waters, this portion was always considerably flooded in every heavy fall of rain, and the whole bore much the appearance of a rich English meadow. Here a herd of wild cattle (originating from a stray bull and two cows) was first discovered by a runaway convict, and backwards from this the largest herds are still found. It was this circumstance which suggested to the acute mind of Mr. Macarthur the idea of selecting a grant here, – conceiving that cattle, being the best judges of their own food, would naturally graze upon the land which produced it in greatest abundance and most suitable to their taste. A forty miles' remove from Sydney, through a line of country where no human habitations were then fixed, was, in those days, counted such a piece of thoughtless boldness, that some pitied and most laughed at Mr. Macarthur, for taking the step: but perceiving ere long the rapid increase of his stock in these fine pastures, where all had free range of food without being crippled by a neigh-bour's encroachments, – they soon saw it was true wisdom on his part, and that the *folly* rested only with *themselves*.

It was while ruminating deeply on the future prospects of his adopted country, that Mr. Macarthur was led to conceive the Merino sheep-husbandry as peculiarly suitable to it. . . . From three ewes and a ram, with which he began the breed, his stock of pure Merinos exceeds now two thousand, and from their produce he has sold upwards of forty rams annually, these many years back, at an average of 17*l.* sterling per head, besides improving his other flocks by crossing, until many of the cross-breds are quite equal to the pure bloods.

Neither has the breed of horses and cattle passed un-noticed by Mr. Macarthur; his cattle partaking much of the Devon peculiarities, being mostly of a deep red with large spreading horns, and appearing to answer this climate par-ticularly well, from being hardy feeders; fattening easily; giving a good supply of milk; and standing well, as working oxen, the fatigue of farm labour. – A thriving vineyard is seen planted upon the face of a rising ground, with an eastern exposure, from which a progressive quantity of wine is yearly making; while a patch of the various English grasses, cultivated in rows for seed, occupies a site nearer to the river. An excellent pack of fox-hounds are also kept here, afford-ing much enlivening sport when opening in chorus after a native dog.

The success of John Macarthur's enterprise introduced into Australian life a very distinctive character – the squatter. Because of the muddle and inconsistency in official landhold-ing policy, it was best for those who wanted a portion of the wilderness for the breeding of sheep to 'squat' on unclaimed land and wait for time to clear up the niceties of legal title. Judge Therry, whose court duties had made him an expert, explained how the system worked:

Suppose, then, the history of a 'run' to be this – the run being a tract of land which with the sheep upon it yields a net income of from three to six thousand pounds a year, and often double that amount. Jones is or fancies himself to be the first occupant. He finds the land vacant; he stocks it, he pays a licence-fee to the Crown for use and occupation of it, he employs a superintendent and shepherds to whom he pays wages. The 'run' is known by the neighbours as 'Jones's run.' He thus enjoys apparently an undisputed right to it for six or eight years. At length, from embarrassment or other reasons, he sells his run to Mr. Brown, it may be for 1000*l.*, the price varying according as he sells the run with or without stock upon it. This surely has all the aspect of a fair transaction where first occupation determines the right. But no such thing. As soon as Brown goes to take possession of the land, he is told by Robinson (Jones's servant and superintendent) that the land belonged to him (Robinson); that he took Jones's and other people's cattle for agistment to graze on the land; and that, in fact, he had sold the land to a Mr. Smith for 1000*l.* Now begins the litigation between two *bonâ fide* purchasers, Brown and Smith, each having invested say 1000*l.* in 'good moneys numbered' in the purchase. The case of Brown *v.* Smith comes on then for trial at a Circuit Court. On the day previous to the trial the two litigant parties enter the town like two candidates at a contested election. Each party litigant is attended with a retinue of witnesses. Brown puts up, with his 'volunteer band' of witnesses, at the Red Lion. Smith, with his host, patronises the Green Dragon, at the opposite end of the town. The respective superintendents of the belligerents provide free living on a liberal scale for their respective troops, where, from morning to night during the assize week, libations, not of Rhenish, but of 'the best Jamaica' and other spirituous liquors, 'are washed down.' Occasionally banners are displayed at the respective headquarters of the combatants, who fight sometimes less for justice than for victory. . . . To the judge the whole proceeding is one that taxes his toil and patience to a greater extent than almost any other kind of action.

Men risked these legal tangles because the rewards from squatting could be very great indeed. When Mark Twain visited Australia at the end of the nineteenth century he reflected on this peculiar phenomenon of the Australian past:

With us, when you speak of a squatter you are always supposed to be speaking of a poor man; but in Australia, when you speak of a squatter, you are always supposed to be speaking of a millionaire; in America the word indicates the possessor of a few acres and a doubtful title, in Australia it indicates a man whose land-front is as long as a railroad; ... in America you take off your hat to no squatter, in Australia you do.

In Australia it takes about two acres and a half of pasture-land (some people say twice as many) to support a sheep; and when the squatter has half a million sheep his private domain is about as large as Rhode Island, to speak in general terms. His annual wool crop may be worth a quarter or a half million dollars.

He will live in a palace in Melbourne or Sydney or some other of the large cities, and make occasional trips to his sheep kingdom, several hundred miles away in the great plains, to look after his battalions of riders and shepherds and other hands. He has a commodious dwelling out there, and if he approve of you he will invite you to spend a week in it, and will make you at home and comfortable, and let you see the great industry in all its details, and feed you, and slake you, and smoke you with the best that money can buy.

And to illustrate just how riches such as these were won, Judge Therry recounted the case of a young man aged 20 who arrived from Glasgow in 1832 with £50 in his pocket:

By the advice of Mr. M'Leay, I placed the 50*l.* which I had received from my father for the purpose of paying my expenses back to Scotland in the savings-bank in Sydney; and in eight or ten days I left Sydney for his station, situated between Gouldburn and Yass. On arriving at the station, the person in charge handed over to me about 2000 sheep, with some stores, and about a dozen of assigned servants; and he left for Sydney the same day.

I now found myself, without any colonial experience, placed in a position of great responsibility, alone, and without any one to assist me. In the first place I made myself acquainted with the nature of the country, the sheep, and the servants I had to deal with; and I soon ascertained that about five years before Mr. M'Leay had lost as large a number of sheep as were then upon the run. As an illustration of the mismanagement that had been going on, I was shown by the shepherds piles of bones, the remains of sheep that had died of scab and starvation. I applied myself to ascertain the cause of this want of increase, and I found that it arose from the prevalence of scab among the sheep, and the great careless-ness of the shepherds, who were all assigned servants. I though it might be well to apply to those servants the inducements to good management which were held out to myself by my agreement with Mr. M'Leay, by which I was to receive a commission upon the gradual increase of the wool sales; and I accordingly gave additional allowances to those servants who proved themselves honest and careful. The result of this system, together with a careful and economical management, was a rapid and steady increase in the flocks. . . . I had observed that even when in perfect health the sheep were fond of licking rock-salt, and that they evidently im-proved upon it. I resolved upon forming a station on the Murrumbidgee, where I had heard of the existence of salt-bush plains; and having suffered so much from the catarrh near Goulburn, I took up a tract of country with thirty miles of frontage to the Murrumbidgee river (farther out than any other squatter) for Mr. M'Leay, and about ten miles of frontage for myself, for which I had to pay 10*l.* a year, and Mr. M'Leay had to pay about 30*l.* for his stations. These proved excellent and healthy runs, but I found at first some difficulty with the natives, who were inclined to attack the shepherds and drive off sheep. By treating them with kind-ness, however, I succeeded in making them useful in sheep-washing, and such-like work. I had also then, being 400 miles from Sydney, great difficulty in getting up provisions – a difficulty which was increased when, a few years afterwards, I pushed out 100 miles farther, and took up additional stations on the Lachlan river, which I still retain.

Upon these new runs the sheep and cattle increased in numbers and quality, and at the end of fifteen years, when I gave up the management, I counted over for Mr. M'Leay, from whom I had received the 2000 sheep, above 30,000 thriving healthy, and well-bred sheep, the gradual increase of the 2000 I had received, exclusive of from 10,000 to 12,000 fat sheep that had been sold during that period. The quality of the wool, and the manner in which it was got up, were so good, that for several years it had fetched the highest price in the London market.

During the last few years whilst I was in charge of Mr. M'Leay's stations, I had been also engaged in purchasing sheep for myself. Upon my ceasing to act for him, and confining myself to the charge of my own station, he made me a present of 1000 picked ewes as a proof of his appreciation of the judicious manner in which I had managed his flocks, and the consequent improvement in the value of his property. From these ewes I had the following year a return of 1500 lambs from two lambings, which, with the sheep I had already purchased for myself, gave me a considerable stock to go on upon. . . . The present stock upon my stations consists of about 100,000 sheep, from 7000 to 8000 head of cattle, and from 700 to 800 head of horses. This is the amount independent of the annual reductions by the sale of a considerable portion to the butcher for meat, and of supplies to new squatters, and support of the men employed on the stations.

Few squatters were as fortunate as this young Glaswegian. Many, particularly those at the limit of colonization, led the rugged life of pioneers, for they were as much explorers as settlers. Here is a squatter's home near Port Phillip, in 1840:

Having unsaddled and tethered our horses in one of the gullies on some coarse grass, we entered the overseer's hut, the interior of which was scarcely an improvement on its outward appearance. It consisted of three rooms, one of which was a store, in which were kept the flour, tea, sugar, meat-cask, &c., of the establishment; another was the bedroom of the overseer's female servant; whilst the principal apartment did duty as kitchen, dining room, and overseer's bedroom. Against the walls, around which were hung a pair or two of horse-hobbles, a gun, stock-whip, some tin dishes, pannikins, a rickety looking-glass, and other odds and ends appertaining to the gentle craft of squatting, were set three rough stools; and on the mantelpiece were disposed, evidently with some regard to effect, a couple of Hall's powder canisters, of a flaming red colour; a horse's hoof; some blue paper boxes containing seidlitz powders (the overseer's substitute for sodawater); a meerschaum pipe, with a large glass-stoppered druggist's bottle as a centre-piece, containing some three pints of a sherry-coloured liquid, and labelled *butyr of antimony*. In one of the walls of the hut there was an aperture of about a foot square, cut through the slabs as a window, before which was drawn, on strings, a little curtain of white calico. The outer door, which always stood open by day, was secured at night by a bar; and a couple of wool-packs, nailed to the tie-beams and reaching the ground, supplied the place of door to the two smaller apartments.

'As tight as a nut, sir,' said the overseer, interposing and looking up at the ridge pole, evidently pleased. 'I had it new barked in the spring. You'll find everything very comfortable and dry,' continued he, addressing me. 'A grand thing, sir, a dry hut; a grand thing! My old one at Western Port used to leak like a sieve, and we were always wet. But, I dare say, gentlemen, you are hungry after your ride.' And, turning to the servant, he ordered supper.

In due time the sea-chest table was covered with a clean towel; three willow-pattern plates, in more or less dilapidated plight, were placed on it; an old pint pannikin, partially filled with clay and topped up with mutton fat from the frying-pan, with a bit of old shirt wrapped round a stick stuck in the centre for a wick, did duty as a lamp; some odd knives and forks made their appearance from the store-room, whilst a round wooden box (marvellously like a lather box) supplied the place of a salt-cellar. Beside each plate the servant laid a pint tin pannikin and a slice of damper; and a large tin dish was placed in the centre of the table. Everything was clean at least, and the tinware bright as silver.

The atmosphere of the room, the fire, the vapour, the odour of the 'fat lamp', the scalding hot tea and reeking mutton, were neither pleasant nor inviting; but as there was no preferable alternative we did 'sit in' to the edge of the sea-chest on our three-legged stools, and, setting to work man-fully, acquitted outselves as well as could have been expected of novices under the circumstances. '*Messieurs, vous êtes servis!*' said one of my friends, laughing, as we began our meal.

And here is another from the northern lands of Moreton Bay:

Captain Griffin's house was of the same primitive character as those of squatters generally, consisting of rough slabs fixed in sleepers below, and in a grooved wallplate above, and roofed with large sheets of bark, supported by rough saplings for rafters. Mahogany tables, chairs, sideboards, &c., and the other moveables of a respectable family in a town, appeared rather incongruous articles of furniture in such an extempore structure; but they gave promise at least of a better house, which I was told it was intended to erect as soon as the more important out-door operations of the establishment should afford the requisite leisure for the purpose, the present house being intended eventually for the barn. I was amused at the ingenious nautical expedient that had been had recourse to to form an additional apartment. The carpet which the family had had in use in their dining-room in Sydney was 'triced up' to use the nautical phrase, during the day, to the wall-plate of the slab-house; but on the usual signal of 'Let go the Haulyards,' being given at the proper hour for retirement at night, the carpet descended like the curtain of a theatre, and not only formed a partition between the sitting-room and a commodious bed-room but stretching, as it did, along the whole extent of the slab-wall of the latter, served to exclude the cold night wind which would otherwise have found a thousand entrances by the interstices between the slabs. . . . On the whole, I was much gratified with my visit to this recently formed Squatting-Station so far to the northward; as it showed how very comfortably a respectable family could be settled in the bush, with comparatively moderate means and exertion, in Australia, with all their flocks and herds around them, like the patriarchs Abraham, Isaac and Jacob of old.

The richer a squatter became the more likely he was to be an absentee, leaving his sheep-runs in the hands of shepherds and stockmen who were either poor immigrants or assigned convicts. And if the early life of the squatter himself was likely to be hard, the whole working career of his lonely shepherd was often on the verge of the unendurable. In 1835, James Backhouse stumbled on a sheep station near the Molong River:

Being much fatigued in the evening, with our walk of thirty-two miles, we had concluded to make a fire, and sleep in the bush, when it began to rain, lighten, and thunder. We therefore made our way, which was now become difficult to find in the dark, to a mean, dirty hut, at a place called Newry, belonging to a settler, and occupied by a ticket-of-leave stock-keeper, and an assigned prisoner-servant. These men entertained us hospitably with milk and damper, fare such as was offered to us at every station at which we called, on our way, and sometimes with the addition of tea and meat. There were two black youths residing in the hut with the stock-men; we were informed that they made themselves useful in minding the sheep, milking the cows, &c. The stock-keeper observed that these Blacks stopped with them better than their countrymen generally do with white people, because they treated them more like companions, and gave them a part of such provision as they themselves eat, instead of throwing scraps to them, as if to dogs.

19th. Our accommodation last night, though the best the place afforded, was such as we but seldom have had to put up with. Our bed was more sombre than would be found in the meanest, mendicant lodging-house, in England; it was only outdone by a blanket, generally used by one of the Aborigines, which was folded to add to the width of the bed. Another such bed, spread on the uneven clay floor, served our hosts; the two Blacks coiled themselves up on some sheep-skins, near the fire, pulling a blanket over them. My companion was driven from his resting-place, by bugs, which were very numerous. He tried to rouse the Blacks, in order to obtain more fuel, to revive the fire, but his efforts proved in vain; he therefore sat down on the best seat he could find: it was an uneasy, narrow stool, which did not stand level. At length, he was obliged to return to bed, by cold and faintness, which overcame all obstacles, and he fell asleep.

These stations, as they are called, usually belong to opulent settlers, living in or near towns, who derive a great part of their wealth from their large flocks of sheep, and herds of cattle. These are tended by their servants, many of whom are prisoners, on their extensive locations, or on unoccupied, contiguous lands, in the interior of the Colony. Many of them also send flocks beyond the boundaries of the located part of the Colony, which is, in many directions for a great distance, low, open, grassy, forest hills, with here and there clear flats, or plains. In such situations, some of the less wealthy settlers feed their own flocks, foregoing, for a few years, most of the comforts of life.

Around this time, Alexander Harris was also trekking into the interior bush to the south-west of Sydney and he was able to give a more exact account of the shepherd's life:

Up a creek which fell into the river close to our hut, on a fine swelling bare hill amidst a tract of forest which had here become almost table-land, stood the sheep station of Mr. —— which I have already mentioned. He had many others in various parts of these mountains, and others again in other parts of the colony. ... At the station were two shepherds who took out the sheep over the adjacent hills by day, and a hut-keeper was responsible for them by night. The flocks themselves were each about 800 strong, fully twice as many as a shepherd can manage in a thickly timbered and mountainous country. The master grumbles if the flock is not allowed to spread; he says the shepherd must be keeping them together by severe dogging, and that running so close they cannot fill their bellies; for this, if the shepherd is a free man, he will often refuse to pay him his wages; if he is a prisoner, he takes him before some other sheep-holding settler in the commission of the peace and flogs him. On the other hand, if the shepherd suffers the flock to spread, in these mountainous runs especially, they get into creeks and hollows; and he loses sight of them and leaves them behind; or a native dog sneaks in among them, and, as it is the habit of these animals to bite as many as they can before beginning to prey, 20, 30, 50 get bitten, most of them mortally, before the shepherd sees or hears the stir and comes to their rescue. By this time the whole flock perhaps is scattered in all directions by the panic to which sheep are so liable. For these mishaps again, if the shepherd is free, the master refuses to pay his wages, and tells him to go to law and get them if he can; which he knows, in nine cases out of ten, the man will not do from want of confidence in the administration of justice: if he is a prisoner he flogs him. . . .

So that the gist of the case is just this: – The New South Wales sheep-master throws the grand and insuperable risk (in such a country) of his trade on his labourer's shoulders: if bond, the man pays for it by having right only to half wages; if free, by being cheated out of half what he agrees for. And let the point I started from be here recollected, that all this wrong is mainly founded on another – that of making each man do two men's work; of giving men 800 sheep where 400 would be a full flock to give fair play to.

To add to the loneliness and pain of life, there was also, for the shepherd, constant danger from wild dogs and snakes, from bushrangers and aborigines, from drought, fire and flood. And when the exhaustion of the range forced the flocks to move on, the weary existence began again amid the trials of the drove:

As Steele's Creek was rather overstocked with six thousand sheep, according to the notions of those times (when people entertained somewhat princely ideas on the subject of feed for their flocks), it was decided to reduce their numbers, and I accordingly started for Tongala with two thousand of the ewes. My road was by what we now know as Pyalong, Egan's Creek, Redcastle, and Colbinabbin. The summer – for it was the month of December – was hot and dry, and at Mount Camel, or, as the Blacks call it, Yiberithoop, my sheep got their last drink, the distance from Tongala being about fifty-five miles. From Yiberithoop down the Colbinabbin Creek, and across the plains to Tymering, took me, I remember, two days and a half of tedious driving, the sheep being in one lot with two shepherds. . . . Towards sundown that evening we arrived at Tymering, and camped amongst the she-oaks, and so far everything went on well.

The whole party, however, was a good deal fagged, as our drive of eight miles, which was all we could accomplish, was over treeless plains, under a burning sun, so that nothing but the most constant efforts on our part could keep the sheep moving. It was Christmas-eve, I remember, and a furious hot wind had been blowing the whole day in our faces. Weary, begrimed and half-choked with the dust, with blood-shot eyes and sunburnt faces, the three of us sat at the camp, after having had a pot of tea and something to eat, our thirst but half-quenched, each one by himself, with his back against the leeward side of a tree. The mournful wailing of the wind as it streamed through the she-oak scrub, and our fatigue together, made us disinclined to talk; so we sat in silence, each, I suppose, occupied with his own thoughts. The fierce sirocco was driving before it sticks and leaves; and, in the distance, quantities of peculiar red-coloured bushes were rolling away to the southward, tumbling over and over before the gale. The horizon had that singular wavy appearance which is common to the plains in such weather; no birds were to be seen, but here and there moving colums of dust, grass, and leaves, the result of whirlwinds, towered high in the air; whilst, close at hand, covered with ashes from the small fire, which, though lately kindled, had already burnt itself out, lay our kettle, frying-pan, and pannikins, and the bag containing our gritty meat and damper. To complete the scene there were the panting sheep, and bullocks with protruding tongues; the close-on-setting sun bathing the landscape in a dull red light, suggestive of an eclipse. Altogether it was a melancholy camp that night, and the more so from the reduction in our little party.

Nor were hardship and natural dangers the only worries. In the mid-1840s, a depression made many sheep-masters bankrupt, and left nothing to be done with surplus sheep but to boil them down for fat, a process that 'diffused such an effluvia that was almost overpowering at a half mile's distance'. In 1843, a settler in Maitland recorded his woes:

Bankruptcy is almost universal and confidence in mercantile matters lost entirely – I consider Dickson, Dee and R.P. Cummins the only 3 solvent men left in Maitland, and it would be difficult to name three in the neighbourhood of the town of whom so much may be said.

(1846 Cummins took to drinking and died insolvent. The other two weathered the storm.)

On the 3rd April I was obliged to file my schedule and take the benefit of the Insolvent act, I was arrested for my bill given to release a friend from the same case a year before.

So valueless has property of all kind become that no monied engagement can be met but at most dreadful sacrifices – sheep are sold at 6d and 7d each, stations given with them, horses £7 each and cattle any price, picked cows for dairy of good kinds 2 guineas each, fat cattle 50/- and hardly to be sold at this price, a company has been started in Sydney for the purpose of salting beef for exportation and is now putting about 25 per day away. Many proprietors are also salting, and the establishment is now going, boiling fat sheep for the fat, wethers are sold in Sydney for 3/- to 5/- – the whole community seems horror struck and nothing that can be now foreseen can avert general bankruptcy. . . .

Nov. 15 – 1843

Bankruptcy has now overtaken or is upon the heels of almost the whole community.

1 Jan. 1844.

Mr. Wentworth of Windermere has established a large boiling concern to get rid of fat stock, it is sinking daily 200 sheep . . . all the large properties of sheep and cattle are getting down their stock by this process – the destruction is immense.

Yet despite all these troubles, and the history of suffering, the success of the squatters and their wool trade was astonishing. Roger Therry set out just how important this trade was to the growing nation of Australia:

In 1803 Mr. Macarthur brought with him to England but a small sample, yielded from his own first successful experiment.

In the year 1811, the first year in which Australian wool is noticed in official returns, the export was 167 lbs.

The official returns of 1835, which represent the quantity exported in 1834, give the quantity from Australia 4,347,610 lbs., whilst the average annual importation from Spain into England during the three years 1833, 1834, and 1835, was 2,428,650 lbs.

In the year 1834 Mr. Macarthur died; his life thus closed at a point of time that admitted of his witnessing the realisation of his ardent hopes that Australia would throw Spain into the shade as a source for the supply of wool to the mother country. It may be said he died at the moment of the triumph of the great design he had planned.

How the infant sample of 1803 grew into gigantic dimensions in 1862, recent returns exhibit. The importation of wool from Spain in 1805 was 6,895,525 lbs.; the importation from Australia in that year was *nil*. In 1861 Spanish wool fell off to 1,268,617 lbs.; the quantity exported in 1861 from the Australian Colonies (New Zealand inclusively), was *sixty-eight millions, four hundred and twenty-eight thousand pounds!!* Prodigious as has been the increase thus shown, these returns do not represent the total amount of this exported commodity, for, as the principles of free trade have thrown open the ports of the Continent to Australian wool, large quantities have been exported to France and other nations of Europe.

At last, the new land was freeing itself from its unhealthy dependence on a penal economy; for as the Quaker James Backhouse said: 'The state of a Government which depends upon the continuance of the sins of the people for the support of its revenue, is truly an awful state.'

*

Young countries are generally anxious for respectability, and the colony of New South Wales was no exception. The inhabitants faced a number of social fences and hurdles. Peter Cunningham, that tireless observer of the social scene, made an effort to sort out colonial ranks and precedence:

> Our society is divided into circles as in England; but, from the peculiarity of its constitution, still farther differences naturally exist, which have at various times received colonial *baptisms*. We have, as I said before, first, the *sterling* and *currency*, or English and Colonial born, the latter bearing also the name of *corn stalks* (Indian corn), from the way in which they shoot up. This is the first grand division. Next, we have the *legitimates*, or *cross-breds*, – namely, such as have *legal* reasons for visiting this colony; and the *illegitimates*, or such as are free from that stigma. The *pure Merinos* are a variety of the latter species, who pride themselves on being of the *purest blood* in the colony. We have likewise our *titled characters*, who bear 'their blushing honours thick upon them,' in the decorations of P.B. and C.B. which profusely adorn their persons; and the *untitled*, who, like myself, have neither '*mark* nor *character*' impressed upon our outward man. The *titled* are all *official* characters employed under the government, in street mending, brick-making, and suchlike, – the titular letters not portending that they belong to any such illustrious order as *the Bath*, but merely that they claim the Prisoner's Barracks or the Carter's Barracks for their respective domiciles.
>
> Our Currency lads and lasses are a fine interesting race, and do honour to the country whence they originated. The name is a sufficient passport to esteem with all the well-

informed and right-feeling portion of our population; but it is most laughable to see the capers some of our drunken old Sterling madonnas will occasionally cut over their Currency adversaries in a quarrel. It is then, 'You saucy baggage, how dare you set up your *Currency* crest at me? I am *Sterling*, and that I'll let you know!'

The native-born made up for their inferior status with a healthy amount of pride and colonial prejudice. They despised farm labour, or employment with the government, for those were *convict* sort of jobs. And they were sure that England had nothing better to offer than Australia:

The Currency youths are warmly attached to their country, which they deem unsurpassable, and few ever visit England without hailing the day of their *return* as the most delightful in their lives; while almost every thing in the parent-land sinks in relative value with similar objects at home. . . . A young Australian, on being once asked his opinion of a splendid shop on Ludgate Hill, replied, in a disappointed tone, 'It is not equal to *Big Cooper's*,' (a store-shop in Sydney,) while Mrs. Rickards' *Fashionable Repository* is believed to be unrivalled, even in Bond Street. Some of them, also, contrive to find out that the English cows give *less* milk and butter than the Australian, and that the choicest Newmarket racers possess *less* beauty and swiftness than *Junius, Modus, Currency Lass*, and others of Australian turf pedigree; – nay, even a young girl, when asked how she would like to go to England, replied with great *naiveté*, 'I should be afraid to go, from the *number of thieves* there,' doubtless conceiving England to be a downright hive of such, that threw off its annual swarms to people the wilds of this colony. Nay, the very miserable-looking trees that cast their annual coats of bark, and present to the eye of a raw European the appearance of being actually *dead*, I have heard praised as objects of incomparable beauty! and I myself, so powerful is habit, begin to look upon them pleasurably.

It was a rather prickly society; polite people were strong on etiquette, as Cunningham soon learnt:

While strolling once with an acquaintance, on my first arrival in the colony, we chanced to encounter a couple of our men of rank, with one of whom my friend walked aside, to hold some private conversation, leaving the other and me standing together. As the gentleman was known to me by sight, and I knew him also to have lately come down the country in a direction which I was about to take on the morrow, I incautiously asked of him the state of the roads. But what was my surprise when, drawing himself up with a most self-important air, he replied in the exact terms of the lawyer before-mentioned, 'Upon my word I don't know you, sir.' Being yet a novice with respect to colonial dignity . . . I naturally began to marvel who this *great man* could be, and should doubtless have set him down as the Duke de las Sierras, or the Marquis of Aquaro at least, had I not been afterwards assured that he was nothing more than a retired subaltern of infantry some time rusticated here. 'Then,' said I, 'this must be a land of high aristocratical feeling, indeed!

And although the colony was, as is usual in pioneer lands, an hospitable place where the traveller was sure of a bed and a welcome, it also had a reputation for sharp practice and too many rogues:

An opinion has, I know, been put forth that free emigrants become gradually inoculated with roguish propensities after their arrival here: this I have not been able to perceive; though certainly no *vast scrupulosity* is manifested by some of them, which may as justly be ascribed to *former habit* as *recent corruption*. Not so, however, thought Samshoo, an East-Indian servant-boy belonging to a merchant here, who had been detected by his employer in purloining a large bag of dollars. 'Samshoo!' said his astonished master, 'what has made *you* turn such a rogue? *you*, that have been so long in my service, and always shown yourself before such an honest lad;' 'Massa,' blubbered Samshoo, shrugging his shoulders, 'when Samshoo come here, Samshoo very good boy; now Shamshoo dam rogue; *every body*, massa, turn rogue here! by and bye, massa turn rogue too!'

Living was expensive, both in Sydney and in the countryside, for so many commodities still had to be imported over very great distances. There was a shortage of housing, unless you were a pioneer settler and put up your own hut. If the newly-landed immigrant did not find a job immediately, prospects were grim. A young man from England, who later became a well-known statesman, remained bitter about his first days in the colony, in 1839–40:

There was no place for the emigrants to go till such time as they could engage with masters, or otherwise provide for themselves. When they left the ship they had to do as best they could. Poor Clarinda, in her weak state, had no one to do the least thing for her – not even dress her baby or make her bed, and in a few days she was obliged to go ashore with her new-born infant in her arms and to walk a mile across the town of Sydney to the miserable place I had been able to provide her as a home, which was a little low, dirty, unfurnished room without a fireplace, at 5/- per week rent. When she sat down overwhelmed with fatigue, on a box which I had brought from the ship, within those wretched walls, I had but 3d. in the world, and no employment.

For more than two weeks I kept beating about Sydney for work, during which time I sold one thing and another from our little stock for support. At length, being completely starved out, I engaged as a common labourer with Sir John Jamison, Knt., to go about 36 miles up the country. Sir John agreed to give me £25 for the year, with a ration and a half of food. This amounted to weekly:

10½ lbs. Beef – sometimes unfit to eat.
10½ lbs. Rice – of the worst imaginable quality.
 6¾ lbs. Flour – half made up of ground rice.
2   lbs. Sugar – good-tasted brown.
¼ lb. Tea – inferior.
¼ lb. Soap – not enough to wash our hands.
2   figs Tobacco – useless to me.

This was what we had to live upon and not a leaf of vegetable or a drop of milk beyond this. For the first four months we had no bed other than a sheet of bark off a Box-tree, and an old door laid on two cross pieces of wood, covered with a few articles of clothing. The hut appointed for us to live in was a very poor one. The morning sunshine, the noon-tide shower, and the white moon-light of midnight gushed in upon us alike. You will perhaps think had you been us you would have had a few vegetables at any rate, for you would have made a bit of garden and cultivated them for yourselves, but you would have done no such thing. The slave-masters of New South Wales require their servants to work for them from sunrise to sunset, and will not allow them to have gardens lest they should steal a half hour's time to work them.

But the well-established had created for themselves a comfortable airy sort of life, not without its own casual easy style, and well-suited to the hot summers and mild winters of New South Wales:

The doors and interior fittings-up of the better description of our houses are of colonial cedar, kept polished in the manner of mahogany, the tables and chairs also being usually of the same. Rush-bottomed chairs, manufactured here, supply the place of the latter for common purposes. – The India cane mat is generally substituted for the English carpet, on account of its superior coolness, while *white* is for a similar reason our domestic costume; the gentlemen, however, exchanging the *white* jacket for a *blue* one when the weather is cool, or on riding out; – blue jackets, over light summer vests and trowsers constitute indeed the common dress of the majority of our respectable tradesmen, and the Sunday garb of the more lowly; straw hats being generally worn in summer, either imported from Manilla, or of colonial manufacture, the finest selling at 12s. apiece.

That may have been the respectable city dress, but when the men from the bush came to town, they amazed the gentlefolk with their homespun looks and behaviour, and they cut uncouth, centaur-like figures with fierce appetites and simple pleasures:

Of the gentlemen one saw, a good sprinkling were *squatters*, who had brought their flocks and herds from New South Wales or Tasmania. As a variety of the *genus homo* they were distinguishable by their hirsute appearance; whiskers, beards, and moustaches being decidedly in the ascendant among them. Many of them, I noticed, indulged in blue serge shirts in lieu of coats, cabbage-tree hats, belts supporting leather tobacco-pouches, and in some few cases a pistol, which, with breeches, boots, and spurs, completed the costume. The horse, too, seemed an animal all but inseparable from the young gentlemen I am attempting to describe. . . . One young squatter, I remember, was particularly noticeable, as it was his custom to have a black boy in livery mounted on his horse's croup. Nor did such little eccentricities seem to surprise the residents or attract much notice, the accepted idea seeming to be, that bushmen were not by any means amenable to the slow ways of the dwellers in towns, and that many things were proper enough in them which might have been esteemed strange, or even objectionable, in others.

The squatters of that period – generally new arrivals from home, and young men who had brought with them more cash than experience – were a good deal discussed by the townsfolk, and more especially by the ladies, who, it struck me, had vague and curious notions concerning them. As far as I could gather, the prevailing notion seemed to be that the squatters' *habitat* in all cases was some fearfully remote and lonely locality which it would be quite impossible for ordinary persons to reach; that without his horse the squatter could not exist; that he wore habitually Hessian boots and spurs, of which it was uncertain whether he ever divested himself; that he was much given to emu and kangaroo hunting; had constant encounters with hordes of blacks; rode as a rule fifty miles a day, chiefly at a gallop – a performance which seemed as necessary to his horse as to himself – and at night slept anywhere, with his saddle for a pillow. It was also surmised that some sense, peculiar to the young squatter, enabled him to find his way in the most unerring manner through trackless forests and waterless wastes; that (when out of town) he lived solely on tea, mutton, and damper, and enjoyed, when in the saddle, a perfect immunity from fatigue. All this of course was mere surmise; what townspeople really did know about the squatter was, that in town he was lavish in his expenditure, affected tandem driving, had a decided *penchant* for beer and brandy, smoked continually, and was not as a rule over-punctual in his payments, or versed in the ways of merchants or bankers. His peculiarities, however, real or imaginary, did not survive the very early days of the colony; he was too lively a bird for our forests, so that eventually, lawyers and courts of justice put out many a shining light of those times. In the early days the young men took to the bush and the neighing steed, as naturally as they now become bank clerks, lawyers and cricketers.

It was a common complaint in the early colony, and even until the mid-nineteenth century, that there was little to do other than work. Cunningham, writing of the 1820s, was critical:

Agreeable amusements are still much wanted, to relieve the dull monotony of a town like Sydney, forming the capital of a small territory, and cut off, in a manner, from all communication with the other parts of the civilized world. – In *all* small communities, where people know too much of each other's private affairs, and where consequently idle gossipings and retailings of personal scandal creep in to fill the blanks occasioned by the flagging of other subjects, some such innocent recreation as theatricals, balls, and evening parties are of manifest utility. – But in a place so long distracted with private and party feuds as New South Wales, – with few subjects 'of a day' either of foreign or domestic interest furnished us to talk about, such inoffensive sources of enjoyment would become objects of paramount importance, both as respects the security of the peace and furtherance of the prosperity of our infant community.
A theatre has long been wanted here, to serve such purposes; and a building is now in course of erection, which is spoken of as being intended for one, by Mr. James Underwood. – No regular subscription balls have yet been set on foot; but private ones are occasionally given; and also *three* annual public balls and suppers, by the respective sons of St. George, St. Patrick, and St. Andrew, as their regular jubilee days arrive; – while the bachelors of Sydney usually make up a splendid *fourth*, where '*bachelor's fare*' forms certainly no portion of the evening's entertainment. Our worthy governor has now however commenced giving his public dinners; and his good lady her even more social *soirées*.

But there was music. John Macarthur's wife, by some accounts, brought out the first piano in 1790. Thereafter, pianos were common enough among prosperous settlers and should, according to the moralistic James Backhouse, have been put to better use:

In the houses of most of the prosperous settlers, from whatever rank they may have risen, piano-fortes are to be seen. Next to drinking and smoking, they seem to be resorted to, to relieve the mind from that sense of vacuity, which ought to lead it to seek to be filled with heavenly good; and thus these instruments of music are made a means of truly injurious dissipation.

In June 1827, the Governor gave the first ball since the founding of the colony 'in which the ladies *equalled* in numbers the gentlemen'. Balls were not frequent, and perhaps more popular with the ladies than with the outdoor menfolk. For these hearty fellows, sport was the thing. To begin with, there was little else for them. The first primitive theatre burnt down in 1798. Then 'the sources of amusement have been confined to cricket, cards, water-parties, shooting, fishing, hunting the kangaroo etc.' These habits persisted. Australians liked life in the sunshine. The girls could 'swim and dive like dab-chicks.' All the English sporting tastes were imported and indulged. Boxing and horse-racing were popular, so too was gambling.

But intellectual life was not completely abandoned. The first newspaper, the *Sydney Gazette*, was founded as a government propaganda sheet in 1803, written, edited and printed by George Howe, a Creole convict from St Kitts. Other newspapers followed and even (by 1825) biweekly and weekly journals. And the habit of reading lightened many a long, lonely day in remote settlements. Around 1840, a settler in Victoria recalled that quiet pleasure:

> In the matter of books I believe we were better off than most of our neighbours, though those in our possession had been got together in a haphazard sort of way, at various times and without any idea of making a collection for the bush. However, from a pair of stout wooden pegs in the wall-plate of the sitting-room of our rough, but not uncomfortable, slab hut at Tongala, surrounded by a miscellaneous collection of fire-arms, foils, masks, wooden sabres, fencing gloves, stock-whips, spurs, and other articles which embellished the walls, hung, in the place of honour, some shelves made of bark, on which were ranged our literary treasures. These volumes, our great resource for years against *ennui*, for want of

something new, were read, re-read, and discussed, I cannot say how often. In fact, several of them became studies in our small circle.

There were several of the Waverley Novels, some of them in French translations, 'Travels in the East', by Lamartine, Stephens, and Chateaubriand; Silvio Pellico's 'Le Mie Prigioni', Horace's 'Odes', Pope's 'Iliad', Junius's 'Letters', some of Florian's works, Sterne's 'Sentimental Journey', 'Blackstone's Commentaries', Adam Smith's 'Wealth of Nations'; two or three elementary works on natural science; 'Youatt on the Sheep and Horse'; and a pile of old magazines, chiefly Blackwood's, and amongst them those in which the 'Noctes Ambrosianae' had appeared. We had, besides, a few colonial works, such as 'Major Mitchell's Explorations'; and the 'Memoirs of Jorgen Jorgenson, ex-king of Iceland,' whom I remember to have seen when a clerk in my father's office.

Yet even in rural solitude, Australians easily had enough of that, and our Victorian settler was soon hurrying out of doors once again. Swimming, hunting, climbing trees, throwing spears, yarning with the locals – that was what the lads in the bush really liked.

Sport, hunting, gambling, reading, theatre, even dancing, they all had their place. But there was one pastime universally liked by the majority of the population and just as universally condemned by the preachers and moralists. Drink had been an understandable temptation in a penal settlement, and the desire did not slacken as the colony moved towards a free society. Surgeon Cunningham found a general unsteadiness all the year round in Sydney:

Sobriety, however, by no means ranks among the conspicuous virtues of our general population; – many, very many, of our dear citizens, keeping up devoutly the religious festival of St. Patrick from year's end to year's end. 'Why, Dennis,' said I to a sottish Hibernian, whom I had seen for some weeks in a state of *oblivion*, 'surely St. Patrick could not be born on *every day* of the last *month*!' – 'Och, it is only my own bad memory that makes me so *particular*, sir; for having a mighty love for the saint, you see, I always begin keeping his birth a fortnight beforehand, lest I should *forget* the day, and after it is over, why the devil burn me but I always *forget* to leave off!'

Nor was the life of the countryside any more sober; for if there were good reasons to be drunk in town, there were even better reasons to be drunk amid the hardships of the bush. The government surveyor, Clement Hodgkinson, discovered scenes of lively debauch among the cedar sawyers of the MacLeay River:

Men and women, (for many of the sawyers have wives), lying day and night on the bare grass in a state of intoxication, and only recovering to renew their orgies; casks broken in, and the contents passed round in buckets; men fighting; native blacks, who have been supplied with liquor, yelling and screeching like demons, under the influence of alcohol. Such are a few of the accompaniments of the cedar sawyers' drinking bouts. At length, when they have drank enough to *balance their account*, they wend their way once more to the brushes with their rations, there to remain until the next time of settlement.

Alexander Harris, who had come across cedar sawyers, stockmen and shepherds in his wandering life, describing the stockman on a cattle-station, wondered at this feckless, alcoholic life:

We had fine weather, and drove our 'mob' wide of the settlement (Bathurst township): the man went three days' stage with us and returned: we would gladly have taken him forward with us as our stockman, but he preferred sticking to the beds, blankets, cooking utensils, &c., which we had given him. Besides, though a good man in other respects, he was a great 'Lushington'; and when these fellows once get disturbed from their regular work, and the notion of a 'spree' gets into their head, they are never easy till they have their 'break out' over, and take the road again to look for some other service, without a penny in their pockets, or, to use their own phrase, 'without a feather to fly with'; or, again 'without a mag to bless themselves with'. What this blessing themselves is unless it be getting another glass of rum, I never could divine. I have known scores of them spend 2o*l.*, 3o*l.*, 5o*l.*, 7o*l.* in Sydney in the course of a few days, and then, as in a sort of desperation, take to one of the great roads up the country, on which there is none of that hospitable entertainment that there is in the bush, and walk for two or three days right ahead without a bit to eat or a drop to drink

Hunting for kangaroo. From Clement Hodgkinson, *Australia from Port Macquarie to Moreton Bay*, 1845

except the water on the road side, sleeping at night a little way off in the bush, by a fire that some more fortunate traveller had left or themselves had kindled, for every working man carries his tinder-box for lighting his pipe. Such, it is very likely, was our stockman's next adventure, I never saw him again.

With habits like this, both in town and country, the colonists made the tavern a prominent feature of their lives. No sooner had Harris set foot in New South Wales than he was inside a public house, viewing with some astonishment the crowd within:

In the large tap-room of the Market-house (which we entered more for the purposes of curiosity than anything else) we

213

found a strange assemblage; and stranger still were their dialect and their notions. Most had been convicts: there were a good many Englishmen and Irishmen, an odd Scotchman, and several foreigners, besides some youngish men, natives of the colony. Amongst them was present here and there a woman, apparently the wife of a settler. The few women were all sober and quiet, but many of the men were either quite intoxicated or much elevated by liquor. The chief conversation consisted of vaunts of the goodness of their bullocks, the productiveness of their farms, or the quantity of work they could perform. Almost everybody was drinking rum in drams, or very slightly qualified with water; nor were they niggard of it, for we had several invitations from those around us to drink. I could not however, even at this early period of my acquaintance with this class of people, help observing one remarkable peculiarity common to them all – there was no offensive intrusiveness about their civility; every man seemed to consider himself just on a level with all the rest, and so quite content either to be sociable or not, as the circumstance of the moment indicated as most proper. The whole company was divided into minor groups of twos, threes, and fours, and the *dudeen* (a pipe with stem reduced to three, two, one, or half an inch) was in everybody's mouth. I think there was not an individual in the room but one female, who did not smoke more or less, during the brief time we sat there.

In Sydney there were 'twice as many unlicensed grog-shops as licensed public-houses,' and Harris admitted that there was a close connection between drinking and crime. But neither rising crime, nor police action, nor the call of morality and religion curbed the consumption of alcohol. In the mid-nineteenth century, Roger Therry, who in thirty years had peered at many a drunkard from the judicial bench, found alcohol, tobacco and tea still greatly in demand:

By calculations lately made, it appears that upwards of a hundred thousand gallons of spirits are annually consumed in the colony, and the same quantity of wine and malt liquors: that also about sixty thousand pounds of tobacco, on average, are of late yearly imported; while the value of tea imported during a single quarter amounted to 14,168*l*.

*

Sydney was the centre of the Australian colonial world; it was the first settlement, the finest harbour, the hub of agricultural and ranching development. The economy flowed through its docks. For twenty-five years, Sydney and its surrounding countryside *was* the colony, despite the penal off-shoots in Norfolk Island and Van Diemen's Land.

For a quarter of a century the circle of containment held. But the sailors had been preparing the way. George Bass charted the southern coast, establishing Van Diemen's Land as an island. In the next few years, Matthew Flinders circumnavigated the whole continent; and before 1820 Phillip King, the son of Governor King, had re-mapped the north. Then the Blue Mountains were pierced and men like John Oxley, Charles Sturt, Allan Cunningham and Clement Hodgkinson, some surveyors and some merely land-hungry pioneers, were on their way into the open interior and the coasts beyond the Sydney heartlands.

They stepped out under expansive southern skies into lands that were sometimes exhilarating but often intimidating. When the first mountains had been left behind there were still wilder ranges sweeping on, depths beyond depths. Travelling in these lands was a manly life, calling for endurance, good sense, self-reliance and improvisation. It also helped to have some guidance and aid from the aborigines. Hodgkinson described the start of a typical journey:

> *March 6th*, 1841. – Got ready a small sack of flour, ten pounds of cooked bacon, a bag full of tea and sugar mixed together, a stone bottle of rum, some tobacco, three hatchets, and a pair of blankets. Having arranged these articles securely on the back of the most sure-footed pack-horse I had, I started on the excursion, with Miles our stockman, both of us being mounted on strong bush horses, and well armed with carbines, pistols, and swords.
>
> Having left our cattle station, at Yarra-Bandini, late in the day, we did not get further, before dusk, than twenty miles from it. We stopped for the night at a brushy water-course, a few miles on the other side of the main range, dividing the basin of the MacLeay river, from that of the Nambucca river, to the north of it. The country thus far was grassy forest land,

thickly timbered with gigantic black-butt gums, and other eucalypti, and abundantly watered with numerous permanent chains of water-holes, and gravelly water-courses in brushy hollows. Having unloaded the pack-horse, tethered out our horses, and lit a fire, we suddenly heard the loud shrill *coo-ee* of the natives, who turned out to be some old friends of mine belonging to the Tanban tribe. Having heard that they were now at peace with the tribes we should have to encounter on our journey towards the Bellengen, I persuaded a couple of them to accompany me, by the promise of a red shirt each, and plenty of *smoke*, (tobacco,) whilst they remained with me; for I was well aware that they would be of great utility in searching out the best crossing places for our horses over the creeks, cutting a passage through the entangled creepers of the brushes, and acting as interpreters to the wild blacks. They had just succeeded in killing a kangaroo, and good naturedly offered us some of it. Having finished our supper, we laid down to sleep with our saddles for pillows, but were much teased during the night by the clouds of musquitos which issued forth from the dense brush to attack us.

March 7th. – Having boiled our tea, and breakfasted on toasted bacon, and *bush biscuit*, (thin cakes of flour and water baked on hot embers,) I started on our journey soon after six o'clock. After a ride of half an hour, we crossed the first large brook which flows into the Nambucca river. I gave it the native name of Oankihi creek; it was flowing on a bed of dark blue rock, which appeared to be limestone. In the thick brushes which skirt this stream, I saw a great number of gigantic ferns, which are common enough at Illawarra, and many other parts of the colony, but which I had never seen in the MacLeay river brushes. After proceeding a few miles farther, over a country of alternate low ranges, and gravelly water-courses in brushy hollows, we crossed a high leading range of grassy forest hills; a descending spur of which brought us to the brink of a rapid stream, dashing along in a very irregular bed of slaty rock, the strata of which had a great inclination. We had some trouble in getting our horses across the jagged and pointed rocks, which rose out of the water. . . . On entering the brush bordering on this river, we experienced considerable annoyance from the great quantity

Travellers in the bush. From Clement Hodgkinson, *Australia from Port Macquarie to Moreton Bay*, 1845

of nettle-tree saplings. My hands and arms soon ached from the poisonous touch of its leaves, and our horses suffered very much; one of them threw himself on the ground, snorting convulsively with pain. The nettle-tree attains a very large size at the MacLeay and Nambucca, being often six feet in diameter, and of a corresponding height; its wood is very soft and spongy, and its leaves, which are of great size, resemble in shape the leaves of the mulberry, and at the same time possess the bright green velvet appearance of the geranium leaf. The slightest touch of one of these leaves occasions a most acute stinging pain; but horses suffer infinitely worse than men from contact with the leaves of the nettle-tree, as their skin rises in large blisters, and great temporary constitutional derangement seems to take place. Our blacks killed a large carpet-serpent near here, which was carefully preserved for their next repast.

Sometimes the days went well in 'the wonderful diversity of climate'; sometimes the rains crashed down; then the storm abated and the travellers retreated into the silent fellowship of the night:

> Hour after hour we sat by the fire, and smoked, and listened, and made tea; then walked about, and stood and strained our eyes to pierce the darkness, and our ears to collect every sound. The small rain fell spraylike, cool, refreshing, and with the open breast and bare neck habitual to the working class in the colony, this is quite a luxury when the skin is fevered with over-exertion. The sky was starless, black, and still. The bush kept up that long indefinite sound that it makes beneath the passage of a mighty wind; something between a roar and a deep hiss, mingled strangely, and one could fancy, awfully with sudden passing intonations like a fitful music. The gale ruffled and howled, and swept away from the fire far across the grass a long train of sparks, which, viewed from the distance as we walked to and fro, looked like the tail of some monstrous comet that had fallen and lay blazing away amidst the darkness on the side of the great slope of country down which the creek coursed.

Nothing could be taken for granted, for after the rains there was likely to be drought. Mark Twain recounted this story of drought:

> As we proceeded the altitude became less, and the heat proportionately greater until we reached Dubbo, which is only 600 feet above sea level. It is a pretty town, built on an extensive plain. After the effects of a shower of rain have passed away, the surface of the ground crumbles into a thick layer of dust, and occasionally, when the wind is in a particular quarter, *it is lifted bodily from the ground in one long opaque cloud.* In the midst of such a storm nothing can be seen a few yards ahead, and the unlucky person who happens to be out at the time is compelled to seek the nearest retreat at hand. When the thrifty housewife sees in the distance the dark column advancing in a steady whirl towards her house, she closes the doors and windows with all expedition. A drawing-room, the window of which has been carelessly left open during a dust storm, is indeed an extraordinary sight.

A lady who has resided in Dubbo for some years says that the dust lies so thick on the carpet that it is necessary to use a shovel to remove it.

Yet despite all these difficulties, what surprised Twain most, among the many Australian surprises, was the rapidity of colonial development:

In 1829 South Australia hadn't a white man in it. In 1836 the British Parliament erected it – still a solitude – into a province, and gave it a governor and other governmental machinery. Speculators took hold now and inaugurated a vast land scheme, and invited immigration, encouraging it with lurid promises of sudden wealth. It was well worked in London, and bishops, statesmen, and all sorts of people made a rush for the land company's shares. Immigrants soon began to pour into the region of Adelaide and select town lots and farms in the sand and the mangrove swamps by the sea. The crowds continued to come, prices of land rose high, then higher and still higher; everybody was prosperous and happy, the boom swelled into gigantic proportions. A village of sheet-iron huts and clapboard sheds sprang up in the sand, and in these wigwams fashion made display; richly dressed ladies played on costly pianos, London swells in evening dress and patent leather boots were abundant, and this fine society drank champagne, and in other ways con- ducted itself in this capital of humble sheds as it had been accustomed to do in the aristocratic quarters of the metro- polis of the world. The provincial government put up expen- sive buildings for its own use, and a palace with gardens for the use of its governor. The governor had a guard and maintained a court. Roads, wharves, and hospitals were built. All this on credit, on paper, on wind, on inflated and fictitious values – on the boom's moonshine, in fact.

This went on handsomely during four or five years. Then all of a sudden came the smash. Bills for a huge amount drawn by the governor upon the Treasury were dishonour- ed, the land company's credit went up in smoke, a panic followed, values fell with a rush, the frightened immigrants siezed their grip-sacks and fled to other lands, leaving behind them a good imitation of a solitude where lately had been a buzzing and populous hive of men.

Adelaide was indeed almost empty; its population had fallen to 3,000. During two years or more the death trance continued. Prospect of revival there was none; hope of it ceased. Then as suddenly as the paralysis had come, came the resurrection from it. Those astonishingly rich copper mines were discovered, and the corpse got up and danced.

South Australia was not the first expansion of the colony. In 1803, David Collins had been sent to establish a penal settlement in Van Diemen's Land. Having tried and rejected Port Phillip on the mainland, Collins settled his party of convicts on the present site of Hobart and started a history of patchy development that was more gloomy and sad than triumphant. The island colony (renamed Tasmania in 1856) was too closely attached to its penal role, for it was here the difficult convicts were sent, especially after the closing of the Pacific out-post on Norfolk Island. The settlers were disaffected, despite good soil and a hopeful start to a whaling industry. And in the saddest act of all, the aborigines were almost exterminated.

Soon the unhappy island settlers, in particular those with an eye to the profits of the wool trade, were viewing enviously the wider ranges they had left behind at Port Phillip. A number of families crossed the Bass Strait in 1835 and after squatting in the vicinity, and wrangling a good deal with the authorities in Sydney, established the settlement of Melbourne. It grew astonishingly fast. Its prosperity was based on fine wool country and on a speculative free enterprise that was none too fussy. The Quaker James Backhouse, who visited the place within two years of the arrival of the first squatter, was not pleased:

> The town of Melbourne, though scarcely more than fifteen months old, consists of about a hundred houses, among which are stores, inns, a jail, a barrack, and a school-house. Some of the dwelling-houses are tolerable structures of brick. A few of the inhabitants are living in tents, or in hovels resembling thatched roofs, till they can provide themselves with better accommodation. There is much bustle and traffic in the place, and a gang of prisoners are employed in levelling the streets. The town allotments, of half an acre, were put up for sale, a short time since, at £5 each, the Surveyor thinking £7 too much to ask for them. But the

fineness of the country has excited such a mania for settling here, that they sold for, from £25 to £100 each!

Eighty thousand acres of land, suitable for cultivation, and for the sites of dwellings for opulent settlers, have already been surveyed, and are expected soon to be put up for sale, by the Government, in sections of from fifty to one hundred acres each. Larger tracts will also be sold, as soon as the survey is sufficiently forward.

At this place we met several of our acquaintance, from other parts of New South Wales, and from Van Diemens Land, who had removed hither from various motives. Some from an unsettled disposition, others from dissipated habits, others with the hope of improving their circumstances, and others from greediness of gain. Some of the great holders of sheep and stock say, that they do not think their removal hither has been, in the aggregate, advantageous. Though they have increased their property, it has been at a great risk, from the greater untowardness of their servants, and from the enmity of some of the Blacks. A few have lost their lives by the latter, and one had eight of his servants murdered, either by them or by their fellow-servants.

Business was at this time, conducted on a very disagreeable and unsound plan, at Port Phillip. Almost every thing, including labour, was paid for by orders on Sydney, or Van Diemens Land; the discount required by the few persons who had cash, was from £20 to £40 per cent! A mechanic received half his wages in goods, charged at about 30 per cent. profit, and the rest in an order, on which he paid his employer 10 per cent. discount for cash!

Such, then, were the spurs that drove on colonial expansion: penal needs, land hunger, and the profits of the wool trade. Allan Cunningham had opened the way to Moreton Bay. The convicts and the animals (not only sheep but cattle too) followed him through. A penal settlement was established in 1824. It grew slowly into Brisbane, an up-country station known for deadly boredom and rustic manners, but with its semi-tropical climate and lazy life much more pleasing to Backhouse than frantic, money-mad Melbourne. He visited Brisbane in 1836:

It is prettily situated, on the rising, north bank of the Brisbane River, which is navigable fifty miles further up, for small sloops, and has some fine cleared, and cultivated land, on the south bank, opposite the town. Adjacent to the Government-house, are the Commandant's garden, and twenty-two acres of Government-garden, for the growth of Sweet-potatoes, Pumpkins, Cabbages, and other vegetables, for the prisoners. Bananas, Grapes, Guavas, Pine-apples, Citrons, Lemons, Shaddocks, &c. thrive luxuriantly in the open ground, the climate being nearly tropical. Sugar-cane is grown for fencing, and there are a few thriving Coffee-plants, not old enough to bear fruit. . . . Coffee and sugar, will probably at some period, be cultivated here, as crops. The surrounding country is undulating, and covered with trees. To the west, there is a range of high, woody hills, distant, in a direct line, five miles.

Within the next two years, Backhouse also visited the two further colonies of Western Australia and South Australia. The first started with disaster from which it took many years to recover. Settlement on the Swan River was a private scheme for riches, put together by speculators in England, which foundered on its impracticability, though Backhouse darkly thought that drink had a good deal to do with it. It pleased him even less than Melbourne:

It is difficult to estimate the ruin that has been brought upon this Colony, by the consumption of spirits. The whole revenue of the Government, amounting to about £7,000 a-year, is derived from spirits, in the form of duty on the imports; so that the amount of capital, annually paid for them, must be much more considerable. The Colony is so poor, as to be unable to import sheep in sufficient quantity, to stock its lands, so that the holders of grants of from 5,000 to 100,000 acres, have little stock of any kind upon them. Such grants are consequently, of so little value, as to occasion land to be sold, as low as from 1s. 6d. to 2s. 6d. per acre! Had the money expended in spirits, since the foundation of the Colony, been occupied in the importation of sheep, it is not improbable that land might now have been ten times its present value; and had no grants originally exceeded 5,000 acres, many more persons would have had the means of maintaining flocks, of about 1,000 sheep each. The wealth of the Colony would probably have been thus increased, so as to have rendered grants of this size, by this time, as valuable as those of 50,000 acres each, now are. Spirit drinking, and avarice in obtaining grants of large extent, have paralyzed the country, which, beyond a doubt, is naturally very inferior to what was originally represented.

The persons, who have improved their circumstances by emigration to this country, are labourers, store-keepers, and a few others, into whose hands much of the capital that was originally in the possession of other Colonists, has passed; but by this transition, the capital of the Colony is not increased. Its population is said to be now, only about 2,000, or one third of what it was, three years after the Colony was first settled. Death, frequently the result of drinking, and emigration to Australia and Tasmania, have been the chief causes of this reduction.

If Western Australia was founded on private greed, South Australia was planned according to a well-defined theory of colonization and set on foot, in 1836, by an Association that was community- as well as profit-minded. It staggered for a while and had its financial troubles but eventually achieved the success that Mark Twain noted. It was the only planned colony uncontaminated by convict labour or penal policy. It celebrated the free association of farmers and townsmen (the native inhabitants, unfortunately, were not included), and thus breaking irrevocably from the convict past, it pointed the way for the future development of the whole continent.

*

The colonies of Australia, growing out of an association of convicts sent abroad, under conditions of shame, by an uncaring motherland, rose rapidly into worldly success. But not everyone wholeheartedly applauded the achievement. There was something forced about it, a hothouse exotic of development whose rapid progress had been paid for in too much pain, misery and greed. This sudden flowering was unnatural. The people themselves had a sense of this, as one citizen, returning to Sydney, put it to Mark Twain:

It *is* beautiful, of course it's beautiful – the harbour; but that isn't all of it, it's only half of it; Sydney's the other half, and it takes both of them together to ring the supremacy-bell. God made the harbour, and that's all right, but Satan made Sydney.

To many, the characteristic marks of this new society seemed to be extravagance, wastefulness, aggressive materialism. Clement Hodgkinson, during the mid-nineteenth century recession, reproached Australians for 'the boundless extravagance of all classes of the community, and the consequent enormous importation of mere articles of luxury.' And to complete this extravagance, there was a general thoughtless waste of natural resources for short-term profit. This was what Harris found in the cedar forest:

> As I have already hinted, the costly and fragrant cedar was at this time a common forest tree in the shady recesses and beside the cool stony creeks of this vast old mountain. When I add that at the time of which I write, nearly a hundred pair of sawyers had gradually come down from Sydney and gathered into this mountain, and were (as they also continued to be for years afterwards) slaughtering away in all directions, it will not be wondered at that the pride of the Five Island Cedar Brush is long since gone.

All this was evidence of an attitude of mind characterized by Hodgkinson as 'the speculative mania which pervaded all classes of the community':

> This rage for speculation was very much encouraged by the loose un-English system of transacting business in New South Wales; long extended credit at high interest was readily accorded on the slightest security. . . . As to the land mania, it was in a great measure produced by the system of selling Crown lands by public auction, and thereby exciting an unfortunate spirit of competition, which drained the colonists of that money which ought to have been employed in the more legitimate objects of colonization, such as agriculture, vineyards, &c. Old settlers and newly arrived emigrants, merchants, and mechanics, all hastened to outbid each other at the Government sales by auction, and purchased at exorbitant rates, sections and allotments of land which they had probably never seen, and which were often hundreds of miles from Sydney, and in situations such, that if they had

only listened to the dictates of common sense, they must have perceived that they were often paying for their land ten times more than it was worth. When the Government thus set the example of exciting competition for land, the same spirit, of course, prevailed in all private land sales. Indeed, in the prosperous times, three or four years ago, scarcely any one purchased land for its fertility, or capability of being converted into good farms; for not one person in a hundred built on, or improved the ground he had bought; the principal motives which influenced these speculators in their purchase of land, was because it was near some Government village, reserve, or else possessed a frontage to some river or road, which would cause it to look well on paper, and consequently resell to advantage, if redivided into small lots, and called '*a town*,' with some grand euphonous appellation. Many persons also threw away their money in the purchase of land they had never seen, and were totally unacquainted with, with no other reason for so doing than the notion that all land in the Australian colonies must go on increasing in value, whatever might be the price originally paid for it.

Not even the vastly profitable wool trade was safe from 'speculative mania'; it was a bubble which expanded and was finally burst by 'the great influx of emigrants of capital from Great Britain, who all eagerly purchased flocks of sheep at any price, under the idea of making rapid fortunes'.

These are serious criticisms. But the greatest stain on the early history of Australian society was the treatment of the aborigines. There was never a policy towards the native inhabitants, only a general contempt and oppression tempered slightly by a loosely directed benevolence in high places. In 1817, the *Sydney Gazette* reported a meeting with Governor Macquarie:

On Saturday last the 28 ult, the town of Parramatta exhibited a novel and very interesting spectacle, by the assembling of the native tribes there, pursuant of the Governor's gracious invitation.

The Governor, attended by all the members of the Native Institution, and by several of the magistrates and gentlemen in the neighbourhood, proceeded at half past ten to the meeting, and having entered the circle, passed round the whole of them, inquiring after and making himself acquainted with the several tribes, their respective leaders and residences. His Excellency then assembled the chiefs by themselves and confirmed them in the ranks of chieftains to which their own tribes had exalted them, and conferred upon them badges of distinction; whereon were engraved their names as chiefs, and those of their tribe. He afterwards conferred badges of merit on some individuals in acknowledgement of their steady and loyal conduct in the assistance they rendered the military party, when lately sent out in pursuit of the refractory natives to the west and south of the Nepean River.

By the time the ceremony was over Mrs. Macquarie arrived and the children belonging to, and under the care of, the Native Institution, fifteen in number, preceded by their teacher, entered the circle, and walked round it; the children appearing very clean, well clothed and happy. . . . Several of the little ones read; and it was grateful to the bosom of sensibility to trace the degrees of pleasure which the chiefs manifested on this occasion. Some clapped the children on the head; and one in particular, turning round to the Governor with extraordinary emotion, exclaimed, 'Governor, that will make a good settler – that's my Picaninny' (meaning his child). And some of the females were observed to shed tears of sympathetic affection at seeing the infant and helpless offspring of their deceased friends, so happily sheltered and protected by British benevolence. The examination being finished, the children returned to the Institution, under the guidance of their venerable tutor; whose assiduity and attention to them merit every commendation.

The feasting then commenced, and the Governor retired amid the long reiterated acclamations and shouts of his sable and grateful congress.

This was high comedy, but it hardly made up for the massacres of the Black War in Van Diemen's Land or for the total usurpation of a vast continent where the aborigines, a primitive, peaceful and ingenious people, had lived undisturbed since the mists of time. When John Batman tried to strike a bargain with the aborigines for the territory of Melbourne he was severely reprimanded since all Australian land was considered to belong to the British Crown.

Although aborigines occasionally, under extreme stress,

retaliated and killed a small number of white men, they did not even constitute the enemy. There were merely objects for use:

An elderly woman, named Boatswain, by the sealers, to whom she had long been in bondage, informed us, by means of signs, and a few words in broken English, of the manner in which these men flogged the women who did not pluck Mutton-birds, or do other work to their satisfaction. She spread her hands to the wall, to shew the manner in which they were tied up, said a rope was used to flog them with, and cried out with a failing voice till she sank upon the ground, as if exhausted. The statements of this woman were confirmed by others, several of whom have escaped to the settlement.

The cutter's boat happened to go to Green Island about a year since, when two women, called Isaac and Judy, took the opportunity of escaping by it, while the sealers were asleep. – Two other women waded and swam from Green Island to the Settlement – a distance of three miles. Most of these women were originally kidnapped. Boatswain says, she got into a boat when a girl, and the sealers rowed away with her.

That story of outrage, which James Backhouse heard in Van Diemen's Land in 1832, was endlessly multiplied from coast to coast. The ordinary status of the aborigines was revealed most tellingly by the complaint of the white settlers convicted of murdering twenty-eight aborigines at Myall Creek in 1837. 'We were not aware that in killing the blacks we were violating the law,' they said, 'as it has been so frequently done before.'

When aborigines were not being casually displaced, intimidated, used or slaughtered, they took their place as figures of fun for the white man. Civilization, far from redeeming them, had reduced them to this:

All the natives round Sydney understand English well, and speak it too, so as to be understood by residents. The Billingsgate slang they certainly have acquired in perfection, and no white need think of competing with them in abuse or hard swearing, a constant torrent of which flows from their mouths as long as their antagonist remains before them; it is of no use for him to reply, his words being quickly drowned in the roar of cursings and contemptuous appellations. I have often stood for a considerable time witnessing contests of this kind, our native satyrs invariably forcing their opponents to retrograde, while the instant *blacky* perceives *whity* beating a retreat, he vociferates after him – 'Go along, you dam rascal; go along, you dam scoundrel; go along, you dam blackguard!' exalting his voice as his enemy retires. But should this volley of abuse provoke 'white fellow' to run up and offer to strike him, '*blacky*' would dare him 'to the scratch,' threatening him with *the jail* and *Massa Wenta*, [the magistrate] if he attempted it. The wisest course, perhaps, is to turn a corner and get out of sight as quickly as possible, for even escaping into a house and shutting the door is no protection, as some of the most *steely-tongued* will sometimes halloo in at the window, or even through the key-hole, as long as they think you are in hearing. Their common practice of fighting amongst themselves is still with the *waddie*, each alternately stooping the head to receive the other's blows, until one tumbles down, it being considered cowardly to evade a stroke. Most of them, however, can 'show off' in the true Belcher style; and indeed I once witnessed a battle in the streets where the attitudes and *squaring* would have done honour to the London ring, many well-put-in blows too being exchanged, though certainly there was much more *chaffing* than *fighting* in this case, – an active humorous little boy appearing to turn the whole into ridicule by dancing round and between the combatants with uncouth grimances and gestures, flourishing his waddie and singing in accompaniment to his pranks.

As beggars, the whole world will not produce their match. They do not attempt to *coax* you, but rely on incessant importunity; following you, side by side, from street to street, as constant as your shadow, pealing in your ears the never-ceasing sound of 'Massa, gim me a dum! massa, gim me a dum!' (dump). If you have the fortitude to resist *firmly*, on two or three assaults, you may enjoy ever after a life of immunity; but by once *complying*, you entail upon yourself a plague which you will not readily throw off, every gift only serving to embolden them in making subsequent demands, and with still greater perseverance. Neither are their wishes moderately gratified on this head – less than a dump (fifteen pence) seldom proving satisfactory.

But what was there in European civilization to attract the aborigines? If they rejected the white man's world (Alexander

Harris wrote), though it was partly from the strength of their own traditions:

> It must certainly also be equally imputed as an effect to the abominations of the white man's character, and to his conduct towards the members of his own race; and to the bitter feeling which the blacks all experience, though they very generally veil it, against us as a nation of robbers, robbing out of mere wantonness, and not from the pressure of necessity. They understand no theories about capital and labour, and pauperism and emigration: all they feel is that they are wronged; all they see, the fact that it is done by those who are rich already, and do not want the soil for subsistence; not by the poor, who might be justified.

These were the dark reflections of a man who had sampled immigrant life and judged it harshly. But what else should we expect? The rank colonial tree, said Harris, had grown out of the foul convict humours of the penal settlements. Harris wrote at the start of the mid-nineteenth century recession, lamenting present discontents and recalling past wrongs. Had he stayed longer he might have found more virtues than vices to portray. The fuller picture showed lives that radiated courage, endurance, energy and almost limitless hope.

The *facts* of the achievement, after all, were astonishing. From the European point of view, at first there had been nothing in an empty land and then, within a short time, there was a resounding plenty. And all this had been done by ordinary men and women. This was the fable of Australian life, the secret history, as it presented itself to Mark Twain in the 1890s:

> Here is this man who laid Melbourne's first brick. His history is history, but one cannot tell it from romance. His name was Buckley; and some day Melbourne's name will be changed to Buckleyville, or Buckleytown, or Buckleyburg – Buckleyville, I think; the present injustice cannot last for ever. Buckley was a young English giant. He had been a brickmason first, later a soldier. He was in the wars in Holland, and bore all his life the decoration of a wound honourably come by. Later, in England, he was convicted of receiving

stolen goods – probably six shillings' worth – and was doomed preliminarily to the hell known as the hulks, for awhile. You note how richly his young life opened, as to incident and episode. Next, he was shipped for Australia along with a cargo of other convicts, to serve – but the length of his term is not stated. This was in 1803, when he was twenty-three years old. The expedition was at sea five months and a half; then it set itself ashore not very far from where Melbourne now stands. It was a bush country, wild and forbidding, and peopled by aboriginals solely. There was not a white man nearer than the little colony at Sydney, hundreds of miles away. A convict station was begun (soon to be abandoned), and Buckley laid the first brick.

Buckley abhorred the shame and the slavery of his new life, and was not well satisfied with the climate by and by, when January brought midsummer, and he had to do his hard day's work in a temperature of 110° in the shade. So he made a break for freedom, and was successful. He had companions when he started; one was shot by the guard, the others got away, and wandered with Buckley in the bush during six miserable days in a famishing condition; then, preferring convict sufferings with food to these without, they set out on their return-trip, leaving Buckley alone, for he would not go with them. There was good stuff in Buckley.

He and his comrades had originally thought of walking to California; for they were not educated men, and their geography was weak; but when Buckley was left solitary, he made no such attempt, because of the distance partly, and partly because he was in doubt as to California's precise whereabouts. He resolved to try for Sydney, but made a mistake, and went from it instead of toward it. He lived on berries and mussels and such things a long time, but was finally captured by the savages. He had just had a stroke of good luck that morning, although he was not aware of it at the time. He had pulled a spear out of a grave, and it was in his hand when the aboriginals came upon him. They believed that he was the occupant of the grave come to life again, so he was among relatives and friends. They were glad to have him back, and so he was at once provided with food, and wives, and a nephew, and other necessaries of life, and made welcome and at home.

He became a savage, and an important and infuential man in the tribe. He lived the tribe's life, he learned the tribe's language, and in time forgot his own. And without ever seeing a white man or hearing white man's speech, this Crusoe lived this strange life, utterly lost to the world, during the amazing term of *thirty-two years!*

It takes Australia to beat the record. The other Crusoes are gone four years, and come back ostentatiously gotten up in goat skins for effect, but the Australian kind are gone a generation and come modestly back without anything on at all, so as not to attract attention.

Thus Buckley began Melbourne.

In our day the telegraph, the newspaper, and the illustrated magazine would take a newly discovered find like this Buckley and fill the world with his name, and make his fortune; but the Buckley of that old day could not close the romance of his life in this splendid way. It was 'clover' for him to be appointed personal servant to the colonel in command of the new colony and have clothes to wear. Also he acted as constable and detective. Presently he resigned and went to Van Diemen's Land (now Tasmania), and through 'interest' got himself appointed assistant-storekeeper to the Hobart Immigration Home. Finally, he got the post of gate-keeper to the Female Nursery. He married the widow of a mechanic in 1840, when he was sixty years old. When he was seventy he was retired on a pension of $60 a year, and enjoyed it six years. Then Death, jealous of his prosperity, took him. It was a sufficiently colourless tapering off of a unique and wonderful career.

Whether strictly true or not, Twain's humorous fancy was based on many careers and romances no less remarkable. And they were all typically Australian. The history of the land was the story of thousands of Buckleys – men and women who, in the spirit of adventure and hope, had pushed on 'beyond the black stump' into the unknown. In the face of this, Mark Twain could only throw up his hands in admiration and wonder:

Australian history is almost always picturesque; indeed, it is so curious and strange, that it is itself the chiefest novelty the country has to offer. It does not read like history, but like the most beautiful lies; and all of a fresh new sort, no mouldy old stale ones. It is full of surprises and adventures, and incongruities, and contradictions, and incredibilities; but they are all true, they all happened.

A SHORT BIBLIOGRAPHY

CONTEMPORARY

General sources:
Clark, C.M.H. (ed), *Select Documents in Australian History, 1788-1850* (Sydney, 1950)

Discovery, the First Fleet and the early settlement:
Barrington, G., *A Voyage to New South Wales* (London, 1793)
Beaglehole, J.C. (ed), *Journals of Captain James Cook* (London, 1955)
Cobley, J., *Sydney Cove, 1788* (London, 1962)
Collins, D., *Account of the English Colony in New South Wales* (London, 1798)
Phillip, A., *Voyage to Botany Bay* (London, 1789)
Tench, W., *Narrative of an Expedition to Botany Bay* (London, 1789)
———— , *Complete Account of the Settlement at Port Jackson* (London, 1793)
Thompson, G., *Slavery and Famine* (London, 1794)
White, J., *Journal of a Voyage to New South Wales* (London, 1790)

The development of the colony:
Backhouse, J., *A Visit to the Australian Colonies* (London, 1843)
Cunningham, P., *Two Years in New South Wales* (London, 1827)
Curr, E.M., *Recollections of Squatting in Victoria* (1884)
Harris, A., *Settlers and Convicts* (London, 1852)
Hodgkinson, C., *Australia from Port Macquarie to Moreton Bay* (London, 1845)
Onslow, S.M. (ed), *Some Early Records of the Macarthurs of Camden* (Sydney, 1914)
Therry, R., *Reminiscences of Thirty Years in New South Wales* (London, 1863)
Twain, Mark, *More Tramps Abroad* (London, 1897)

LATER WORKS

Barnard, M., *A History of Australia* (Sydney, 1962)
Barton, G.B., *History of New South Wales* (Sydney, 1894)
Bateson, C., *The Convict Ships, 1787-1868* (Glasgow, 1959)
Mackaness, G., *Admiral Arthur Phillip* (Sydney, 1937)
O'Brien, E., *The Foundation of Australia* (Sydney, 1950)
Roberts, S.H., *The Squatting Age in Australia* (Melbourne, 1935)
Rutter, O., *The First Fleet* (Sydney, 1937)
Sharp, A., *The Discovery of Australia* (Oxford, 1963)

INDEX

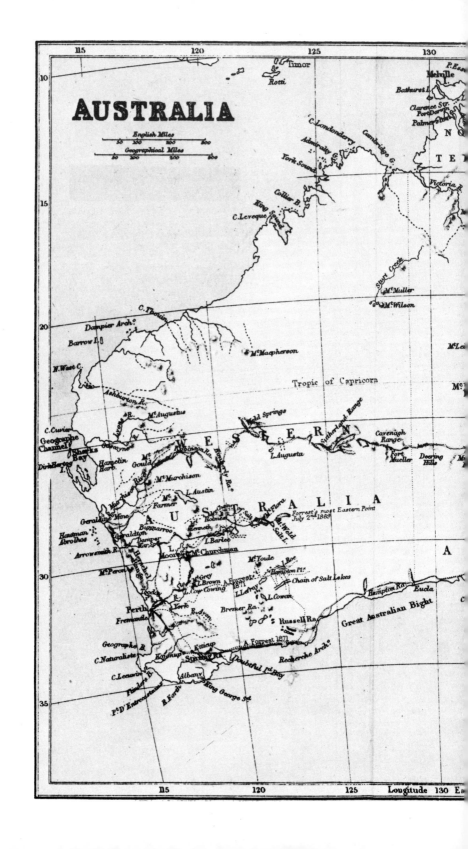